G000068324

MEXICO ON MAIN STREET

LATINIDAD

Transnational Cultures in the United States

This series publishes books that deepen and expand our knowledge and understanding of the various Latina/o populations in the United States in the context of their transnational relationships with cultures of the broader Americas. The focus is on the history and analysis of Latino cultural systems and practices in national and transnational spheres of influence from the nineteenth century to the present. The series is open to scholarship in political science, economics, anthropology, linguistics, history, cinema and television, literary and cultural studies, and popular culture and encourages interdisciplinary approaches, methods, and theories. The series grew out of discussions with faculty at the School of Transborder Studies at Arizona State University, where an interdisciplinary emphasis is being placed on transborder and transnational dynamics.

Matthew Garcia, Series Editor, School of Historical, Philosophical, and Religious Studies; and Director of Comparative Border Studies

For a list of titles in the series, see the last page of the book.

MEXICO ON MAIN STREET

Transnational Film Culture in
Los Angeles before World War II

COLIN GUNCKEL

RUTGERS UNIVERSITY PRESS
NEW BRUNSWICK, NEW JERSEY, AND LONDON

Library of Congress Cataloging-in-Publication Data
Gunckel, Colin, 1975–

Mexico on main street : transnational film culture in Los Angeles before World War II / Colin Gunckel.

pages cm. — (Latinidad : transnational cultures in the United States)
Includes bibliographical references and index.

ISBN 978-0-8135-7076-1 (hardcover : alk. paper) — ISBN 978-0-8135-7075-4 (pbk. : alk. paper) — ISBN 978-0-8135-7077-8 (e-book)

1. Mexican Americans in motion pictures. 2. Motion picture industry—California—Los Angeles—History—20th century. 3. Motion pictures—California—Los Angeles—History—20th century. 4. Motion pictures—Social aspects—United States—History—20th century. I. Title.

PN1995.9.M49G86 2015

791.43'65203678073—dc23

2014027523

A British Cataloging-in-Publication record for this book is available from the British Library.

Visit our website: http://rutgerspress.rutgers.edu

Manufactured in the United States of America

For Lucio

This and all else is for you.

CONTENTS

ACKNOWLEDGMENTS

The genesis of this project goes all the way back to my first extensive exposure to Mexican cinema as an undergraduate at the University of New Mexico. As a student of Latin American literature, I was astounded to discover decades of entertaining and compelling works of cinema that had somehow been excluded from my education to that point. I immediately dove in and never looked back. Susan Dever's courses at UNM's Department of Media Arts sparked and fueled my obsession, and she graciously shared her extensive VHS collection of Mexican cinema rarities. Of course, I always relished any opportunity to talk about my favorite films and stars. In a number of conversations with my friend Ester Guajardo and her parents, however, it became apparent that the theaters they attended were often the actual focus of a story or memory. Indeed, they seemed to affirm a contention that has become widely accepted within cinema studies: that the social experience of cinema might be just as significant or as memorable as the film showing on-screen. Curious about this dimension of Mexican American movie going in the United States, I began doing research on this dimension of film history that, at the time, had received decidedly scant scholarly attention.

I wrote my first research piece in Elizabeth Cohen's UCLA graduate seminar on film sound. From its original inception to its current form, this project has taken a number of iterations, and my perspective about my object of study has changed multiple times (and to be honest, so has the object of study). I obviously owe a great deal to those whose advice and guidance have informed the final shape of this book. Most obviously, my mentors at UCLA—Eric Avila, John T. Caldwell, Kathleen McHugh, and Chon Noriega—provided crucial insight and support at every stage of process. Professor Noriega in particular offered me a tremendous amount of support and professional experience during my time as a graduate student. I owe a great deal to his ongoing mentorship. I am also indebted to Edward Dimendberg and his insightful comments on the manuscript in its early stages. I would also like to thank all of those who offered feedback during my 2011 manuscript workshop at the University of Michigan: Giorgio Bertellini, Gregory Dowd, Mary Francis, Markus Nornes, Matthew Solomon, Jacqueline Stewart, and Larry La Fountain-Stokes. I have relied generously on the support and advice of staff at Michigan, including Mary Lou Chlipala, Mary Freiman, Judith Gray, Orlandez Huddleston, Carrie Moore, Marlene Moore, Mariam Negaran, Brooklyn Posner, Tabitha Rohn, Marga Schuhwerk-Hampel, and Tammy Zill. Lastly, I am eternally grateful to the insightful and constructive feedback provided by the anonymous readers and the assistance and support of Leslie Mitchner and Matt Garcia at Rutgers University Press.

The research entailed in this sort of project naturally required the assistance and generosity of multiple archivists and librarians. At the Margaret Herrick Library of the Academy of Motion Picture Arts and Sciences, I would like to thank Clare Denk, Barbara Hall, Janet Lorenz, and Jenny Romero. Robert Dickson in particular has been remarkably and consistently generous since the inception of this project. Not only has he introduced me to collections that I would not have otherwise discovered, but his own research represents an important landmark in this area. I would also like to thank Sheryn Morris at the Los Angeles Public Library for her help with theater materials. Terri Garst at the LAPL has also offered valuable assistance with image acquisition. And, to all the various librarians at the Central Library who humored my incessant requests for microfilm and printouts, I will forever appreciate your patience. Big thanks also go to Sandra Joy Lee Aguilar at the USC Warner Bros. Archive. At the Seaver Center for Western History Research, John Cahoon provided crucial assistance in the final stages of manuscript research. I also would not have been able to complete the final manuscript without the assistance and input of the following individuals: Daniel González, Claudia Hernandez, Orquidea Morales, and Wendy Sung. The final stages of my research were also generously supported by the University of Michigan's College of Literature, Science, and the Arts and the Departments of American Culture and of Screen Arts and Cultures. Thanks also to Indiana University Press for allowing me to reproduce material from my article "The War of the Accents: The Reception of Hollywood Spanish-Language Films in Los Angeles."

Aside from those involved in the production of this book, I would never be at this point in my career without the support and guidance of a number of individuals too numerous to mention here. At the University of New Mexico, Nina Fonoroff, Ira Jaffe, Brian Konefsky, and James Stone instilled in me a love for the study of film history and analysis. At UCLA, I benefited tremendously from seminars by Janet Bergstrom, Stephen Mamber, and Steven Ricci. It should also be mentioned that, if I am successful at all, partial credit goes to my incredibly supportive PhD cohort at UCLA, all friends for life: Eric Mack, Ross Melnick, Candace Moore, Sudeep Sharma, Eric Vanstrom, and Laurel Westrup. And at the University of Michigan, I have been surrounded by a number of incredibly supportive colleagues in American Culture, Screen Arts and Cultures, and Latina/o Studies: Richard Abel, Evelyn Alsultany, Stephen Berrey, Amy Sara Carroll, Bruce Conforth, Maria Cotera, Daniel Herbert, Shazia Iftkhar, Victor Mendoza, Anthony Mora, Lisa Nakemura, V. Prasad, and Matthew Solomon. There are also so many friends who have been part of this journey in one way or another, people who have made it hardly seem like work at all: C. Ondine Chavoya, John Cheney-Lippold, Ramón García, Olga Giller, Lamar Glover, Daniel González, Ana Guajardo, Fatimah Guajardo-Glover, Candace Moore, Gronk Nicandro, Ariana Rosas, Kristen Schilt, Darling Sianez, Pilar Tompkins Rivas, Maria Vazquez, Jessee Vidaurre, and Antonio Vigil.

The only reason you are currently holding this book in your hand is because of my family. My parents, Cindy and Les Gunckel, have always encouraged and supported my strange and incredible journey, even when at points when it probably seemed perplexing. I owe to them my constant curiosity, my love of education, my obsession with popular culture, and my incessant work ethic. I grew up in a family where those things mattered, and it has made me who I am. My sisters, Emily Manning and Allison Wagoner, have also been incredibly supportive and understanding of the twists and turns that have always been a part of my life. Lucio Matías Gunckel, one of my only aspirations is to provide you with the support necessary to pursue your passions, whatever they may be. I want to give you what my family was gracious and patient enough to bestow on me, because it made an incredible difference. And finally, while I was finishing this book, I was fortunate enough to meet my wife, Liaa Raquel Cruz. I've never been involved in a more hilarious, loving, productive, and mutually supportive collaboration. We've already proven that together we can do absolutely anything. I know that the reward for all our hard work and sacrifice is on the horizon. No matter where we find ourselves, there will never be any greater happiness in my life than being with you and Lucio.

MEXICO ON MAIN STREET

INTRODUCTION

A Mexican immigrant attending a theater on Los Angeles's Main Street from the 1910s to the 1930s might have paid admission to see an impressively wide range of entertainment: a second- or third-run Hollywood film, a Mexican or Argentine feature, a dramatic play, a vaudeville performance, or a musical concert. Depending on the year, any or all of these might have shared the same stage for an evening. Even a cursory survey of theater listings during these decades reveals an incredibly diverse and ever-changing array of leisure options and venues along this corridor. This vibrant, transnational Mexican film culture along Main Street—the epicenter of social and cultural life of Mexican Los Angeles before World War II—functioned as an arena through which immigrants contributed and responded to the making of Los Angeles, of Hollywood, and of Mexican cinema at pivotal moments in their respective, intersecting histories.[1] At the same time, by participating in this entertainment landscape, immigrants negotiated emerging conceptions of race, nation, community, and identity through changing formulations of transnational Mexicanidad (Mexicanness) beyond the boundaries of Mexico. Latinos, while being represented by and responding to cultural products of multiple origins during this period, also employed elements of film culture in surprising ways to generate alternative representations, mostly (and perhaps paradoxically) without access to the means of cinematic production.

Mexican immigrants in the United States were subjected to and engaged with conceptions of themselves shaped by overlapping hierarchies of race and class in both countries. The images and discourses circulating through local film culture continually constructed them as audiences and generated an array of representations across texts. To understand the place of Latinos within histories of Mexican cinema and Hollywood, it is essential to look at the complicated ways that Mexicans (and by implication, other marginalized groups) have historically been represented by, responded to, and participated in culture industries. More than simply talking back to mainstream representations, for instance, Mexican cultural authorities mobilized practices of cultural production, reception, and consumption to articulate and contest ideas about what it meant to be Mexican in the United States. While scholarship on media reception usefully situates audiences as active, historically situated participants in the creation or shaping of meanings, the agency of viewers and critics in such instances should not necessarily be defined only by their reaction to cinematic texts. In other words, beyond the question of individuals making meanings from specific films, the reception of cinema in Mexican Los Angeles constituted a significant aspect of alternative formations of identity and community, not to mention ways of engaging the broader institution and experience of cinema. So while Charles Ramírez Berg's assertion, for instance, that "the participation of Latinos in silent Hollywood cinema was negligible" may remain indicative of the racial politics of industrial labor practices in the early decades of the twentieth century, broadening our focus beyond the sphere of production allows us to understand participation in more expansive terms.[2]

Mexico on Main Street begins with the emergence of Main Street as an epicenter of Mexican culture in the early twentieth century, coincident with a massive influx of immigration and the rise of Hollywood. To examine representations and constructions of Mexicanidad across a diversity of texts, it is necessary to trace the ways in which the connections between media changed over time *and* how these transformations intersect with changing notions of race, identity, urban space, and nationality. Each chapter consequently foregrounds a particular form of cultural production—from the Mexican immigrant press to theater and Hollywood films—while articulating its position within the broader frame of local Mexican film culture. While proceeding chronologically, five historical flashpoints make these relationships apparent in Mexican Los Angeles: the expansion of the Mexican immigrant press and the consolidation of Hollywood; the explosion of Mexican theater production and criticism; the transition to sound and Hollywood's Spanish-language films; the emergence of a Mexican film industry; and Hollywood's production of Pan-American films and the emergence of a Mexican theater district in East Los Angeles. At each turn, debates about cinematic representation and Mexicanidad are impacted as intermedial arrangements, industrial conditions, and exhibition practices adjust and transform. The eventual decline of Main Street as a site of Mexican movie culture by the late 1930s also coincided with another set of fundamental changes in urban development, film industrial practices, the downtown exhibition landscape, global politics, demographics, and the Mexican immigrant press.

The very existence of Mexican film culture—which encompassed a range of media including film criticism, theatrical production, exhibition practice, musical performance, and serialized novels—was the product of the intertwined growth of Los Angeles and its immigrant population. Naturally, the inextricable nature of these trends impacted emerging conceptions of both. After the arrival of a transcontinental railroad connection in the late nineteenth century, Los Angeles experienced tremendous and rapid expansion in population and size, fueled by the concerted promotional efforts of real estate interests and local investors. With a population of slightly more than eleven thousand in 1880, it had grown into a modest-sized city of one hundred thousand within a span of just twenty years. By 1930 Los Angeles had exploded into a major metropolis of more than one million people. This population increase was driven by a constant influx of native-born arrivals from the Midwest and other regions within the United States, along with a diverse group of immigrants—Japanese, Chinese, Italian, Filipino, Russian, and Mexican—recruited or otherwise attracted to the city to work primarily as laborers in either an industrial or agricultural capacity. While drawn by such opportunities, Mexicans were also compelled to migrate northward because of their homeland's economic instability, the widespread expropriation of agricultural land, and the profound impact of the Mexican Revolution (1910–1917). As a result of these factors, the city's Mexican population would approach one hundred thousand by 1930.[3]

By the mid-1910s Main Street near the Plaza (the site of the original Spanish settlement) had transformed into a bustling cultural and social corridor that hosted a number of Mexican-oriented businesses and venues: restaurants, hotels, grocery stores, medical offices, theaters, pool halls, saloons, penny arcades, record stores, photo studios, and a pharmacy. This area also served as the headquarters of the period's most widely distributed Spanish-language dailies, both of which published extensive cultural criticism: *El Heraldo de México* and *La Opinión*. Given the diversity of immigrants that contributed to the city's spatial and demographic growth, the first decades of the twentieth century also witnessed the parallel emergence of other downtown ethnic districts that often combined housing with culturally specific leisure and commerce. The burgeoning African American population (more than fifteen thousand by 1920) would increasingly congregate around the Central Avenue area south of downtown.[4] The city's original Chinatown was located on North Alameda just east of the original Plaza, before being razed in the 1930s to make way for the construction of Union Station. Little Tokyo was located along First Street near Alameda and served as a cultural and commercial center for the city's Japanese population (which numbered eleven thousand by 1920 and would grow to more than twenty thousand by 1930).[5] Even as early as 1900, there were "many Japanese-owned restaurants, hotels, food shops, bamboo shops, etc." in or near Little Tokyo; by 1907 this would include a movie theater, the International.[6] A slightly later influx of Filipinos would give rise by the early 1920s to a Little Manila near Second Street (between Main and Los Angeles) that included barbershops, restaurants, a newspaper office, and an employment agency.[7]

While all these areas coexisted simultaneously and Main Street served as the epicenter of Mexican commerce and culture, this corridor also regularly attracted

an incredibly diverse audience with its myriad of entertainment options. Within
both popular and academic discourse produced in the first decades of the twentieth century, Main thus became widely synonymous with downtown's racial and
ethnic heterogeneity and the flourishing of working-class leisure. As such, its
reputation suggests how the proliferation of these immigrant entertainment cultures shaped the growth and development of Los Angeles, while contributing
in multiple ways to prevailing conceptions of a city in transition. Perhaps most
obviously, those areas and persons racialized as nonwhite served as a foil against
which boosters and civic leaders framed Los Angeles as a "white spot." *Los Angeles Times* publisher Harry Chandler and his cohort often used this term rhetorically to distance the city from the problems supposedly facing East Coast cities
(including overcrowding, large immigrant populations, and labor activism).
As Mark Wild points out, however, this term also accrued racial connotations:
"the white spot was seen by some Angelenos as a racially pure space, a city built
by white Americans for white Americans."[8] In concrete terms, this meant that
immigrant neighborhoods were frequently characterized as blighted, ripe for
redevelopment and revitalization in the name of progress. In turn, areas removed
from or replacing such enclaves were able to claim respectability premised on
exclusionary constructions of whiteness. Beginning in the second decade, Main
Street functioned as the confluence of all that the city's power structure would
like to disavow or eliminate from the civic imagination: lowbrow entertainment,
racial heterogeneity, a substantial (and often vocal) working class, and the continually growing presence of Mexicans.

Within this process of "othering" through which a particular notion of civic
identity was formulated, the Mexican immigrant population occupied a peculiarly
prominent yet ambivalent position. As William Deverell has argued, "Los Angeles
came of age amidst (and in part because of) specific responses to Mexican ethnicity and Mexican spaces."[9] This is not to suggest that other immigrant groups
were not instrumental to this process. Chinatown during this period, for instance,
functioned as a maligned other against which the city's power structure defined
the identity of the city, an enclave whose place within urban space intersected with
cinematic images and multifaceted anxieties about an impending "Yellow Peril."[10]
But it is the ascendancy of Mexicans as the largest immigrant group during this
period *and* their peculiar positioning relative to the city's history and identity that
prove particularly revealing of the role that local entertainment cultures played
in shaping and reflecting conceptions of race and urban space. As the city was
founded as a Spanish colonial outpost in 1781 and had been part of Mexico until
the signing of the Treaty of Guadalupe Hidalgo in 1848, the power structure of Los
Angeles continually struggled to reconcile the city's Mexican past with the reality
of its Mexican present. Exacerbating this was the fact that by 1930 the Mexican-
descent population constituted an estimated 20 percent of Los Angeles County
(higher than any other immigrant group).[11] On both counts, the Mexican presence
would become a central yet contested element of the city's development, growth,

and civic identity. For instance, while elements of the city's power structure continually wrung their collective hands about the supposed Mexican problem, they also
celebrated its so-called Spanish past as a considerable asset, a marketing tool and
tourist attraction. In his study of the Padua Hills Theatre in Claremont, Matt Garcia describes this apparent contradiction as "a simultaneous process of celebration
and subordination that validated the existing racial and political order in Southern California and 'Greater Mexico.'"[12] During the first decades of the twentieth
century, these ambivalent and even paradoxical conceptions greatly informed the
representations of Mexicans on-screen and as a presence in urban space. Mexican
film culture constitutes a key site through which to gauge the ways in which these
pervasive, entrenched notions were variously negotiated, appropriated, reshaped,
and rejected by various constituencies.

If the very idea of Los Angeles as an urban white spot relied perhaps paradoxically on the simultaneous presence and disavowal of a racialized or immigrant
working class, Hollywood's own bid for respectability in the 1910s hinged on a
similar mechanism. Drawn by year-long sunshine, nonunion labor, the availability of land, and a diverse range of landscapes, a number of studios relocated
there from the East Coast during the 1910s, just as Los Angeles grew into a major
metropolis.[13] By the 1920s Hollywood had become internationally recognized
both as a concept and as the undisputed epicenter of film production in the
United States, accounting for 84 percent of the nation's film production by as
early as 1922.[14] Speaking specifically about the mutual dependency between Los
Angeles and Hollywood during this period, Mark Shiel contends that "the city
shaped films and films shaped the city in symbiotic, incestuous, and interne-
cine ways."[15] Hollywood became a key component of an urbanizing Los Angeles,
projecting the city to the world. Los Angeles became the nation's primary location for film shoots and as a result, cinema became perhaps the primary vehicle
through which representations of the city, not to mention the United States, were
mediated. It is hardly coincidental that the position of immigrants (and Mexicans in particular) within dominant conceptions of the city paralleled efforts by
an emerging film industry to produce a cinematic experience suitable for white,
middle-class audiences.

The transition of cinema from an entertainment once associated with immigrants and the working class to one generally considered a "respectable" medium
reveals the multifaceted role that Mexican immigrants would assume in the
operation of Hollywood as an institution. Significantly, the industry's bid for
respectability occurred at the level of both production and exhibition. In the
first instance, the nature of this transition relied on conceptions of a coveted
audience, notions of all-Americanism tied to whiteness and the textual content
deemed most suitable for both. Within the literary adaptations, historical epics
(including, most notoriously, *The Birth of a Nation*, D. W. Griffith, 1915), and
other cinematic exaltations of Western civilization, characters racialized as nonwhite quite frequently functioned as the others against which white American

identity was formulated. Mexicans, for instance, were often cast as the *bandidos*, "greasers," and half breeds who threatened the chastity of white womanhood and antagonized the triumphant white hero.[16] While this dynamic is perhaps hardly surprising, this representational economy had its correlation in the sphere of exhibition. If theater chains attempted to attract a more affluent clientele, they did so by constructing the first generation of movie palaces, replicating a physical environment associated with legitimate theater and opera. As the case of Los Angeles demonstrates, this elevation of cinema required an explicit physical and discursive distance from immigrant-oriented entertainment and neighborhoods. The respectability of new theaters constructed along Broadway relied to some degree on a distinction from Main; the popular press and sociological studies reiterated this distinction by characterizing Mexican audiences along Main as unruly, unsanitary, and decidedly nonwhite. In both realms—and in the places where they converged, whether on-screen or in the urban sites of film exhibition—Mexican immigrants as audiences and textual representations were central to the mutually dependent development and discursive construction of Los Angeles and Hollywood and, by proxy, conceptions of American national identity.

In tracing the role of Mexicans in the formation of Hollywood and Los Angeles, this book thus considers the ongoing interrelation between conceptions of them as textual representations and cinema audiences. That is, conceptions of the Mexican audience historically projected by film industries, the popular press, and academic discourse were in a multifaceted dialogue with cinematic representations on-screen. While the birth of Hollywood constitutes a key and formative instance of this dynamic, examining the ongoing interplay between these two registers provides a nuanced understanding of Hollywood's relationship to Mexicans (and other marginalized groups), while also shedding light on the stakes of battles over cinematic representations and the interventions that proposed to combat or transform them. For instance, Hollywood's version of the greaser as a mixed-race mongrel during the silent period coincided with the mainstream press's fascination with racializing portrayals of North Main Street's audiences, the Americanization of cinema, the growth of Los Angeles, and the relationship of all of these to the Mexican Revolution. As a result, the Mexican press was not only involved in protesting such disparaging representations on-screen and beyond but also aspired to rehabilitate the image of Main as a bastion of elevated Mexican cultural expression and community. While there is already substantial scholarship on the historical representation of Latina/os in U.S. cinema, less understood are the changing relationships between competing conceptions of urban space, varying perceptions of the city's Mexican presence (as audiences), and the cinematic representation of Mexicans (as textual figures).

In addition to shedding light on localized cultural battles over race, urban space, and cinematic representation, examining Mexican film culture in Los Angeles reveals how Hollywood and Mexican cinema—in the spheres of production, exhibition, and reception—functioned as transnational industries. As perhaps the largest domestic "foreign" audience in the United States, for instance, the city's Mexican population offers insight into the transnational dimension of Hollywood studios' productions and their reception. Here again, the history of Latino representation is inextricable from the simultaneous history of Hollywood's construction of its various audiences. Hollywood's consolidation and international dominance meant that by the early 1920s studios incorporated global appeal and regional censorship concerns into its productions. This process entailed policing representations of specific groups as well as constructing a conception of specific audiences and their tastes for the purposes of marketing. If the greaser and bandido were the products of an industry that initially disregarded the Latin American market, its subsequent desire for that market then affected changing constructions of that audience, prevailing representational conventions, and the responses to both. As I detail in chapter 3, during Hollywood's transition to sound production in the late 1920s and early 1930s, Hollywood included Mexicans within an overarching conception of the coveted Latin American market. In the eyes of Mexican cultural authorities and critics, this produced a generalized notion of the Latin audience that produced a de-Mexicanizing erasure of cultural and linguistic specificity in Spanish-language film. Rather than only talking back to these on-screen representations (which they certainly did), Mexican cultural authorities also launched a sustained critique of the industry's discriminatory hiring practices, arguing for the increased presence of Mexicans as labor and talent to alter the nature of on-screen representations. Through tracing Hollywood's various conceptions of the Mexican via Los Angeles, we can gauge the representational tensions (and contradictions) negotiated by a globally dominant culture industry and the ways in which local audiences worked to transform the images and discourses by which they were positioned.

As the reactions and proposed interventions of Mexican critics in Los Angeles suggest, Mexican immigrants functioned not only as perpetual others against which dominant conceptions of Los Angeles and Hollywood were defined nor only as potential audiences. Rather than only constituting a representational "problem," Mexican immigrants—cultural authorities and journalists in particular—actively participated in the construction of alternative conceptions of Los Angeles and its Mexican presence. Mexican individuals and institutions engaged in practices akin to the "reconstructive spectatorship" that Jacqueline Najuma Stewart has identified during the same period in Chicago, whereby "African Americans used the cinema as a literal and symbolic space in which to rebuild their individual and collective identities in a modern, urban environment."[17]

If Mexican immigrants exerted an impact on the city and its film industry (directly or otherwise), they simultaneously used entertainment culture as an arena through which to forge emerging notions of identity, community, and urban space. With the rise of commercialized leisure and mass culture in the early twentieth century, Mexicans were certainly not alone in sustaining a complex and sometimes ambivalent relationship with this realm of production and consumption.[18] In the case of Mexican America, Douglas Monroy, Vicki L. Ruiz, and George J. Sánchez have all demonstrated how Mexican immigrants often mobilized cultural practices to foster community formation and cultural retention, as younger generations brokered new conceptions of identity in part through various engagements with commercialized leisure.[19] As their work reveals, the relationship to cinema was undeniably colored by factors of generation and gender. These complex relationships with popular culture were also inextricable from the broader construction of a transnational Mexicanidad that occurred through film culture and cultural consumption. Laura Isabel Serna has argued that through the exhibition, reception, and distribution of U.S. cinema in the silent period, "moviegoing and film culture nurtured a sense of what it might mean to be Mexican on both sides of the border."[20] Expanding on this considerable insight to examine these dynamics in the context of Los Angeles—during the silent and sound periods—reveals a cultural environment whose constituent elements were simultaneously local and transnational in nature, both echoing and shaping emerging articulations of identity that also adopted this dual focus.

The particular conception of transnational Mexicanidad as the basis for individual identity and collective formation in Los Angeles was clearly in dialogue with and influenced by discourses of Mexican nationalism emerging from a nation in transition. The substantial exodus of Mexican immigrants to the United States and the socioeconomic disorder spurred by the Mexican Revolution posed challenges to the maintenance of a cohesive national identity. In the aftermath of the revolution, the Mexican State engaged in a multifaceted nation-building project calculated to unite a heterogeneous population divided by region, class, race, and even language. This initiative encompassed everything from the nation's famous mural program to extensive rural education drives. Mexicans in the United States were implicated in this process through the notion of *México de afuera* (Mexico outside of Mexico), which framed the U.S. immigrant population as Mexican nationals temporarily living abroad. More than incorporating these individuals into a preexisting concept of a Greater Mexico that transcended the confines of geopolitical borders, those included in México de afuera also actively contributed to the national project as a work in progress and helped to define the terms of Mexicanidad.

The development of a transnational Mexicanidad through film culture, however, drew more from Mexican nationalism than the intertwined emphases on allegiance to nation, the retention of Spanish, the embrace of common cultural markers coded as traditional, and the resistance to Americanization or assimilation. Mexican nationalism's adamant fixation on these factors often belied the fact that conceptions and constructions of Mexicanidad, as they circulated across borders and through multiple media, were fundamentally transnational in nature. In simple terms, discourses of Mexican nationalism typically adopted a bifurcated address. To an internal audience they stressed collective unification of national community through a cohesive conception of identity, while simultaneously projecting an image of the nation for external consumption as a way of stimulating investment, trade, and tourism.

Typically embracing the already-transnational foundations of Mexican nationalism, critics and cultural authorities responsible for formulating notions of transnational Mexicanidad also adapted its bifurcated address to a Los Angeles context. That is, the array of media and practices within local film culture was often implicitly directed to at least two potential audiences. Focused internally, Mexican cultural authorities strove to bring the working class in line with a prevailing brand of Mexican nationalism. A key component of such efforts in the cultural sphere involved encouraging immigrants to resist Americanization by avoiding certain kinds of leisure while using others as the basis of community formation. Focused externally, these same individuals worked to fashion a notion of Mexicanidad in dialogue with the racial landscape of Los Angeles, where the working class faced discrimination at multiple levels, was forced to operate within localized hierarchies, and competed within a stratified labor market. This effort on the part of journalists and other advocates included an outcry against discrimination and efforts to racially and culturally "elevate" the image of the city's working-class Mexicans.

As was the case with other groups classified as nonwhite in Los Angeles, culture became a venue through which to make a bid for respectability and potentially to transcend the limitations of local racial hierarchies. While the local Filipino press, for instance, exhorted their readership to avoid behavior and leisure options (including gambling establishments) that only reinforced prevalent stereotypes, Japanese theater owners encouraged their clients to engage in consumption habits that corresponded to class-based notions of respectability and hence "project a favorable international image of Japan as a civilized modern nation."[21] On both counts, leisure was connected to how a particular group was represented through particular media (as in, for example, cinematic images) and how members of that group might work against disparaging stereotypes by representing themselves (as audiences) differently to outsiders through acts of cultural consumption. As in these cases, Mexican cultural producers worked to impact mainstream representations of Mexicans both as cinematic characters and as consumers.

As I detail in chapter 2, the efforts of Mexican critics to promote and sustain theatrical production in the 1920s were premised on similar formations of national audience and community through the consumption of "respectable" entertainment that would supposedly transcend divisions of generation and class while mobilizing associations of high culture to elevate the perceived status (racial and otherwise) of immigrants. As a result, theatrical critics advocated the production and consumption of works that could not only transcend class-based notions of taste but that also projected to multiple constituencies a palatable image of Mexicans as both textual characters and audiences with cultivated tastes. As this example suggests, the Mexican immigrant population continually navigated a contested cultural space between dominant perceptions of Mexicans and multifaceted constructions of transnational Mexicanidad. Examining these particular articulations of identity and community allows us to understand the complex relationships between Mexican immigrants and at least two transnational cultural industries, while also accounting for the unique nature of their position as national subjects *and* as foreigners with ambivalent legal and racial status in the United States.

While fostering alternative conceptions of identity specific to Los Angeles, however, Mexican cultural producers and critics did not necessarily generate subversive, oppositional, or radical representations. Key players within this cultural sphere (many of them of the expatriate elite) consistently advocated constructions of Mexican identity and community that in fact frequently betrayed anxiety about the intertwined issues of racial heterogeneity, working-class behavior, immigration patterns, Americanization, and cultural uplift. Indeed, their construction of transnational Mexicanidad often situated working-class Mexicans as a problem, both as textual representations and as a hypothetical audience for downtown entertainment. Borrowing again from Mexican nationalism, these individuals proposed notions of cultural elevation, even superiority, that would work against (or reverse) the position of Mexicans in the city's racial hierarchy, while often disavowing conceptions of the working class conjoined to nonwhiteness and immorality. To this extent, working-class immigrants often functioned again as the other; the construction of transnational Mexicanidad was often implicitly premised on the kind of exclusions undergirding middle-class whiteness. Accordingly, it is impossible to posit sharp distinctions between competing conceptions of Mexicanidad or to simply characterize transnational Mexicanidad as an oppositional stance. Rather, the city's power structure and the immigrant press at times unwittingly adopted parallel, hierarchical conceptions of race, class, cultural production, and urban space.

If elements of Mexican Los Angeles mobilized criticism and cultural production as a way of fashioning transnational notions of identity and community, this conceptualization also informed the exhibition practices and critical reception that accompanied an emerging Mexican cinema in the early 1930s, a national industry that was undeniably transnational at its inception. Following Andrew Higson's foundational proposal that national cinema histories attend to conditions of distribution, exhibition, and reception, my own study of local film culture reveals the intermedial nature of cinema as both institution and experience, as well as various articulations of national expression across these spheres of activity.[22] Considering Mexican cinema along these lines requires departing from a conventional approach that "typically privileges production *as* cinema, neglecting the equally important modalities of distribution and exhibition," as Serna has proposed.[23] From this perspective, Spanish-language press in Los Angeles worked as a discursive site wherein theater publicity, film promotion, and cultural criticism were part of a broader effort to formulate and debate conceptions of Mexicanidad. By the same token, movie theaters constituted the physical sites that hosted the various performances and displays of Mexicanidad that surrounded the films: live theater, musical performance, star appearances, radio broadcasts, theater decor, and other components of exhibition practice. As constitutive elements of this film culture, these all participated and contributed to changing conceptions of identity and community in Mexican Los Angeles.

As did other cultural forms of Mexican cultural production in the postrevolutionary era, Mexican cinema and the discourse surrounding it already assumed the importance of a bifurcated cinematic embrace of nationalism. In the context of Los Angeles, this twin emphasis on internal and external reception positioned Mexican cinema as a force capable of sustaining Mexican community and affecting attitudes, representations, and perceptions of the city's Mexican presence. But while film producers and the cultural critics were generally in agreement about the necessity of aligning Mexican cinema with the broader impulses of cultural nationalism, a decided lack of consensus lingered about what constituted cinematic Mexicanidad.

As I demonstrate in chapter 4, even the film regarded as the epitome of cinematic nationalism, *Allá en el Rancho Grande* (*Over on the Big Ranch*, Fernando de Fuentes, 1936), pioneered conventions that quickly became a matter of contention. Desirée J. Garcia has compellingly argued that the film's success in Los Angeles can be attributed to the fact that it "fostered feelings of nostalgia and longing for *nuestro México* (our Mexico) that, however idealized, served to ease the sense of alienation and isolation experienced by migrants in the United States." As an element of community building aligned with official nationalism, "the film encouraged Mexicans in the U.S. to strengthen their ties to each other and their homeland."[24] Despite its apparent popularity with audiences, however, *Rancho Grande* (and the *comedia ranchera* genre that it spawned) was not uniformly received as a successful expression of nationalism. At issue within critical debates was the other facet of nationalism: the value of the film as public relations for an external audience. The question of whether the genre properly embodied Mexicanidad hinged precisely on its transnational dimensions and whether its particular vision of Mexico perpetuated or refuted existing stereotypes circulating simultaneously in tourist literature, Hollywood films, and fanciful evocations of the folkloric past at local sites like Olvera Street.

Because these two processes—the formulation of transnational Mexicanidad through cinema and as a way of thinking about community—were operating not only parallel to each other but in constant dialogue, each holds the capacity to shed light on the other. In other words, understanding Mexican cinema on these terms reveals it not as a stable set of texts but instead as a discursive category created, adjusted, and sustained through ongoing criticism and debate. This book thus resonates with discursive histories of national cinemas, such as Aaron Gerow's recent study of early cinema in Japan, which "refuses to take borders as given, but considers instead how they are defined and redefined at crucial conjunctures through the words and meanings attached to them."[25] Such an approach to Mexican cinema productively examines the development of this category that does not depend exclusively on cinematic texts (but rather their circulation and reception), while also moving beyond national confines to explore its transnational nature and operation. Conversely then, historical debates about Mexican cinema suggest the stakes of cinematic representation and their relation to emergent terms of identity. Expectations for this cinema in Los Angeles, in keeping with the dual focus of nationalism, included the sustenance of a social and cultural milieu (including movie theaters) and its potential to alter intertwined perceptions of Mexicans as cinematic representations and residents of the city. Again, what makes this film culture Mexican is not a predetermined body of texts, nor a stable set of cultural characteristics, but the ongoing struggle to define Mexican identity and cinema between two nations, a process that is undeniably still under way.

To understand Mexican film culture's relation to conceptions of Los Angeles, formations of identity or community, and the politics of cinematic representation, this book engages a range of textual artifacts, including archival collections, publicity, newspaper criticism, films, trade journals, sociological studies, and serialized novels. Given the focus of this book, however, it necessarily relies on the abundant Spanish-language press coverage of the entertainment landscape in Los Angeles as a primary discursive site. As few archival traces of these theaters remain, such dailies—which include *El Heraldo de México* and *La Opinión*, in addition to other less prominent publications—constitute the most extensive source of information about film culture in Los Angeles. Aside from providing basic information through reviews, theater publicity, and editorials, these papers were at the epicenter of film and theatrical culture, producing reams of cultural criticism. Their staffs also worked as playwrights, organized mutual benefit organizations, and held positions (to a limited extent) in Hollywood. These newspapers were the nexus of a multimedia Mexican cultural scene and as such served as the crux of a middle-class and elite cultural and economic network. Not coincidentally, the analysis of this print culture presented here constitutes one of the most extensive studies of entertainment culture in Los Angeles and of the U.S. Mexican immigrant press to date.

To return to the hypothetical immigrant theatergoer that opened this introduction, it should be apparent that the tensions that structured Los Angeles's Mexican film culture meant that choosing which theater to attend amounted to more than a matter of personal taste or preference for a certain form of entertainment. Rather, the range of options referenced earlier was indicative of the multiple, intertwined dilemmas that confronted Mexican immigrants in the cultural realm before World War II: negotiating competing conceptions of Mexicanidad alternately connected to Mexican nationalism and the local terms of racialization; competing constructions of Mexicanidad generated by two film industries (not to mention other cultural forms); the ambivalent positioning of Mexicans within the urban fabric of downtown; and the ongoing dialogue between these different registers. In reconstructing the experience of cinema in Mexican Los Angeles and the discursive horizons that may have shaped it, however, these working-class immigrants remain a representational and analytical problem of sorts. Namely, although implicitly placed at the center of this book, the relationship they had to these images and discursive formations remains uncertain and, indeed, essentially unknowable. To this extent, *Mexico on Main Street* can ultimately only trace the horizons and expectations that structured this particular experience of cinema in Los Angeles. In the codas that conclude each chapter, I briefly examine the dilemmas that confront any effort to reconstruct the history of a film culture from which the audience is undeniably central yet conspicuously and unavoidably absent.

CHAPTER 1

CONSTRUCTING
MEXICAN LOS ANGELES

COMPETING VISIONS OF AN
IMMIGRANT POPULATION

The transformation of downtown Los Angeles in the twenty-first century has been fundamental and remarkably rapid. While it had experienced periodic bouts of revitalization and development throughout the twentieth century (inevitably fueled by narratives of blighted slums in need of razing), recent development demonstrates a combined emphasis on work, leisure, and residence.[1] In other words, downtown has suddenly emerged as a desirable neighborhood, particularly for the young and upwardly mobile. South Main Street is now lined with wine bars, bistros, art galleries, dog boutiques, and old hotels converted into lofts. This apparently successful overhaul of Main Street is of no small significance; for decades (and despite previous revitalization efforts) it had consistently served as an emblematic point of reference for downtown's decline, an area perpetually in need of "improvement." While renowned during the first half of the century as the epicenter of morally suspect leisure and racial heterogeneity, in more recent decades it had become synonymous with downtown as a haven for drug addicts and the homeless. Just as the centrality of Main Street to downtown's physical and conceptual geography was established with its original designation as Calle Principal during the Spanish colonial period (where it also functioned as the western border of the central Plaza), it has also functioned as both a material and symbolic synecdoche for broader trends in the city. And, as it is currently emblematic of widespread gentrification and the concurrent displacement of poor residents in neighborhoods in and around downtown, conceptions of Main Street in the early twentieth century were likewise tied to narratives of the city's development and its relation to local dynamics of race and class.

In the first decades of the twentieth century, a number of fundamental transformations swept Los Angeles: a tremendous demographic growth (including that of the immigrant and African American populations), accelerated industrialization, and the consequent transformation and expansion of urban space. These developments coincided with the widespread explosion of commercialized leisure nationwide so that changes in the urban fabric of Los Angeles were shaped by and inextricable from the rise of the feature film and big-time vaudeville, the consolidation of Hollywood, and a concurrent expansion of ethnic entertainment and press cultures. Because Mexicans, as the largest immigrant population, were clearly a crucial component of these processes, multiple forces within the city struggled to define or comprehend the exact nature of their presence relative to these rapid developments. All these transformations were interdependent to varying degrees and generated an ongoing dialogue across multiple institutions and media; to grasp the varying constructions of Mexicanidad they generated during this period, none of them can be held in isolation. Instead, competing characterizations of Mexican immigrants relied precisely on the ways in which discursive formations were mobilized and orchestrated between these spheres of activity. Just as important, these formations were inextricable from the broader representation of Los Angeles and its residents by multiple parties.

During the 1910s we can identify at least two distinct conceptualizations of the Mexican presence downtown. The geography of cultural production and consumption in this area was central to both. Indeed, this chapter serves as an introduction to the key forces responsible for the generation of these constructions of Mexicanidad in Los Angeles and the central role that Spanish-language newspapers will occupy in Mexican cinema culture for decades to come. On the one hand, mainstream cinema, exhibition practice, press accounts, and reform efforts collaborated indirectly to frame the population as threatening, pathological, and racially inferior. These notions were intimately tied to representations of the immigrant district surrounding North Main, and the questionable nature of the leisure available there. On the other, elements of the Mexican expatriate community alternately countered such conceptions through a concurrent yet divergent discourse that occurred on multiple fronts, including theatrical production, cultural criticism, and conceptions of urban space. This construction of Mexican Los Angeles included a reframing of North Main as respectable through cultural elevation and nationalistic consumption.

While ostensibly at odds with each other, these representational regimes framed Mexicans through prevailing notions of race, class, and economic expediency. On both counts, working-class Mexicans posited a special problem. For the Euro-American power structure, they threatened to undermine the well-being of the burgeoning metropolis. For the Mexican elite and middle class that operated local newspapers and other institutions, the working-class population was in constant need of elevation as consumers, as Mexican citizens, *and* as textual representations in the name of forming and projecting a morally sound and unified Mexican community within the United States. Ultimately, cultural production and criticism would serve as arenas through which these individuals crafted a transnational Mexicanidad in conversation with Mexican nationalism and local dynamics of race and class.

From Main to Broadway: Mapping Mexicans Downtown

The expansion of Mexican-oriented commercial entertainment downtown coincided with the wide-ranging transformation of Los Angeles at the beginning of the twentieth century. The transition was indeed drastic and surprisingly swift in terms of population alone. Los Angeles grew from a small city of 100,000 in 1900 (and 350,000 in 1910) to a sprawling modern metropolis of more than one million by 1930. The Mexican population itself would approach 100,000 by 1930.[2] In fact, the number of Mexicans residing in the city during this period grew approximately 1,000 percent between 1900 and 1920, compared to 500 percent for the overall population.[3] For mainstream journalists, reformers, and social science researchers, the area along the North Main Street district in particular became an important site through which the multiple implications of these shifts and their interdependence might be understood. Such individuals situated the consumption habits of the multiethnic population along this corridor to represent the so-called Mexican problem in a way that intersected with broader concerns about the impact of commercialized entertainment. In turn, the perception of these venues and their audiences became central to articulating the coincidence between urban development, demographic shifts, and the transformation of leisure in Los Angeles (including the rise of Hollywood). Mexicans constituted a key element of this entertainment landscape, while the construction of them as an immigrant audience played a central role in the conceptual and physical remapping of a rapidly growing downtown in the 1910s. Not coincidentally, visual conceptions of Mexicans circulating in Hollywood films of the period reinforced these ideas and were also instrumental to the establishment of the film industry as a "respectable" enterprise.

Since the annexation of California to the United States in 1848, immigration from Mexico had remained relatively constant through the remainder of the nineteenth century, although the Mexican descent population was no longer the center of civic or political power as it had been during the Spanish and Mexican periods. The late nineteenth and early twentieth century, however, witnessed a substantial influx of Mexican immigration to Southern California, a phenomenon spurred by the push of land policy and revolutionary violence in Mexico and the pull of labor shortages occasioned by the explosive expansion of industrial agriculture in the southwestern United States.[4] During the regime of dictator Porfirio Díaz during the late nineteenth century, many rural Mexicans had been forced off their land by speculators or had their ancestral or communal holdings expropriated and sold to large agricultural interests (many of them owned by foreign investors). Those Mexicans seeking work in the country's industrializing economy often faced continual periods of unemployment and inflation.[5] While this spurred an initial wave of immigration to the United States, the Mexican Revolution that began in 1910 added considerably to the number of migrants coming from Mexico. While a full account of the details and vicissitudes of this multifaction civil war lies beyond the scope of this project, it is sufficient to note that an estimated 10 percent of the nation's population left Mexico during this period as a result of the revolution's devastating economic and social impact. Although the conflict technically ended in 1917 with the signing of a new constitution, violence and economic instability persisted through the 1920s, ensuring a steady influx of Mexican immigrants to Los Angeles and other destinations within the United States.

If these factors account for the pushing of Mexicans into the United States, immigrants were also drawn by the expansion of industrial agriculture, urban industry, railroad lines, and mining in the Southwest, and the reliance of these on a cheap and flexible labor pool. Mexican immigrants emerged as the preferred labor force in these industries by the early twentieth century, as passage of the Chinese Exclusion Act of 1882 had curtailed the availability of Chinese workers. A subsequent influx of Japanese laborers had likewise been all but halted by Theodore Roosevelt's Gentlemen's Agreement with Japan in 1907. Not only did railroad connections with Mexico facilitate the arrival of a new supply of cheap labor from south of the border, but the notion that Mexican labor was temporary (an idea promoted primarily by proagricultural interests) was intended to allay nativist anxiety about the possibility of permanent Mexican population settling in the United States. Because Los Angeles was conveniently located in proximity to multiple areas of agricultural activity and became a recruiting center for railroad work, Mexican immigrants were drawn to the burgeoning metropolis, at least as a place to secure employment. As the region and its agricultural and industrial productivity grew (partially as a result of the demands of World War I), the city became an even more attractive destination for these immigrants.

From the last years of the nineteenth century through the second decade of the twentieth, a number of areas located in downtown Los Angeles served primarily as spaces of transition for recent arrivals seeking employment that was often itinerant and temporary in nature. In particular, the central Plaza area (the site of the original Spanish settlement) and Sonoratown (or Little Mexico) neighborhood to the north of downtown became residential epicenters for the Mexican immigrant population, many of them single men. More permanent settlement was initially hampered by low wages and geographic segregation that restricted the range of housing options available to Mexican immigrants and because many of them harbored the intention of eventually returning to Mexico. Significantly, Mexicans were part of a surprisingly multiethnic population that settled in and around the Plaza during this period. In fact, this area provided residence to a working class composed of approximately twenty ethnic groups, including Italians, Chinese, Japanese, Jews, Molokan Russians, and African Americans.

Los Angeles at the turn of the century was a modestly sized city of a hundred thousand occupying roughly one hundred square miles that had yet to expand into the sprawling city of suburban enclaves designed around automobile traffic. As Ricardo Romo notes, "the residents of Los Angeles at the close of the century still clustered together in what might be called a 'walking city' environment" that gave "Angelenos ample opportunity to interact and work together, despite racial and class differences."[6] Indeed, Mexican immigrant enclaves were initially located in close proximity to the city's economic, commercial, and civic centers located on Main and Spring (particularly near First), in the immediate vicinity of the original Plaza. By the 1910s and 1920s a number of ethnic districts would emerge in concert with the broader growth of the city.

The dynamics of urban space downtown would begin to change by the mid-1910s, however, as the city's population grew rapidly and the direction of development (particularly by increasing suburbanization) placed greater physical and discursive distance between immigrants and native-born Euro-American populations arriving in droves from other parts of the United States. As Mark Wild has argued, real estate developers, boosters, and city officials during this period perpetuated these distinctions in the interest of promoting a vision of Los Angeles that contrasted with the congestion and ethnic heterogeneity of East Coast cities (despite the fact that the city had the largest nonwhite population outside of Baltimore).[7] Josh Sides has explained spatial dynamics of race that increasingly obtained as the city grew: "Los Angeles was clearly divided by a color line, but on one side of that line was a white (and largely Protestant) population while on the other was a large and vibrant patchwork of races and ethnicities."[8] One of the key factors that facilitated these distinctions was the increase of new civic and private construction away from the original center of the city and farther south along Broadway by the early twentieth century. Initiating this shift, a new city hall building was constructed in the 1880s between Second and Third on Broadway, and the Mason Opera House opened in 1903 at 127 South Broadway. Thus despite the fact that Broadway (particularly south of Third) was primarily residential before the 1890s, it quickly emerged as the main center of commerce and entertainment in downtown Los Angeles by the 1910s, and this trend would only accelerate in the following decade.

The direction of this development coincided with the emerging dominance of the feature film and the concerted efforts of exhibitors and producers alike to convert cinema into a respectable medium suitable for white middle-class audiences. In terms of exhibition, the career of Thomas Lincoln Tally was typical in its conjoining of notions of respectability with location. After opening the Electric Theater nickelodeon in 1902 at 212 North Main near the Plaza in 1902 (which many regard as the first dedicated motion picture venue in the country), he opened Tally's Broadway along the Broadway corridor by 1905, which he would soon move even farther south (on Broadway between Eighth and Ninth) by 1909.[9] From this point forward, the Electric (under new management) would be operated as the Teatro Eléctrico and attract a Mexican immigrant audience.[10] This change in location for Tally accompanied a change in format and conceptions of audience composition, from the working-class, immigrant associations of nickelodeons to the middle-class aspirations of feature films (often advertised as high quality "photoplays") and big-time vaudeville. Likewise, William H. Clune closed his first theater on Fifth and Main and inaugurated Clune's Broadway in 1910, which one contemporary commentator described as "one of the finest motion picture houses on the West Coast."[11] John A. Quinn's Colonial Theater (opened in 1912) "presented six acts of vaudeville, first-run movies and augmented orchestra," a programming policy approximating the other major theaters along Broadway.[12] Thus within less than ten years, the venues operated by Tally, Clune, and Quinn had distanced themselves spatially and in terms of presentation from their former locations along Main Street (see fig. 1).

The notion of cultural elevation that accompanied this transitional era in cinema was thus also mapped on to emerging conceptions of urban space downtown and proved inextricable from concurrent class-based and racial and ethnic hierarchies. As a result of this new construction and development, the blocks near North Main and Spring, once central to the commercial and entertainment landscape of downtown, subsequently flourished as a site of businesses and institutions geared toward immigrant populations. This demographic and spatial transition occurred at a remarkable pace. For example, as one study claimed about the former "centrality" of Main Street, "during the period from 1878 to 1900, if one wished to establish business or social prestige it was necessary to have either residence or business quarters in the Baker Block" (at 346 North Main).[13] Given the direction of development by 1915, however, the Baker Block had irrevocably lost this reputation and status among the Euro-American population and was home instead to a number of Mexican-oriented institutions, including *El Heraldo de México* newspaper and the San Antonio–based Mayo y Compañía department store (see fig. 2). This trend also facilitated a more decisive segregation of entertainment downtown, including the emergence and expansion of immigrant- and Mexican-oriented entertainment venues (including the establishment of the Teatro Plaza in 1911, the Teatro Metropolitan in 1911, and the Teatro Hidalgo in 1912 on North Main).[14] Archival photographs of the area surrounding Grand Opera House at 110 South Main clearly demonstrate the way this area transformed into a Mexican-oriented commercial and entertainment district (see figs. 3 and 4). Surrounding the Grand here are multiple businesses addressing a Spanish-speaking clientele: a tailor, a dentist, and a notary public. In fact, by the 1920s the Grand would be rechristened the Teatro México to reflect the entertainment it offered and audiences it hoped to attract.

In the eyes of many Angelenos, the multitude of businesses and amusements serving a Mexican constituency near the Plaza epitomized an area in definitive "decline," as they were often housed in buildings abandoned by previous

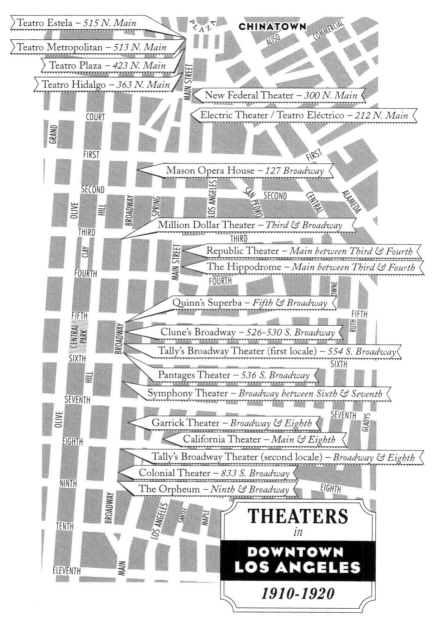

Teatro Estela – *515 N. Main*
Teatro Metropolitan – *513 N. Main*
Teatro Plaza – *423 N. Main*
Teatro Hidalgo – *363 N. Main*

PLAZA

CHINATOWN

ALISO

COMMERCIAL

New Federal Theater – *300 N. Main*
Electric Theater / Teatro Eléctrico – *212 N. Main*

MAIN STREET

COURT

GRAND

FIRST

FIRST

Mason Opera House – *127 Broadway*

SECOND

OLIVE

HILL

BROADWAY

SPRING

LOS ANGELES

SAN PEDRO

SECOND

CENTRAL

ALAMEDA

Million Dollar Theater – *Third & Broadway*

THIRD

THIRD

CLAY

MAIN STREET

Republic Theater – *Main between Third & Fourth*
The Hippodrome – *Main between Third & Fourth*

FOURTH

FOURTH

TOWNE

Quinn's Superba – *Fifth & Broadway*

FIFTH

CENTRAL PARK

BROADWAY

FIFTH

RUTH

Clune's Broadway – *526-530 S. Broadway*
Tally's Broadway Theater (first locale) – *554 S. Broadway*

SIXTH

SIXTH

HILL

Pantages Theater – *536 S. Broadway*
Symphony Theater – *Broadway between Sixth & Seventh*

SEVENTH

Garrick Theater – *Broadway & Eighth*

SEVENTH

GLADYS

OLIVE

California Theater – *Main & Eighth*

EIGHTH

Tally's Broadway Theater (second locale) – *Broadway & Eighth*
Colonial Theater – *833 S. Broadway*

NINTH

BROADWAY

The Orpheum – *Ninth & Broadway*

EIGHTH

THEATERS
in
DOWNTOWN
LOS ANGELES
1910-1920

TENTH

LOS ANGELES

SANTEE

MAPLE

ELEVENTH

MAIN

Fig. 1. Map of major vaudeville and movie theaters in downtown Los Angeles, 1910–1920. Designed by Daniel González.

Fig. 2. The Baker Block on North Main, ca. 1920. At this time it housed the offices of the newspaper *El Heraldo de México*, the Liga Protectora Mexicana, two dentists' offices, and the Mayo y Compañía department store. Los Angeles Public Library Photograph Collection.

occupants in favor of the Broadway district. As one historical account suggests, it was at this point that the Plaza area and its theaters confirmed to many that "the Plaza area was no longer the commercial or social center of the city."[15] By the early 1910s multiple nickelodeons, dance halls, burlesque houses, brothels, saloons, and other supposedly "bawdy entertainments" serving a heterogeneous population of laborers provided evidence of a clear division of urban space that marked differences of race and class.[16] The mainstream press and social science literature of the period increasingly framed Main Street as Broadway's unseemly other, generating a discourse in which notions of race, class, and taste converged to characterize an emergent Broadway corridor as a locus of respectable entertainment suitable for middle-class whites. Whether pathologizing Mexicans and other immigrants or arguing for their protection, such entities referred to their presence and behavior to map emerging notions of cultural distinction. This constituted a key element of an analogous reformist discourse that at the turn of the century had situated predominantly Mexican Sonoratown "as a spatial and racial category, a counterimage to an emerging 'progressive' Anglo city."[17]

Figs. 3 and 4. These two photos indicate the kind of transformations that occurred along Main Street during the first decades of the twentieth century. Tom B'hend and Preston Kaufmann Collection, Margaret Herrick Library, Academy of Motion Picture Arts and Sciences.

As in other urban areas experiencing a convergence of dramatic population growth, industrialization, and immigration, these transformations in Los Angeles gave rise to a number of reform initiatives in the early twentieth century. During this period, cultural elites and adherents of the reform movement across the country expressed a general anxiety about commercialized leisure, constituting one element of a broader concern for immigrants and their impact that encompassed a range of issues: Americanization, education, labor practices, gender norms, sexual behavior, alcohol consumption, and domestic habits. As perhaps the most prominent of these reformers, Jane Addams, and her Hull House organization in Chicago, believed that Americanization through Victorian values was central to equipping immigrant families to function properly in an industrialized society.[18] She and others regarded commercialized leisure as an impediment to this process and a threat to the moral fiber of immigrant communities. Reformers in urban environments across the country regularly monitored dance halls, amusement parks, nickelodeons, vaudeville theaters, and other amusements patronized by immigrant youth.[19] They often regarded cinema in particular as a potential corrupter of immigrant youth and, alternatively, as a force for proper Americanization, if produced according to the strictures of Anglo Saxon Protestant morality. Pressure from reformers resulted in the establishment of the National Board of Censorship in 1909, and the first proposals for a Federal Motion Picture Commission in 1914, a body that would regulate cinematic content on a national level.[20]

In Los Angeles, a specific brand of reformist discourse and policy emerged in response to the contours of the city's entertainment landscape and its multiethnic population, including Mexican immigrants. As in other cities like Chicago and New York, the early years of the twentieth century witnessed calls to regulate amusement venues on the part of reformers, police officers, and local newspapers (including the *Los Angeles Times* and the *Los Angeles Express*). Adopting what Jan Olsson has characterized as the "school-of-crime discourse," these institutions accused vaudeville theaters and cinemas of providing instruction in criminal behavior and promiscuity to impressionable audiences, through the content of their actual presentations and street advertisements. Those spectators seen as particularly impressionable in this context included children and immigrants (Asians and Mexicans in particular).[21] This coincided with a broader conception and representation of cinema audiences in the early twentieth century. Drawing on works in crowd psychology, as Richard Butsch points out, individuals from reformers to psychologist-cum–film theorist Hugo Munsterberg "considered women, lower classes, and certain races to be more susceptible" to the influence of cinema.[22] In Los Angeles this conception of audiences on the part of multiple parties spurred regulatory measures that mirrored those in other urban centers: the prohibition of unaccompanied minors from theaters, the institution in 1911 of a Board of Film Censors, a 1911 city ordinance that established interior lighting requirements for theater auditoriums, and the hiring of the policewomen charged particularly with the "supervision of young girls' amusement habits."[23]

During this period, the behavior of immigrant cinema audiences held a particular ethnographic fascination for the local press that embraced this reformist impulse, echoing the earlier "tourist-cum-slumming" literature produced by organizations like the Los Angeles Settlement Association.[24] Daily newspapers during this period were indeed engaged in a concerted, ongoing effort to represent the city's immigrant population and their environs. As Phoebe Kropp has noted about this extensive textual production, "when the plaza area, a multiethnic immigrant neighborhood, found mention in the *Los Angeles Times*, it was as a vice or health problem, and it lay outside the everyday paths of Anglo residents."[25] In fact, a number of Los Angeles newspapers from 1907 to the mid-1910s conducted multiple investigations of the North Main district and its centers of amusements in particular, generating an identifiable "Main Street discourse," according to Olsson. From the perspective of these articles, "Main Street's daily display of carnivalesque business hoaxes and cheap entertainment outlets attracted audience groups framed by the city reporters as primitive and child-like in their responses."[26] A 1915 *Los Angeles Times* article by Henry Christeen Warnack, for instance, painted a lurid portrait of the area for an ostensibly Euro-American readership, describing a district of "Cherokee gypsy fortune telling booths and of shooting galleries, with pretty, dark girls who will take you on for a match . . . the Main Street of electric organs and post card galleries, the Main Street of the Century, the Hippodrome, and a hundred lesser amusements." Significantly, Warnack also emphasized the multiethnic audience drawn to these attractions (where the "taste of the crowds is bloodthirsty and melodrama reigns supreme"):

> If you will go down to the Plaza Theater you will find yourself surrounded by the representatives of every nation, if not of every station. It will be too dark to tell whether your neighbor in the next seat is Mexican, Hindu or Chinese, but he is one or the other, and he might be a little bit of all three, not that I advocate amalgamation, merely because for the minute I am forced to reflect a little of the color of an amalgamated thoroughfare.[27]

Although such discourses may not have been directly linked to regulation efforts, its consistent mobilization of racial stereotypes did serve to create a contrast with the "sophisticated" entertainment and spectatorship norms in more "respectable" venues in the burgeoning South Broadway district. An illustration that accompanies one such article by Harry C. Carr, for instance, makes a number of these associations apparent. The ethnically heterogeneous Plaza audience in figure 5 is cramped together in an apparently erratic and potentially uncomfortable arrangement, responding openly to the entertainment with laughter. A prominent sign behind them demonstrates the necessity of policing audience behavior in such a venue, reminding patrons in Spanish to remove their hats and to refrain

Fig. 5. A cartoon illustrating an article by Harry C. Carr. *Los Angeles Times*, October 13, 1907.

from smoking and cursing. The drawing also insinuates that, while supposedly unruly and in need of instruction, the clientele and these venues are unsanitary by characterizing a disproportionately large flea as a "regular attendant." While succinctly visualizing the overlapping concerns of the press and reformers relative to this immigrant population, these patrons are placed in direct contrast to a more subdued, orderly, and restrained white audience, whose posture, attire, and decorum demonstrate that "it is different uptown."[28] Another cartoon printed in the *Los Angeles Record* likewise provides a caricature of the multiethnic habitués of Main Street, reiterating racialized divisions of space (see fig. 6). The nature of the diverse Saturday night crowd here is made explicit through the inclusion of a contrasting image, that of a woman representative of mission workers, who are "about the only white people in evidence."[29] As in the previous cartoon, a throng

Fig. 6. A cartoon typical of those that accompanied articles about Main Street and its entertainment options. *Los Angeles Record*, February 25, 1913.

of Asian and Mexican immigrants are represented as stereotypical caricatures and segregated visually from representatives of respectable whiteness. In this instance, the border drawn around the mission worker not only marks racial distinction but also parallels the discursive maneuvers that mapped a strict division of race, taste, and propriety between Main and Broadway.

As this illustration indicates, reformers from missionaries to sociologists expressed anxieties about the nature of cheap amusements near the Plaza. The rhetoric of their accounts frequently coincided with that of journalists to mark similar spatial distinctions. Perhaps the most detailed documentation of the entertainments patronized by Mexicans in downtown Los Angeles before 1920 is provided by the 1914 thesis of University of Southern California sociology student William Wilson McEuen, titled "A Survey of the Mexicans in Los Angeles." This thesis was among the many studies of the Mexican population in Los Angeles conducted from the 1910s through the 1930s, a trend initiated with the appointment of University of Chicago–trained Emory S. Bogardus as the chair of sociology in 1911. Situating themselves as activists and social reformers, Bogardus and his students produced an impressively extensive body of scholarly work that led the "efforts to provide intellectual justification for Americanization" programs during the period. As George J. Sánchez points out, much of this scholarship adopted a "heavily moralistic impetus which had no qualms about mixing Protestant sensibilities, academic research, and public policy."[30]

Typical of such studies, McEuen conducted a detailed survey of housing types and conditions in the Los Angeles area, while also offering a moralizing overview of the leisure options available on North Main Street near the central Plaza. Sketching a portrait of a vibrant entertainment district, McEuen viewed its many establishments through a lens that highlighted their potentially deleterious effects, describing pool halls where "the air is filled with tobacco smoke, vile and obscene talk is prevalent . . . the whole atmosphere is unwholesome and destructive" and denouncing penny arcades that are "cheap and vulgar in the extreme." Within his overview of commercialized leisure, McEuen dedicates the most extensive attention to five theaters along this corridor, all of which had a Mexican descent patronage that exceeded 50 percent and combined live performances with film exhibition: the Hidalgo, the Metropolitan, the Electric (the venue formerly operated by Tally), the Plaza, and the New Federal (see fig. 7). He evaluated each venue on the basis of its "social" and "art" value. Supplementing these measurements with commentary, the author further notes that "films shown in the theaters of the Mexican district, especially along North Main Street, are melodramatic and exciting in the extreme and not infrequently suggestive and more or less immoral," that the advertisements for these venues are generally "lurid and disgusting," and that much of the vaudeville presented is "vile and objectionable."[31]

Fig. 7. An exterior view of the Teatro Hidalgo on North Main. Los Angeles Public Library Photograph Collection.

The assessments of McEuen and other reformers are indicative of the way that Main Street entertainment and its patrons became a key optic through which to understand the relationship between demographic, spatial, and cultural transformations occurring in Los Angeles during the period. Journalists, reformers, and city officials alike aligned the working-class, immigrant population of downtown with disreputable and even potentially dangerous forms of entertainment. If such formulations served to uphold and reinforce the respectability of Broadway, they also rhetorically segregated the Mexican population from the exhibition of the feature-length film, high-class vaudeville and well-appointed movie palaces. As Charles Ramírez Berg has argued, "the Mexican community was marginalized geographically, socially, and economically from Anglo Los Angeles and the burgeoning filmmaking community," an exclusion that exacerbated the industry's tendency to portray "most Mexicans as social, class, cultural, and racial Others."[32] If urban development restricted the access to film industry employment and potentially impacted on-screen representations, as Ramírez Berg contends, the impositions of class-based and racial hierarchies on the entertainment landscape of downtown Los Angeles exerted an analogous impact and generated its own representations. The distinction between Broadway and Main obviously drew on and reinforced notions of Mexicans' racial inferiority while using representations of them as audiences as a way of marking out respectable, middle-class whiteness.

FROM THE AUDIENCE TO THE SCREEN: MEXICANS AND
THE AMERICANIZATION OF U.S. CINEMA

Hollywood's cinematic projection of racial hierarchy during the 1910s relied precisely on such notions of difference, implicitly distancing Mexicans and undesirable others from the conception of its cinema as respectable, American entertainment. The intentional Americanization of cinema by film studios during this transitional period was motivated by a number of interrelated impulses: efforts of the nascent film industry to drive foreign competitors out of the domestic market, the related development of American subjects (like Westerns) that would distinguish U.S. production from foreign cinema, a concerted effort to attract white, middle-class audiences, and the broader orientation of cultural production toward the articulation of a unified Americanism in the face of immigration and World War I. Giorgio Bertellini has compellingly argued that during this period "the film industry's aspiration for the widest popular appeal" inspired the production of films that avoided "alienating either its immigrant or middle-class audiences" and "engaged in the 'realistic' and universalist representation of racial and cultural diversity."[33]

While Italians (per Bertellini) and other groups may have been at least partially incorporated into Hollywood's formulation of American identity, Mexicans remained decisively outside this construction. As Daniel Bernardi has argued, although the industry "attempted to 'upgrade' the actual décor and safety of movie houses as well as 'uplift' the audience to a respectable, more bourgeois level" through the monitoring of content and "'vulgar' representations," it nonetheless remained acceptable "to depict non-whites as bloodthirsty or noble-yet-inferior savages, or to consistently show them as devious wanton threats to white society, white families, and white women."[34] One could push this logic even further: the simultaneous uplift and Americanization of the U.S. film industry actually relied on such representations, inside the theater and out. If images of Mexico and its residents served to bolster conceptions of respectable whiteness and American values on-screen, their positioning within the entertainment landscape of Los Angeles further reinforced these notions. The representations of Mexicans as targets of reform, as subjects of Hollywood film, and as cinema audiences thus became intimately interrelated and perhaps even mutually dependent.

On-screen images thus explicitly resonated with offscreen mechanisms and representations that othered Mexicans in the context of Los Angeles. In particular, the proliferation of greaser and bandido characters in Western films framed Mexicans in the following terms (per Ramírez Berg): "dirty and unkempt, usually displaying an unshaven face, missing teeth, and disheveled, oily hair. Scars and scowls complete the easily recognizable image. Behaviorally, he is vicious, cruel, treacherous, shifty and dishonest; psychologically, he is irrational, overly emotional, and quick to resort to violence."[35] Western films including *Greaser's Gauntlet* (D. W. Griffith, 1908), *The Rattlesnake* (Romaine Fielding, 1913), *Tony the Greaser* (Rollin S. Sturgeon, 1914), *Bronco Billy and the Greaser* (Gilbert M. "Broncho Billy" Anderson, 1914), and *Broncho Billy's Greaser Deputy* (Gilbert M. "Broncho Billy" Anderson, 1915) shared a set of narrative and visual conventions that constructed a particular conception of Mexicans across texts.[36] In *Broncho Billy and the Greaser*, for instance, the titular "greaser" (listed as the "Half-breed" in the opening credits) embodies many of the prevalent qualities of this stereotype: he is portrayed by a Euro-American actor (Lee Willard) wearing dark makeup, he makes unwelcome advances toward the hero's erstwhile love interest, he exhibits a proclivity toward underhanded violence (and knives), he drinks liquor constantly, and, perhaps most important, he is easily dispatched by the white hero.

What proved so obviously objectionable about these representations, as scholars like Ramírez-Berg have pointed out, was the consistent characterization of Mexicans as relentlessly violent, sexually aggressive, and inept. Furthermore, these qualities were inherently linked to notions of racial inferiority vis-à-vis exemplary specimens of "all-American," Anglo Saxon manhood (like Western stars Broncho Billy or William S. Hart).[37] Beginning with the dime novels and conquest fiction of the nineteenth century, greasers or bandidos were identified by their nation of origin and racial mixture. As Arthur G. Petit has noted, such literature refers to such characters as "greasers, Mexes, Mexikins, yallers, [half] breeds, mongrels, and niggers," whose skin tones were alternately described as "dusky, dingy, sooty, swarthy, sallow, inky, pitchy, and greasy" and who were typically representatives of the lower class.[38] Not coincidentally, the racial conception of Mexicans (and workers in particular) through the pseudoscience of eugenics hinged precisely on the problem of racial mixture they embodied. As Ramón Gutiérrez has noted, "in the racialist science of the late nineteenth century half-breeds were believed to inherit all the negative cultural traits of the races they carried in their blood. From such polluted blood, clearly only criminals, imbeciles, heathens, and degenerates could result."[39] The legacy of representations informed by such ideas obviously carried over into cinema (often visualized through "brownface" makeup), as the greaser cycle demonstrates. Reformers in Los Angeles also made distinctions between California's original "Spanish" settlers and recent immigrants that they regarded as "Aztec Indian" or "Mexican half-breed."[40]

The widespread visibility of such images was a product of the Americanization of cinema in the 1910s (often through the Western genre) and the simultaneous obsession with and anxiety about the Mexican Revolution (1910–1920). The mainstream media thus slightly adjusted and updated Mexican stereotypes of the nineteenth century to address this conflict. In essence, the greaser, bandido, and revolutionary quickly became interchangeable terms, particularly in cinema. The general public in the United States demonstrated an apparently insatiable fascination with events in Mexico, often accompanied by concerns about revolutionary violence spilling over the border and reports of insurrectionist violence in Texas.[41] A range of media responded to simultaneously create and fulfill this demand: William Randolph Hearst's yellow journalism stoked hysteria about the conflict; Mutual Film Company produced *The Life of General Villa* (Christy Cabanne, 1914), with Villa himself placed under exclusive contract; multiple film companies released newsreels that covered the conflict; and photographers marketed picture postcards of the revolution's major figures and battles.[42] The first years of the conflict coincided with the onset of newsreel production by multiple studios, the popularity of the Western and the transition to the feature film.[43] Within this representational economy, the victory of the "all-American" over the inferior "half-breed" acquired an additional allegorical dimension informed by the potential role of the United States in the conflict.

Not coincidentally—returning to the presence of Mexicans in Los Angeles—widespread media coverage of the revolution also shaped notions of public space in downtown and the Plaza in particular. Mexican labor and political activism, associated in particular with the radical Industrial Workers of the World (IWW) and the Partido Liberal Mexicano (PLM) led by the exiled Flores Magón brothers, simultaneously stoked fear about labor radicalism and the revolution crossing the border into Los Angeles.[44] As a space of congregation for a heterogeneous working class, "the Plaza was a central meeting place for various working-class social and political movements."[45] Its characterization as an incubator for disease and immorality thus converged with anxiety stoked by the "Brown Scare" and its potential impact on the city's reputation as a white spot free of labor strife and ethnic heterogeneity. Publishers of the *Los Angeles Times*, including Harrison Gray Otis, held extensive investments in Mexico (the Mexican government had granted him 200,000 acres in 1908 alone).[46] Otis was also a member of a corporation, along with *Los Angeles Herald* publisher Thomas E. Gibbon, which controlled more than 850,000 acres of Mexico. Notoriously, Hearst (who owned the *Los Angeles Examiner*) had land holdings south of the border comparable to the size of Vermont.[47] These papers' representation of the revolution and its manifestations in Los Angeles coincided predictably with the broader discursive formations and representational conventions of the period that vilified Mexicans.

At key moments, the problematic nature of popular amusements downtown thus acquired a political valence in journalistic accounts that matched their supposed lack of hygiene and morality. In the aftermath of the so-called Christmas Day Riot that erupted between members of the IWW and the police in 1913, for instance, the LAPD raided "the many restaurants, bars, pool halls, penny arcades, and theaters along North Main" in search of immigrant insurrectionists.[48] As such instances make apparent, the representation of this space from nativist conceptions of race converged with Hollywood production and the language deployed by reformers, journalists, and public health officials in the city. Together, these apparently disparate spheres of activity generated a multifaceted yet rather consistent representational regime across institutions and media, the product of material connections and mutual interests.

To this extent, mainstream journalism served as a nexus where interests of newspapers and Hollywood converged *and* where explicit connections emerged between the agenda of local boosters like Otis and the "slum clearance" efforts spearheaded by real estate interests and reformists alike. The patent racism of journalistic accounts had broader implications than "offer[ing] ethnographic excitement to readers," as Olsson has argued.[49] Notably, they consistently support the characterization of this area as problematic in racial terms, hopelessly heterogeneous in its nonwhiteness and a danger to the health of the city (in a literal and figurative sense). Furthermore, as Natalia Molina has pointed out, the invariable characterization of Mexican and Japanese immigrants as ignorant, unsanitary, and immoral shaped city policy, while also serving to situate these groups within a regionally specific racial hierarchy.[50] Quite expediently, it also framed this part of downtown as ripe for potential redevelopment, providing apparent justification for concomitant displacement of residents that would occur during future phases of civic development. Speaking of the mobilization of the city's "*dark* side" as a key component of the Los Angeles "downtown fable," Norman M. Klein has argued that these constructions have historically served an identifiable function: "the ironic genius of social imaginaries as cities, either of the sunshine variety or the shady: they always wind up selling products, in a culture well adapted to promotion."[51] As will be the case for the remainder of the twentieth century, the product in question is Los Angeles itself as both an investment opportunity and tourist destination. Significantly, this expedient, overdetermined othering of Mexicans within such an economically expedient mythology—whether on-screen or off—generated a multifaceted response and counterrepresentations on the part of Mexican elites in the city.

REMAPPING MAIN STREET: CRITICAL DISCOURSE AND ALTERNATIVE CONSTRUCTIONS OF MEXICANIDAD

As did mainstream press culture, the Mexican immigrant press in Los Angeles served as a nexus of convergence between the interests and operations of multiple entities: Mexican-owned businesses, local theaters, cultural criticism, and social or political organizations geared toward immigrants. This press culture thus facilitated the sustenance of social and economic networks sustained primarily by the elite and middle class, while involving the generation of a counterdiscourse. The Spanish-language press of Los Angeles was in fact perhaps *the* key institution through which mainstream representations of Mexicans were regularly contested and through which an alternative imagining of Mexican Los Angeles emerged as a concerted undertaking. As documents of Mexican entertainment culture in Los Angeles, publications like the daily *El Heraldo de México* (1915–1929) reveal the contours of a Mexican entertainment culture that was inextricable from a number of overlapping and intersecting spheres of activity. As with concurrent discourses generated by dominant institutions, battles over representation occurred here on multiple fronts. Indeed, the Mexican-oriented entertainment landscape (and the criticism attending it) became a key optic through which a particular class of journalists and cultural authorities imagined Mexican identity and community outside of the United States. In particular, these individuals worked to craft an implicitly transnational conception of Mexicanidad that connected to Mexican nationalism and served to contest the place of immigrants within the local racial order.

Newspapers and other publications targeting the Mexican population of the Southwest flourished throughout the nineteenth century. The mass immigration of the early twentieth century, however, spawned a new generation of publications addressing Mexican nationals that would presumably return to their homeland when revolutionary violence subsided. As Nicolás Kanellos has argued, the Spanish-language press in the United States, particularly during the first decades of the twentieth century, promoted the notion of a México de afuera, encouraging readers to "maintain the Spanish language, keep the Catholic faith, and insulate their children from what community leaders perceived as low moral standards practiced by Anglo-Americans," combining this with the defense of the civil rights of the immigrant population.[52] As George J. Sánchez has pointed out, these papers were part of an orchestrated "Mexicanizing" campaign intended to counter Americanization efforts on the part of reformers and others, one that emphasized the moral superiority of Mexican culture.[53] The persistent emphasis on moral standards, as both quotes suggest, was part of the press's broader effort to reverse or at least contest local racial hierarchies that placed Mexicans near the bottom. Part of the papers' protectionist stance also included protests and criticism of racializing stereotypes that justified or perpetuated the mistreatment of the papers' imagined constituency. As Doris Meyer has pointed out, relative to the New Mexican press of 1890–1920, the active correction of stereotypes also often involved the discursive construction or representation of their imagined readership.[54]

In the case of Los Angeles, this resistant stance should not be automatically interpreted as a grassroots expression of subaltern protest or solidarity, nor as evidence of subversive or radical politics. Instead, newspapers typically reflected the worldview and political stances of middle-class and elite Mexicans and their particular conception of Mexican identity. Ignacio Lozano was one of the more prominent members of this exile elite and a key figure in the history of Spanish-language news media in the United States. Having immigrated to San Antonio from Mexico in 1908, he established the daily newspaper *La Prensa* in 1913.[55] It would soon become the most widely distributed Spanish-language paper in the United States, as Lozano sought from the beginning to cultivate a broad Mexican readership-cum-community. His publishing empire would eventually include the opening of bookstores and the publication of novels, which generally coincided with his somewhat conservative view of Mexican politics and the revolution.[56] Considering the incredible demographic growth of Los Angeles, he began publication of the daily *La Opinión* there in 1926, where it is still in operation. Eventually, this paper would eclipse the extant *El Heraldo de México* to become the predominant daily in Los Angeles, with national distribution and influence.

While the news coverage of such papers typically focused on developments in Mexico, they emphasized not only the maintenance of Mexican culture (including the Spanish language) and "resistance to Americanization" but the very imagining of a community united by national culture that was spiritually and morally superior.[57] Indeed, these papers initiated a transition within immigrant press culture from the coverage of local issues to the formation of solidarity among Mexicans on both sides of the border.[58] The upper classes conceived of the press as being central to this process, particularly as a site where multiple elements of Mexican culture and commerce converged and collaborated. As we shall see, this struggle toward the formation of a transnational Greater Mexico was inextricable from the construction of Mexicanidad through cultural production, particularly as journalists and editors maintained the belief that the "spirit of la Raza could best be maintained . . . through everyday cultural activities."[59] More specifically, the exiles that operated such papers focused on "reproducing the homeland in a representational form of their own choosing and one that serve[d] their own needs."[60]

During the period in question, for instance, the Spanish-language press of Los Angeles, and *El Heraldo* in particular, regularly identified Hollywood productions that insulted Mexico or Mexicans and readily connected such representations to an extension of specific political agendas, including the demands for more extensive U.S. intervention in the revolution. With the proliferation of cinematic interpretations of Mexico and its revolution (including the greaser and the bandido stereotypes), this period marks the moment in which Mexican audiences and critics on both sides of the border began an ongoing critical engagement with such representations. As early as 1917, the Mexican government formally complained about offensive images of Mexicans in Hollywood films, prompting President Woodrow Wilson to request that studios remove from circulation any film with the potential to offend friendly nations.[61]

Despite including cinema coverage that coincided with Hollywood publicity and promotion, both *El Heraldo* and *La Opinión* would from this point onward sustain ongoing campaigns against demeaning and "denigrating" images of Mexicans in U.S. films. One particular article in *El Heraldo* alerted readers that the Hearst Corporation was producing newsreels along the Texas-Mexico border that reenacted episodes of Mexican American insurrection as instances of "pillage and banditry" replete with "details of carnage and savagery." The stakes of such films were spelled out explicitly by the author: Mexicans acting in such films out of financial necessity did not realize that such newsreels were taken as fact, ultimately serving as propaganda against the Mexican nation. Actors, he suggests, should instead dedicate themselves to "something that does not leave a dark stain of affront toward la Raza, something that gives honor and credibility, not that which causes lack of prestige, dishonor, and disgrace."[62] Another article endorsed proposals to censor "denigrating" films before they are exported to Mexico but noted that there should be a similar mechanism for film shown within the United States, as they "hurt the feelings of Mexicans, they foment racial prejudice, and offend a friendly nation."[63]

Ongoing protests against such images on the part of journalists, spectators, and government officials alike eventually culminated in Mexico's 1922 boycott against the importation of films from Paramount, Metro, and Famous Players Lasky. According to Ruth Vasey, this incident constituted a watershed moment for Hollywood as an internationally oriented industry, "convincing producers of the need for industry-wide regulation of certain images intended for export."[64] As Laura Isabel Serna has demonstrated, in the wake of the 1922 boycott, newspapers and individual citizens in both the United States and Mexico continued to notify Mexican officials about films they had seen.[65] As John Mraz has suggested, such ongoing concerns were likely an extension of late nineteenth-century battles over the visual representation of Mexico. In particular, concerns about the impact of photography on Mexico's international reputation (and images of poverty and misery in particular) led to proposals to legally ban "obscene and indecent" images from circulating, an effort that clearly resonates with the 1922 Paramount ban.[66] As we shall see, many of these concerns over cinematic representation hinge precisely on the perception of Mexicans as racially inferior, poverty stricken, and culturally backward.

Such complaints and protests colored the paper's subsequent advocacy of film projects that would correct such representations. When critic Luis G. Pinal announced the forthcoming cinematic adaptation of Manuel Acuña's play *El pasado* in 1925, for instance, it praised Enrique Vallejo and actress Ligia de Golconda for undertaking the production, which aspired to present an ostensibly authentic depiction of Mexico. Naturally, Pinal also warned the film's producers "that they MUST choose those beautiful, dignified 'exteriors' that show us as we truly are, and for no reason show pulquerías [bars serving fermented agave juice, popular with the underclass] or the lower classes of the streets that tend to frequent places of vice and idleness."[67] In the same issue of the paper there appeared an article detailing the intentions of director-actor Ben Wilson (who had independently produced a number of Westerns) to film motion pictures in Mexico, emphasizing that "he will study and film our customs, our types, and our way of being in a way faithful to reality, without ridiculously altering our customs or types in a form that would denigrate Spanish-speaking peoples."[68]

While the condemnation or promotion of specific films remained a key component of Mexican-oriented press culture in Los Angeles, entertainment journalists integrated these critical responses into an active re-presentation of Mexican Los Angeles and the construction of a transnational Mexicanidad. On the one hand, they sought to rehabilitate the image of Mexicans in Los Angeles. Accordingly, they regarded demeaning cinematic images as perpetuating a racial logic that justified the discrimination, repression, exploitation, and unequal treatment of Mexicans in the United States. Similarly, Main Street discourse produced and justified a racialized mapping of urban space. Countering the characterizations of reformers, city officials, and mainstream journalists, Mexican dailies were thus extensively involved in establishing a vision of Main Street that "elevated" the status of Mexicans through an emphasis on morally respectable entertainment. But this elevated projection of Mexicanidad also implicitly relied on an elision of the "problematic" multiethnic composition of the area and simply excluded any reference to its less respectable establishments or audiences.

On the other hand, correcting Hollywood stereotypes also comprised one component of an attempt to unite the Mexican population under a single conception of Mexican national identity through proper, cultivated consumption. But this conception of a cohesive Mexican community similarly produced a number of exclusions and even contradictions, as it reflected the interests and ideology of a class of Mexican exiles. The alternative Main Street discourse generated by these newspapers thus recovered the area as a bastion of respectable Mexican culture and commerce; in the process it aspired to construct a cohesive Mexican population *and* to alter its public perception. On both counts, however, efforts to counter dominant racial discourses by instituting an alternative hierarchy of respectable morality that placed Mexican culture on top perpetuated existing divisions of race and class. If critics objected to the production of films that showed (as I mention earlier) the lower classes and their consumption habits, they also strove to excise these very elements from their own collective construction of transnational Mexicanidad.

The efforts of these individuals to generate alternative representations thus constituted a rather paradoxical attempt to simultaneously construct and protect a unified national community across class while implicitly marking class distinctions. That is, protests against negative representations during this period were at least partially driven by the dominant society's assumption that all Mexicans were working class and of indigenous or mixed race extraction. As Emory Bogardus later noted in 1934, "so many people in the United States unfortunately generalize against all Mexicans on the basis of the lowest level Mexicans that the better class Mexicans grow discouraged and pessimistic regarding opportunities in the United States."[69] This view corresponds to the dynamic Gabriela F. Arredondo has identified in Chicago during the same period, where fixed (and not entirely flattering) conceptions of Mexicans were applied uniformly to a heterogeneous population.[70] Elites thus often worked to separate the category of the Mexican from qualities associated with poverty, disease, and nonwhiteness. In cleansing and elevating the representation of Mexicans in Los Angeles, journalists and other educated elites in some respects also disavowed the class they ostensibly claimed to protect. In insisting on a cohesive Mexican identity and community shaped in their own image, the uplift of the working class in this context seemed to require their invisibility, while implicitly marking a poor, racialized other against which this construction of community was ultimately premised.

This apparently contradictory attitude toward class divisions also placed their construction of Mexicanidad in conversation with concurrent conceptions of race on both sides of the border. As Alexandra Minna Stern has pointed out, there existed a common ground between racial discourses in Mexico and the United States, despite important differences. More specifically, "ambivalence existed in both countries about racial hybridity and the significance of the term *mestizo*." I have already provided examples—cinematic, journalistic, and sociological—indicative of reigning attitudes about racial mixture and ethnic heterogeneity (whether on the level of the individual or the neighborhood) in Los Angeles. Concurrent Mexican discourses, however, generally viewed racial mixture, through the figure of the mestizo (a mixture of indigenous and Spanish), as ultimately positive, an agent of "biological enhancement."[71] While this mixture was increasingly seen as the basis of national identity through the 1920s and 1930s, the embrace of hybridity by its proponents ultimately served the interest of producing a homogenous mestizo race, as Stern has argued. That is, the indigenous population was generally to be excluded from or eliminated by this new racial order. Again, as was also the case with class, the formation of a national community was premised on a process of othering, an attempt to make invisible those of lower class or racial status. At any rate, Mexican workers racialized as nonwhite in Los Angeles were simultaneously positioned as problematic by two competing constructions of Mexicanness, two distinct yet overlapping conceptions of race. Although the Mexican press of the city protested stereotypes and re-presented its constituency in the process, its discourse at times intersected uncomfortably with mainstream discourse, despite being motivated by a distinct set of investments.

The motivations for crafting a notion of Mexican identity and community premised on a putative elevation of race and class, while apparently benefiting the upper classes and their self-perception, was also a strategic response to the contested status of Mexicans in a multiethnic city with a complex racial hierarchy. The positioning of immigrants between two different racial regimes, in other words, had implications beyond the crafting of a transnational Mexican identity in dialogue with both. Rather, racial hierarchies had very concrete consequences for Mexicans and others in Los Angeles. This dynamic would become particularly evident within the stratified labor market from the 1910s onward. While native-born Euro-American laborers always earned the highest wages, others competed for jobs on a lower pay scale and faced exclusion from or discrimination within certain industries. As Sides has noted, "the multiracial character of the city . . . actually exacerbated the effects of employment discrimination by increasing competition at the lower end of the labor market."[72] One study described the competitive and at times confusing labor market in which different ethnic groups would often compete with one another by the 1920s:

In certain plants Mexicans and whites worked together; in some others white
workers accepted Negroes and objected to Mexicans; in others white workers accepted Mexicans and objected to Japanese. White women worked with
Mexican and Italian women, but refused to work with Negroes. Mexican and
Negroes worked under a white foreman; Italians and Mexicans under a Negro
foreman; and Mexicans in some places were refused entirely because of plant
policies against "mixing."[73]

The various positioning of Mexicans relative to native-born whites, African
Americans, and Asians suggests at least some of the incentives of Mexican elites
may have had for rejecting and reframing the racial status of their working-class
compatriots during this period, a discursive maneuver that included downplay-
ing the ethnic heterogeneity of Main Street and the Plaza area. Even the concept
of "denigrating" images constituted a telling element of this rhetoric. As the word
most commonly used to describe stereotypical representations in the Mexican
immigrant press during the period, its connotations as a "blackening" of character hold clear racial implications. If Mexicans typically possessed an advantage
over African Americans in at least some of the city's industries in the first decades
of the twentieth century, distancing them from denigrating or blackening images
also represented a rhetorical attempt to protect or enhance the status of Mexicans
within local racial hierarchies.[74] This effort also fortuitously bolstered the self-
perception of the upper classes, along with the racial dimensions of their brand
of Mexicanidad.

In Los Angeles, Mexican cultural authorities were not alone in attempting to
elevate the status (racial and otherwise) of their constituency through recourse
to notions of respectability tied to urban space and cultivated cultural consumption. As Denise Khor has demonstrated, for instance, the local Filipino press
(operated by "elites and the intelligentsia within Filipino communities") encouraged their readership to reject American mass culture, gambling establishments,
and dance halls and instead, "as a means of racial uplift . . . embrace the values of
thrift and cultural respectability."[75] This insistence on morality and respectability,
as in the Mexican case, was also motivated by the way in which Filipinos were
racialized as inferior. Journalists and other Filipino elites often accused their
working-class compatriots of perpetuating such disparaging stereotypes through
their leisure habits, of behaving in a way that only confirmed notions of their
supposed racial inferiority.[76] Khor has also demonstrated that in Los Angeles and
elsewhere, Japanese theater owners were part of an elite class that strove to affect
racist attitudes by encouraging their countrymen to embrace behavior and consumption habits aligned with class-based notions of respectability.[77] In the Mexican case, the racial and cultural elevation of the immigrant working class would
(internally) bring them in line with elite conceptions of Mexican national community, while (externally) improving their status and treatment in Los Angeles.

Promoting Mexicanidad: *El Heraldo de México*

Any attempt to fully understand the relationship between upper-class constructions of transnational Mexicanidad and cultural consumption requires an examination of the intimate interdependence that developed by the late 1910s between Spanish-language newspapers, multiple local businesses (including theaters), and organizations like mutual aid societies (*mutualistas*). All of these constituted distinct yet overlapping elements of a Mexican middle-class and elite presence in Los Angeles and the way they imagined a collective Mexicanness through culture. A brief analysis of *El Heraldo de México* during this period provides a sense of the discourse it generated relative to cultural consumption and how it developed through symbiotic relationships between these institutions. Its appeals to and constructions of the Mexican-descent population struck a curious balance between advocacy and marketing, often blurring the boundaries between them. Not coincidentally, most of these businesses and organizations were located in the area near North Main. They accordingly reconceived the area as a safe haven for immigrants and a bastion of respectable Mexican national culture, a place where consumption ensured continuity of culture (within individuals and as a business enterprise), a formation of national community, and freedom or protection from discrimination. The battle over cinematic representation was hence accompanied by efforts to imagine and re-present the presence of Mexicans in general, particularly within the fabric of downtown.

To begin with, all these Mexican-oriented institutions shared a persistent and rather overdetermined tendency to address their respective readers and patrons *as* Mexican nationals. At a very basic (and most obvious) level of interdependency between such entities, advertisements placed in *El Heraldo* by local businesses supported the financial viability of the newspaper. Both these advertisements and *El Heraldo*'s own self-promotion situated consumption as a potential act of patriotism and loyalty to fellow Mexicans. In this regard, such rhetoric coincides with the practices of other ethnic and immigrant presses (which encouraged patronizing community merchants), while also serving as an early iteration of Latino niche marketing. That is, through a persistent recourse to Mexican nationality and the Spanish language, businesses strove to distinguish themselves within the marketplace while proposing a coincidence between the mutually dependent interests of customers and proprietors. If the current marketing industry "simultaneously serves the multiple interests of those who profit from difference as well as the interests of those subordinate populations whose attainment of presentation is essential to contemporary politics," Mexican newspapers (and the middle-class interests that converged within them) marked perhaps an early attempt to strike this balance.[78] Because the paper relied on advertising revenue, it also had an interest in promoting and perpetuating this brand of nationalism through consumption. And if language was frequently

Fig. 8. A typical example of a print advertisement for Repertorio Musical Mexicano. *El Heraldo de México*, May 19, 1918.

connected directly to cultural maintenance, it also became a central component of advertising and commerce; the existence and viability of the Spanish-language press itself depended on this convergence.

The print ads for the music store Repertorio Musical Mexicano, owned by Mauricio Calderón and located at 408 North Main Street, are typical in their appeal to nationality. This business was indeed one of the more regular advertisers within the pages of *El Heraldo* (along with San Antonio's *La Prensa* and later *La Opinión*). One 1918 advertisement in particular explains to potential customers the specific benefits of patronizing the store: "MEXICANS: This store was established exclusively for your patronage. No other place could serve you better because we, in a word, treat you like MEXICANS and COMPATRIOTS." In this instance, the music store is making an implicit attempt to mark the disadvantages of patronizing stores not owned by Mexicans, where customers might encounter cultural misunderstanding and even discrimination (see fig. 8). Beyond extolling the advantages of shopping at businesses that were so patently Mexican in every apparent aspect, advertisements and newspaper articles alike emphasized to potential customers and audiences that supporting these establishments was a patriotic duty, hence linking proper consumption practices directly to national loyalty. Another advertisement for Repertorio Musical Mexicano, for instance, pleads with readers, "Don't forget and make your commercial preference a Mexican establishment, so that you will give proof of your patriotism and contribute to the betterment of our colony in this country."[79]

Using similar language, articles in *El Heraldo* would also encourage readers to patronize Mexican-owned businesses, and theaters in particular. For a brief period of nearly a year (1918–1919), Mayo y Compañía (a department store and money-transfer service on North Main) operated the Teatro Hidalgo and contracted several theatrical troupes to perform there, including the one featuring actress Angélica Méndez. With two of its major advertisers merging, *El Heraldo* not surprisingly (and repeatedly) extended its gratitude to Mayo and urged its readers to patronize the Hidalgo through recourse to patriotic language: "We recommend that our compatriots don't hesitate to prove their culture and nationalism, attending functions at the Hidalgo, since we rarely have the opportunity to admire a [theatrical] company this good."[80]

These businesses often further emphasized their national credentials through visual illustrations. Advertisements for the Repertorio music store, for instance, regularly featured a singing *charro* (Mexican cowboy) stroking his guitar while sitting atop an oversized phonograph. As Agustín Gurza notes, stickers placed on records sold by the Repertorio displayed the same image and patriotic text. He rightly points out that "the store's sale pitch played on the powerful link between culture, commerce, and community."[81] This particular image also draws connections between charro attire, musical performance, and conceptions of Mexican authenticity, associations that would soon be further consolidated through official versions of postrevolutionary Mexican nationalism and its cinematic manifestations. Advertisements for the Farmacia Hidalgo also provided visual support for its claims of nationalism, showing an eager throng of working-class Mexicans congregating at its doors (as the print copy suggests; see fig. 9). This sea of anonymous men wearing sombreros seems to reinforce claims that the Hidalgo embodies a convergence of a Mexican (working-class) clientele, a Mexican (middle-class) ownership, and Mexican products. Curiously, such ads visualize the Mexican working class in ways that resonate with their representation in English-language newspapers in Los Angeles, complete with oversized sombreros. What differs here is not the rejection of convention or stereotype relative to the visual representation of the working class. Rather, what these ads typically exclude is any reference to other immigrant customers (the Asians depicted or mentioned in the aforementioned articles) or non-Mexican ownership. Proper consumption is framed as an uninterrupted circuit of national pride, community support, and cultural maintenance in a way that denies the "problematic" heterogeneity of the district.

El Heraldo consistently promoted itself in terms similar to other Mexican-owned businesses, as a service to the Mexican population of the city. Supplementing this, however, the paper also aligned itself with entities like the Mexican Consulate by reiterating its dedication to the protection and defense of the

Fig. 9. Advertisement for the Farmacia Hidalgo. *El Heraldo de México*, March 25, 1919.

working class. In multiple ads and articles, the newspaper affirmed its dedication "to the defense of the interests of Mexico and Mexicans in the United States."[82] Certainly, other enterprises made similar claims in their appeals to Mexican immigrants. Mayo y Compañía, for instance, characterized itself as "the establishment that protects the interests of Mexicans."[83] For *El Heraldo*, however, this language of defense and protection amounted to something that seemed to transcend a mere marketing ploy. Perhaps most notably, the newspaper and its staff founded a mutual aid society, the Liga Protectora Mexicana (Mexican Protective League). With both its managing editor (Juan de Heras) and editorialist (Prof. Ignacio Ramírez) serving on the board of directors, the Liga received extensive and regular coverage in *El Heraldo*. Taking as its mission the "material, moral, and intellectual improvement of the Mexican working class," the organization promised its membership assistance with employment, defense against workplace exploitation, consumer protection, legal services, and health insurance.[84]

The efforts of the newspaper, Mexican-owned businesses, the Liga, and the consulate converged on multiple occasions. Perhaps most obviously, all of them contributed to the celebration of Mexican Independence each year. As Richard Griswold del Castillo has pointed out, this celebration (along with Cinco de Mayo) in Los Angeles developed through the collaboration of social clubs, organizations, and the press in the nineteenth century.[85] Moving into the 1910s, as George J. Sánchez has likewise noted, the Mexican Consulate "emerged as the central organizer of community leadership," whose goal "was the preservation of the cultural integrity of Mexican emigrants through the establishment of institutions to foster Mexican patriotism, with the long-term goal of encouraging return migration."[86] As it continued into the twentieth century, this celebration became thoroughly integrated into the city's commercial and entertainment landscape. Just as with other key signifiers of nationalism, the holiday was regularly and prominently incorporated into newspaper advertising of the period. Businesses in this decade and beyond would schedule openings and events to coincide with Mexican Independence celebrations (September 15 and 16) as further proof of their dedication to Mexico. The premier issue of *El Heraldo* in 1915 was, in fact, published to coincide with this holiday, the commemoration of which had already been central part of community life in Mexican Los Angeles for decades.[87] Not coincidentally, the newspaper was among the institutions central to supporting and promoting public celebrations of Independence Day each year.

How, then, did this class-based political orientation and economic network relate to entertainment options, cultural criticism, and conceptions of Mexicanidad in Los Angeles? As I have already demonstrated, music stores and theaters were among the businesses typically owned and operated by elite and middle-class exiles, which collaborated regularly with newspapers, mutual aid organizations, and the consulate. During the week of Independence Day in 1918, for instance, the Teatro Hidalgo (still owned by Mayo y Compañía) hosted a benefit for the Liga Protectora Mexicana, featuring a program of *zarzuelas* (Spanish light opera). That same week, on the fifteenth, the Hidalgo also hosted an Independence commemoration organized by the Liga, which featured a program of "music, speeches, and patriotic lectures."[88] The newspaper itself was also involved in contributing to the festivities this particular year. Managing editor De Heras, in addition to his position with the Liga, also served as secretary of the Mexican Committee of Civic Festivals, which organized a musical procession with the Islas Brothers Mexican Band.[89] The Islas Brothers, it should be noted, also owned a music store that specialized in instruments and sheet music, billing itself as "the Mexican music store for Mexicans."[90] As the events for just this single year indicate, there was a relatively tight-knit social and economic network among these businesses and organizations in which cultural production (theater and music in particular) occupied a prominent position.

If this network of interdependency and mutual support collectively situated itself as a bastion of Mexican nationalism in the United States, charged with protecting working-class immigrants, entertainment was often situated as a central component of this arrangement. One unsigned editorial, in fact, linked education and the progress of humanity with the concerted and interrelated efforts of the local Mexican cultural authorities. Optimistically predicting that after World War I, technological progress will be directed away from killing and toward "increasing the comforts of life, lightening the labor of workers and converting our world . . . into a more beautiful and kinder place, more in line with the aesthetic aspirations of man," the piece asserts that this impetus has already become evident within the Mexican population living in the United States, "even among the most humble class": "the numerous attendance seen at the popular festivals held in the Plaza, the growing increase of members of the elevated institution that bears the name Liga Protectora Mexicana, the current trend that drives Mexicans to the theater to hear good dramatic pieces, and the determination to read newspapers written in Spanish." Further improvement in this regard, according to the editorial, would entail increasing "concerts and spectacles of high culture, full of Mexican workers" so that "there is not a single Mexican inhabitant of California that does not belong to the Liga Protectora."[91]

The collective uplift ostensibly ensured by this convergence of social and political advocacy, community formation, economic benefit, and cultural consumption also entailed particular class-based conceptions of taste. Critics and journalists working for the major Spanish-language newspapers in Los Angeles consistently promoted theatrical presentations that coincided with middle-class notions of high or respectable culture. *El Heraldo*, for instance, regularly made claims about the quality of entertainers based on their reception in the metropolitan centers of Latin America and (less frequently) Europe. Anticipating a performance by the singing group Los Cancioneros, for example, the paper explains that the duo has been enthusiastically received by "the cultured Mexican society made up of honorable families of our beautiful capital, where the young artists are well-known and appreciated."[92] Advertisements for the theaters themselves often emphasized these connections. A grand opening of the Teatro Hidalgo in 1918, for instance, assured readers that the establishment was "dedicated exclusively to spectacles of high morality and culture, in beautiful and sonorous Spanish." It further boasted of presenting performers "of true merit from Madrid, Barcelona, Buenos Aires, Mexico, and Havana."[93] Such rhetoric encouraged adherence to middle-class notions of taste and propriety as it reframed and re-presented North Main Street in a way that challenged its reputation as a breeding ground of vice, depravity, germs, and multiethnic interaction. This "cultivated" version of the Hidalgo, for instance, clearly marks a departure from the lurid characterizations of McEuen's aforementioned study and mainstream journalistic accounts alike. It also posits a moral cultivation that aspired to counteract a representational denigration in racial terms.

The evocation of high culture through press and publicity remained inextricable from a concurrent emphasis on nationalist sentiment and particular notions of Mexicanness. A subsequent article about Los Cancioneros (reprinted in *El Heraldo* from San Antonio's *La Revista Mexicana*) proclaims that they specialize in "Verses pregnant with the spirit of our Race! Hearing them in Mexico is a delight; listening to them in foreign lands is the same as contemplating a portrait of a mother who is far away, something like reading a love letter from an absent girlfriend."[94] This coverage of Los Cancioneros thus points to a broader discursive trend within the press whereby middle-class cultural standards and conceptions of national culture converged, with both being seen as crucial and mutually inextricable facets of sustaining a cohesive feeling of Mexicanness among immigrants in the United States. The omission, within these accounts of Main Street, of any reference to multiethnic audiences or the cheap amusements they actually patronized suggests that the terms of respectable Mexicanness operated in a way analogous to (yet distinct from) the construction of respectable whiteness. If ethnic diversity among working-class immigrants on Main Street provided a field against which whiteness was defined and affirmed, it also remained a structuring absence within the coverage of the Spanish-language press. The equation of proper consumption with Mexican nationality and middle-class notions of taste thus reconceptualized and Mexicanized North Main in a way that consciously disavowed a condemnation of the same street based precisely on the presence of a racially heterogeneous working class and its suspect or problematic tastes. In other words, if the conception of Mexicans (and their environs) as poor, nonwhite, unruly, and violent constituted the central representational problem, the Spanish-language press simply erased such elements from their own construction of Mexican Los Angeles.

These articles from *El Heraldo* further make apparent the construct that linked the protection of workers with Mexican nationalism, conceptions of community, and cultural consumption. More specifically, cultural criticism constituted a key facet of an ongoing attempt to construct a conception of Mexicanidad that was fundamentally transnational, in that it simultaneously worked to reconcile discourses of a bourgeoning Mexican nationalism with racialized notions of what it meant to be Mexican in Los Angeles. It is this bifurcated conception of Mexicanidad that will guide theatrical and cinematic criticism, a logic that conjoins elite and middle-class notions of taste and moral rectitude with the articulation of an "elevated," transnational Mexican identity. In other words, guiding the taste and consumption habits of its readership constituted a cultural extension of the defense of workers in the United States while keeping them within the national orbit. This discourse, in addition to its more altruistic pretensions, also worked to sustain the commercial interests of middle-class businesses framed as the embodiments of Mexico and the cultural authority of journalists and critics. The particular configuration of businesses, newspapers, and theaters will necessarily change over the course of the next two decades, as will the culture industries in both the United States and Mexico. Nonetheless, this discursive formation, and the aspiration on the part of critics for the sustained production of respectable Mexican culture in Los Angeles—as a bastion of nationalism *and* a response to localized racialization—will greatly inform the reception of cinema within the pages of local newspapers like *El Heraldo* and *La Opinión*. Through this emphasis the Mexican working class is consistently positioned as both a problem of representation and an audience in need of guidance and discipline.

Coda: *Calle Principal*

I conclude this discussion of the representation and construction of Mexicanidad through urban space by examining a more contemporary representation of Main Street in the early twentieth century. Located on at 501 North Main near the site of the original Plaza, the LA Plaza de Cultura y Artes is a nonprofit cultural center that opened in 2011 with a mission to "celebrate and cultivate an appreciation for the enduring and evolving influence of Mexican and Mexican-American culture, with a specific focus upon the unique Mexican-American experience in Los Angeles and Southern California."[95] In addition to renovating historical buildings as part of this Mexican American reclamation of the Plaza, the institution houses several permanent exhibitions dedicated to re-presenting the history of the city from this vantage point. While the entire first floor is dedicated to a sweeping historical exhibit titled *LA Starts Here!*, a portion of the second floor houses an interactive reconstruction of Main Street in the 1920s.

Drawing from the Main's original name from the Spanish period, *Calle Principal: Main Street Los Angeles, 1920s*, replicates a small section of the street lined by reconstructions of six historical storefront businesses: Farmacia Hidalgo, Librería Lozano (the bookstore operated in conjunction with *La Opinión*), Repertorio Musical Mexicano (the aforementioned record store), Mercado Plaza (a small grocery store), Plaza Studio (a portrait studio), and the Main Street Department Store. As a nod to the political activism of the period, several soapboxes are arranged at one end of the reconstruction of this street to commemorate the Plaza as a place where "people gathered to exchange ideas and information, to speak about the injustice they encountered, and to protest" (see fig. 10).[96]

If the exhibit "offers visitors a hands-on investigation of daily life during that period, encouraging them to make connections between the past and present," it does so in a way that also neatly replicates Mexican middle-class and elite conceptions of Main Street in the 1920s through the press.[97] That is, the exhibit privileges the middle-class social and commercial networks that emphasized enterprise, class-based notions of respectability, and a cohesive Mexican national identity. While, quite crucially, elements of the Mexican working class are acknowledged as political subjects by the soapbox display, the exhibition seems to make little space for a more nuanced understanding of Mexican immigrants that lies between resistant activism and patriotic consumption. That is, this particular construction of Main Street, consistent with publications like *El Heraldo*, imagines a street free of institutions that would challenge the investment in such representations: pool halls, cheap hotels, penny arcades, dance halls, cheap theaters, bars, and any business owned by non-Mexicans (and there were plenty). As surely as these were a key part of this thoroughfare's vibrant history, they also interrupt a sanitized, celebratory, unitary construction of Mexican (American)

Fig. 10. Detail of *Calle Principal: Main Street Los Angeles, 1920s* exhibition (with exteriors of the Librería Lozano and the Repertorio Musical Mexicano). LA Plaza de Cultura y Artes, Los Angeles. Photograph by Meztli Photography.

identity that either elides or idealizes the working class. Quite significantly, such a construction denies the utter heterogeneity of Main Street, overlooking its multiethnic composition almost entirely. This dimension of the exhibition received comment by journalist Hector Tobar, who noted that the indigenous presence in Los Angeles receives scant treatment in the museum, while the re-creation of Main Street approximates a "Mexican version of Main Street U.S.A. in Disneyland" in its negation of diversity. Summarizing his impressions of the city as person of Guatemalan descent, he laments, "I wish I didn't have to learn about my city's past in such a splintered way."[98]

Without a doubt, such an exhibition serves as a necessary corrective to xenophobic and frankly racist descriptions of this part of downtown. In 1927 for instance, author Louis Adamic (himself an Eastern European immigrant) described the Plaza area in the following terms: "For the most part it consists of cheap wooden tenements occupied by Mexicans and Chinks, of various camouflaged bawdy houses, dance halls, foreign-looking hotels, bootleg dives, hop joints, movie shows, tamale stands, peep shows, shooting galleries, and stores selling rosaries and holy pictures. Main Street North, the principal thoroughfare of the district, is a moron stream, muddy, filthy, unpleasant to the nose."[99] Given the persistent reiterations of the area in sociological, historical, and journalistic accounts, the temptation to recuperate North Main by "sanitizing" and "uplift-ing" are undeniable and obviously persist into the contemporary moment.

It is such an impetus that likely accounts for the exclusion of Mexican-oriented theaters along North Main (along with other cheap amusements) from this his-torical reconstruction. On multiple counts, they disrupt the circuit of cultural nationalism central to the Mexicanized Main Street discourse. First of all, they were certainly the site of presentations that would have violated middle-class notions of respectability and were at times accused of too thoroughly catering to a working-class taste for vulgarity, as I detail in chapter 2. Second, they were not always owned by individuals of Mexican descent. Japanese owners, for instance, converted the Hidalgo into the Sun Ban Theater for a brief period in 1919, while its later resurrection as the Hidalgo occurred under its Jewish manager, Meyer Trallis. Reportedly a controversial figure, Trallis was repeatedly accused of harboring a prejudice toward his Mexican clientele.[100] Last, the Hidalgo (and other theaters in the area) alternated between variety shows, films from Latin America, and Hollywood features, with the latter often dominating its program-ming (depending on the year and its ownership). All these factors make the theaters exceedingly difficult to recuperate into a representation of North Main as an unconditional bastion of Mexican (American) culture, as they point to a decidedly complex and heterogeneous history of consumption and multiethnic interaction, one that has more than a few controversial or potentially unsavory dimensions.

To be sure, as it neatly replicates the Mexican Main Street discourse of the 1920s, this exhibit demonstrates the obstacles inherent in historical reconstruc-tion and representation. More specifically, the Mexican press offers quite simply the most extensive glimpse into Mexican immigrant life during the period, as other historical traces are scant or simply nonexistent. While we must necessar-ily rely on such sources, however, it is crucial to remember that they generated particular representations and held specific investments in such constructions. As Meyer rightly points out in her study of the New Mexican Spanish-language press, "witnesses of the past—especially those relegated to silence by virtue of their class, gender, race, or economic condition—rarely left behind evidence of their 'take' on history."[101] While we must thus maintain a critical distance from the representations generated by this press (as I have attempted to do in this chapter), constructing an alternative vision can be significantly more difficult, given the lack of available archival evidence.

At several telling junctures, *Calle Principal* seems to recognize its own limita-tions in this regard. Inside the re-creation of the photo studio, arranged among actual photos of the period, hangs an empty frame. Above this, a printed sign explains, "Many Mexican immigrants in Los Angeles in the 1920s could not afford to have a professional portrait made" (see fig. 11). It is precisely this lack of

Many Mexican
immigrants in Los Angeles
during the 1920s
could not afford to have
a professional
portrait made.

Fig. 11. Detail of *Calle Principal: Main Street Los Angeles, 1920s* exhibition (re-creation of the photo studio). LA Plaza de Cultura y Artes, Los Angeles. Photograph by Meztli Photography.

working-class self-representation (and archival documentation), along with the concurrent mania for multiple others to represent this class, that makes historical reconstruction and representation so difficult in the present. Nonetheless, it is worth interrogating this "Mexican problem" of representation during the period, remaining attentive to the exclusions consistently perpetuated through these constructions and the way they shape our understanding of the past.

CHAPTER 2

SPECTACLES OF HIGH
MORALITY AND CULTURE

THEATRICAL CULTURE AND CONSTRUCTIONS OF
THE MEXICAN COMMUNITY IN THE 1920S

Combating multiple entities from Hollywood to Euro-American reformers, Mexican press culture in early twentieth-century Los Angeles contributed to a discursive Mexicanization effort that was fought on multiple fronts. By insisting on the moral and cultural respectability of Main Street entertainment, the press worked to reinforce national sentiment while aspiring to elevate the perceived status (racial and otherwise) of Mexicans within the city. As the broader entertainment landscape further transformed in the 1920s, live Spanish-language theater became a key component of the representation and construction of Mexicanidad on a number of levels: as an alternative or corrective to Hollywood films and forces of Americanization; as a source of apparent cultural elevation; as an ongoing part of a middle-class business network; and as a form of external public relations geared toward improving the image and reputation of Mexicans in Los Angeles. Perhaps most significant, for entertainment journalists, theatrical entertainment (if properly executed) held the unique potential to unite all classes under a cohesive sense of Mexican nationality, one that extended to multiple, overlapping registers: spatial, textual, and spectatorial.

Although a distinctly separate medium, theatrical activity participated in an ongoing dialogue with a broad and intersecting range of representations, including those projected by cinema. If Charles Musser has proposed a conception of "'theatrical culture,' which includes both the stage and screen," a usefully expansive notion of this approach would also encompass relevant intertexts and intersecting spheres of activity. This chapter also demonstrates, as Musser further argues, that "in many instances, it becomes obvious that these two affiliated practices interpenetrate to such an extent that to examine one without consideration of the other ensures critical impoverishment."[1] Indeed, the fate of Spanish-language theater in Los Angeles is very much inextricable from histories of film exhibition and production, press culture, urban space, and Mexican commerce downtown. The multifaceted interplay between cinema and theater in this context aptly reflects Robert Knopf's observation that "the economic competition and technological developments of the two media . . . result in their being polarized at times, drawn together at others."[2] Cinema and theater in 1920s Mexican Los Angeles were not always positioned as rival media, nor can we summarize their relationship as one in which cinema merely replaced theater. Rather, their ongoing connections were varied and multiple, with developments in the realm of cinema (in an apparently counterintuitive manner) at times inspiring and stimulating the production of theater.

The multiple facets of Mexican entertainment culture functioned as a generative force that participated in the active representation and construction of identity. The articulation of a transnational Mexicanidad in the 1920s occurred through the ongoing interaction between daily newspapers, theater, music, and journalism—the only representational tools at the disposal of this immigrant population. Examining the multimedia intersections of film and theatrical culture in this context holds implications for the study of Latino theatrical culture and those of other populations for whom theatrical culture in the early twentieth century constituted a key site of community formation *and* alternative representations thereof.[3] The dynamics of this process again generated an implicitly transnational notion of Mexicanidad that aspired to create a cross-class, intergenerational Mexican community while elevating its status within the city. Paradoxically, distinctions of race and class continued to undergird the very foundation of this supposed unifying effort, as Mexican critics worked to create a map of cultural distinction in downtown Los Angeles.

By considering its overlapping cultural, representational, and economic functions, it also becomes apparent that the Mexican theater scene functioned in a way analogous to a national cinema in the absence of its possibility. As a transnational cultural form, its products attempted to address the unique position of Mexican immigrants in Los Angeles. And as a national cinema would, the texts, criticism, and publicity surrounding the theater constituted an attempt to forge an "imagined community" through culture.[4] Mexican theater in Los Angeles, quite appropriately, also struck a delicate balance between an appropriation or emulation of Hollywood and an alternative to it, in a manner similar to other national cinemas during the period. Hence, while multiple points of intersection exist between cinema and theater in Mexican Los Angeles, its approximation of a transnational cinema constitutes one of its defining features. Nonetheless, the ongoing sustenance of this type of theatrical production (and its promises of nationalistic, cross-class unification) remained more of an ideal toward which journalists and cultural authorities aspired. In practice, this history is littered with critical failures, false starts, and short-lived solutions. It is through this contentious and tumultuous history, however, that we can gauge the ways in which live theater briefly became central to cultural struggles over conceptions of Mexicanidad in Los Angeles.

A History of False Starts: Transnational
Mexican Cinema in 1920s Los Angeles

Theater would become central to efforts of community formation through culture at least partially because silent cinema could not be effectively or regularly
recruited into an explicitly nationalist agenda, despite its popularity with immigrant audiences. To fully understand the cultural significance of live theater in
Mexican Los Angeles, it is thus necessary to understand its relationship to cinema and, in particular, the initial failure to sustain a Mexican film culture at the
level of both production and exhibition. As I argue elsewhere, Mexican immigrant audiences sustained a complex and ambivalent relationship to Hollywood
during the silent era that included yet transcended fears of Americanization.[5]
Nonetheless, Los Angeles was witness to multiple attempts to create a transnational Mexican film culture as a viable alternative to Hollywood and its representation of Mexicans. As we shall see, live theater would not only assume a central
role in the cultural formation of transnational Mexicanidad during the 1920s but
would also exhibit its own ambivalence toward Hollywood through a complex
negotiation with mass culture and its appeal to local audiences. Not coincidentally, a renaissance of theatrical production in Mexico (much of it nationalist in
character) provided aesthetic and formal models that could be easily emulated
and adapted by cultural producers in Los Angeles, at a moment when lofty cinematic aspirations only rarely came to fruition.

The production of cinema in Mexico and analogous efforts by Latinos in the
United States was decidedly sporadic during this period, at best. As correspondent Gabriel Navarro regularly pointed out when writing for San Antonio's *La
Prensa*, a general scarcity of regular, ongoing film production from Mexico (or
from Mexican cinema produced within the United States) somewhat thwarted
the impulse to align the expatriate press culture's broader embrace of cultural
nationalism with its cinema coverage in a straightforward or intuitive manner. In
a rather pessimistic assessment, he explained in one column that

> I don't believe that in the near future—nor the distant future—the [Mexican]
> film industry will reach the heights that it has in the United States for many
> reasons. . . . In the first place, in Mexico there are no actors, nor directors, nor,
> more than anything, the capital to make movies. Next, Mexico cannot logically
> have a market for the films it produces, since Latin America is controlled by
> the American Industry, which has invested many more millions of dollars than
> you could count in your entire life.[6]

Indeed, with a few key exceptions, Hollywood increasingly dominated global
screens by the 1920s through a combination of industrial consolidation, vertical
integration, and government intervention in trade. Uneven cinematic exchange
and the manner in which this dynamic handicapped many other national cinemas created a situation whereby the international experience of cinema centered

increasingly on Hollywood. As Richard Maltby has noted, the domination of the U.S. film industry during this period stoked international anxieties about Americanization on three distinct yet interrelated levels: the impact of cinema on immigrants in the United States, the Americanization of younger generations in other countries, and a general fear of a global homogenization through Americanization that would erode cultural specificity worldwide.[7] All these anxieties were perceptible within the Mexican immigrant context during the silent period and beyond. For instance, as Douglas Monroy has demonstrated, immigrant parents in Los Angeles worried about the potential de-Mexicanizing impact of mass culture (including movies) on their children's behavior, appearance, and general morality, while film critics rightly perceived Hollywood's popularity as the primary impediment to the development of a stable Mexican film industry that could generate an ongoing supply of features.[8]

At several moments, independent Mexican production in Southern California emerged as an alternative and potential rebuttal to Hollywood and its supposed Americanizing influence. Given the lack of substantial production from Mexico itself, critics in Los Angeles viewed such production initiatives as particularly promising and urgent. As an extension of the protests that initiated in the 1910s (see chapter 1), a number of independent producers in Los Angeles aspired to create a transnational cinema of their own as early as 1920. Coinciding with the decline of revolutionary violence in Mexico, these efforts were simultaneously framed as part of the nation's recovery, an economic opportunity, and a means of improving Mexico's image to the international community. These initiatives clearly resonated with the impetus of concurrent silent film production within Mexico, as irregular as it may have been. Along with other culture industries, filmmakers often collaborated at least indirectly with the national government and its educational campaigns to create a coherent national consciousness after the divisive and destructive Mexican Revolution (which lasted from 1910 to 1917).[9]

The promotion of a singular national identity, a concept at times as inconsistent and contradictory as its acceptance was uneven, would ostensibly unify a heterogeneous population under the aegis of a national consciousness and also legitimize the postrevolutionary regime. Inextricable from this impetus was a concern for Mexico's reputation among other nations and its ability to project itself as a stable, modernized, and unified entity worthy of, among other things, foreign investment and tourism. This transnational dimension of Mexican nationalism has recently received renewed scholarly attention and is readily apparent in much of the cultural criticism of the 1920s and 1930s.[10] Mexican critics in Los Angeles participated in this cultural project, albeit with the additional mandate of crafting and sustaining a cohesive sense of Mexican identity outside the confines of the nation while elevating the perceived status of Mexicans in the United States. For many, the production of cinema, with its mass popularity and potential for wide distribution, was seen as a crucial component of this impetus.

The substantial Mexican population of Los Angeles, its status as a center of Spanish-language theatrical entertainment, and its proximity to Hollywood technology and training likely informed considerations of Los Angeles as a viable center of Mexican silent film production. As the rhetoric surrounding these nascent (and mostly ill-fated) efforts coincided with the nationalist orientation of local critics, all of them received substantial and enthusiastic attention from the Spanish-language press of Los Angeles. In 1920 Manuel Sánchez Valtierra, a former supervisor at Universal, announced the formation of the Anahuac Film Corporation in San Bernardino. Noting that recent production from Mexico showed potential and featured promising talent, an advertisement for the corporation framed it as a means of bringing much-needed expertise to the fledging national cinema, thus correcting that industry's "neglect of details that reveals deficient art direction and very, very poor technical direction." He also planned to ask the Mexican government for financial support in this endeavor, as the production of quality Mexican films would (in the words of the advertisement) "become a valuable collaborator in the reconstruction of the country" and would not only compete in the global market but "demonstrate to the civilized world, once and for all, the false opinion they have of us from judging us through American films."[11]

A more elaborate endeavor announced its formation in 1921 under the name of Estudiantes, Obreros, y Artistas Latino Americanos Film Co. (Latin American Students, Workers, and Artists Film Company). Much like the Anahuac Film Corporation, this independent production firm based in Los Angeles planned to make films about aspects of Mexico "almost completely unknown to North Americans who denigrate us unjustifiably" as a means of "providing evidence that our Republic is capable of walking among the best nations of the world, despite the difficulties it has encountered."[12] Indeed, the company presented itself as a more comprehensive and complex undertaking that would provide long-term support and training for the foundation of a transnational cinema. With technical expertise provided by the experienced director Francis Ford and Mexican filmmaker and theater director Enrique Tovar, the corporation intended to produce films of strictly documentary and educational nature that would serve as a training ground for technicians, writers, and artists from Latin America and Spain, with a particular emphasis on Mexico. With support from Mexican clubs and organizations in the United States, the titular students, workers, and artists would sell shares of the company door-to-door, with some of the proceeds going directly to the establishment of cultural centers. Evidently, Tovar opened the first of such establishments in Los Angeles shortly thereafter, offering free classes to Spanish-speaking students in "reading, artistic studies, recitation, dramatic elocution, mimicry, and the technical arts of cinema."[13]

A number of Latino actors and other talent trained in Hollywood also emerged as aspiring independent producers during the 1920s, including Manuel R. Ojeda (a silent film actor that would later go on to write, direct, and produce film in Mexico) and character actor Chris Pin Martin (producer of *Tepee Love*, 1922).[14] Perhaps the most successful of these figures during the silent period was Guillermo Calles. Beginning his career as an actor and stunt man in silent films, Calles was cast in films about the Mexican Revolution, as an Indian in Westerns, and as a sidekick to action star William Duncan. He would use the knowledge and connections he gained in Hollywood to produce several films: *De raza azteca* (Of the Aztec race, 1921), *El indio yaqui* (The Yaqui Indian, 1926), *Raza de bronce* (Bronze race, 1927), and *Sol de gloria* (Sun of glory, 1928). As Rogelio Agrasánchez Jr. points out, Calles conceived of these films as "the vindication of our race on celluloid," in keeping with the nationalist impetus of Mexican production during the period. While the success of these various enterprises remains uncertain (but was most certainly limited), all subscribed to the logic of a Southern California–based Mexican film industry, acknowledging the benefit of proximity to Hollywood's technical superiority and emphasizing the potential ability of Mexican productions to affect U.S. opinions and treatment of Mexicans.[15]

The general lack of culturally specific production, however, prevented the silent cinema from being fully integrated into local networks of nationalist consumption. Not surprisingly, most of the theaters around the Plaza and along North Main necessarily relied heavily on subsequent-run Hollywood films. Although the Teatro Hidalgo was dedicated primarily to theatrical and variety performances through the early 1920s (billing these as "spectacles of high morality and culture, in the beautiful and sonorous Spanish language"), for instance, it also regularly screened features.[16] The manager, Meyer Trallis, bragged at one point that he had been "exhibiting very expensive pictures in which the most famous stars of the silent art appear . . . in other words, thirty-six reels in only four days, something no other theater in the city has done, much less at the very low prices the Teatro Hidalgo charges."[17] That week, in fact, the theater had screened *Revelation* (George D. Baker, 1918), starring Alla Nazimova; Charlie Chaplin's *Shoulder Arms* (1918); and *Carmen*, with Geraldine Farrar (Cecile B. DeMille, 1915) (see fig. 12). During the early 1920s the Hidalgo and Estela Theaters occasionally participated in Paramount Week (an annual promotional event in which "thousands of America's finest theatres devote an entire week's program exclusively to Paramount Pictures!") and were subsequently listed in the *Los Angeles Times* alongside other downtown venues showing Hollywood films.[18]

Apparently, a number of establishments in the immediate vicinity of the Plaza, including the Teatro Plaza and Teatro Alegría, screened U.S. productions almost exclusively. And although the Electric Theater (Teatro Eléctrico) on North Main made explicit appeals to Mexicans, assuring them that "we want this to be your theater and we want you to bring your family and enjoy your free time here," the venue (dedicated exclusively to cinema) often advertised its bookings of films like

Fig. 12. Film listing for the Teatro Hidalgo. *El Heraldo de México*, February 21, 1920.

Charlie Chaplin's *The Kid* (1921).[19] The specific appeal of such venues to the Mexican working class apparently resided in a combination of location and pricing (in addition to the allure of Hollywood) instead of any sort of Mexican content.

Theater owners did attempt to capitalize on the rhetoric of national and cultural pride when Mexican or Latino-oriented productions were exhibited, however rarely. In terms of cinema, Plaza area theaters advertised more extensively for films that would somehow distinguish them as venues catering specifically to the Mexican population or appropriately compliment live performances, an attempt to appeal to the cultural loyalty of their preferred clientele. These films in turn received more dedicated attention on the part of the cultural critics working for the Mexican immigrant press. For instance, to commemorate the one hundredth performance by the Cuadro Novel theater troupe at the Teatro Novel, musical performances by Amparito Guillot and Miguel Lerdo de Tejada were accompanied by several short films, including one that documented the most recent Independence Day celebration in Mexico City. Films shown in such contexts were often short documentaries or travelogues like *Mexico bello* (Beautiful Mexico), which one reviewer praised as "the exhibition of a Mexican film that like a perfumed breeze has brought us the memories of some of the most beautiful corners of Mexico."[20] Teatro Columbia on Spring Street offered "A Trip through Mexico!" that consisted of a ten-part film featuring views of Mexico City and a number of other cities, along with footage of historical sites and prominent figures of the Mexican Revolution.[21] In addition to these shorts and actuality films, the Spanish-language theaters of Los Angeles often booked features that were either produced in Mexico or would most likely hold some appeal for Mexican audiences. For the premier of the landmark Mexican silent *El automóvil gris* (The grey automobile, Enrique Rosas, 1919), for instance, the Teatro Princesa advertised the screening of all sixteen episodes over the course of five nights. Other Mexican silent features, including *Cuauhtémoc* (Manuel de la Bandera, 1918) also received substantial promotion.

Even in the case of certain films produced in Hollywood, publicity would emphasize their potential appeal to Mexican audiences based on either textual content or talent. The Teatro Eléctrico, for example, placed an uncommonly large advertisement in *La Prensa* to publicize a showing of *When Dawn Came* (advertised as Al brillar la aurora, Colin Campbell, 1920) starring Colleen Moore, assuring audiences that "many Mexican artists take part in the picture, because the story of this exciting film deals with the first settlers in California."[22] Likewise, the Teatro Plaza atypically placed a full-page ad in *El Heraldo de México* to announce the showing of Ricardo Cortez in *The Spaniard* (advertised as El español, Raoul Walsh, 1925) and *That Devil Quemado* (advertised as Diablo quemado, Del Andrews, 1925) a drama that takes place on the U.S.-Mexican border (see fig. 13).[23] Despite these best efforts of exhibitors and the press, however, cinema during the 1920s would not play a central role in the cultural nationalism and community formation under way in Los Angeles.

This is not to suggest, however, that cinema had absolutely no connection to the conception of Mexican community to Los Angeles. Indeed, it was a force to be reckoned with and potentially harnessed in efforts to redefine cultural standards and attract audiences and readership. *El Heraldo de México*, for instance, regularly traced developments in the U.S. film industry, particularly (but not exclusively) those relevant to or somehow involving Mexican talent or content. The paper also provided general celebrity news, reviews, and production notes, particularly in its regular column "De cinelandia" and its less frequent "La página cinematográfica."

Fig. 13. Advertisement for Teatro Plaza. *El Heraldo de México*, September 12, 1925.

Given the popularity of Hollywood among their readership, cinema coverage proved economically expedient for the papers, despite reservations about its Americanizing impact. It also then necessarily became a factor to be negotiated in any attempt to draw audiences into a cohesive construction of Mexican identity or community through cultural consumption, and theatrical culture in particular.

A History of High Hopes: Los Angeles and the Spanish-Language Theater Boom

While efforts to create a transnational Mexican cinema were largely unsuccessful, the dramatic growth of Los Angeles's Mexican immigrant population and the entertainment options available to them produced a substantial expansion of theatrical activity and criticism in 1920s Los Angeles. Although Spanish-language theater had been performed in Los Angeles since at least the mid-nineteenth century, the city by the 1920s had transformed into a major center of Mexican-oriented theatrical activity; Los Angeles began hosting prestigious touring companies from Mexico and Latin America, becoming an important "manpower pool for Hispanic theater" in which theatrical companies formed to tour the Southwest. According to Nicolás Kanellos, Los Angeles supported five major Spanish-language theaters from the late 1910s into the 1930s, with approximately fifteen others hosting performances on an irregular basis.[24] The growth of this cultural activity and the criticism that attended it would become indelibly fixated on the terms of Mexicanidad, the formation of community across class, and "elevating" perceptions of the Mexican presence in downtown.

This increased activity was facilitated by a number of factors. First, as Los Angeles developed into a populous industrial center, regular employment in manufacturing, railroad construction, and service provided some immigrants the opportunity to purchase land and build houses near the city center or in East Los Angeles. Restrictive policy implemented by the 1917 Immigration Act (enacting measures, including a head tax and literacy test, ironically intended to deter immigration) also compelled many to remain in the United States for longer periods. These factors, among others, stimulated a limited degree of social mobility and at the very least created a more stable and permanent population of Mexicans that called Los Angeles home rather than merely a winter residence between harvest seasons or a site of labor contracting. The Mexican population consequently tripled over the course of the 1920s and would grow to more than ninety-seven thousand by 1930.[25] Although civic construction (including the iconic city hall and Union Station) and industrial growth eventually dispersed the population living near the Plaza and drove up rental prices, the commercial district serving the Mexican population flourished and expanded under these conditions. With the restriction of European immigration following World War I (coupled with ongoing unrest in Mexico), the Mexican population gradually "reclaimed the Plaza" through the 1920s, and an increasing number of businesses in the immediate area emerged to serve this particular demographic, particularly along North Main.[26]

While development in the previous decade had created stratified racial demarcations downtown, the increasing geographic dispersal of Los Angeles (along with restrictive real estate covenants) placed even greater distance between the multiethnic downtown and Euro-American transplants arriving from the South and Midwest. As William David Estrada explains, "Anglo newcomers sought to shield themselves from ethnic newcomers and moved away from downtown altogether," further exacerbating the geographic segregation of the city.[27] Although this area had served at the turn of the century as the center of finance, commerce, and entertainment for individuals of every class, race, and nationality, the growing development of suburbs that privileged automobile traffic diminished the centrality of downtown as an occasional shopping or leisure destination for the Euro-American elite and middle-class population by the 1920s. At this point, as Robert Fogelson argues, downtown Los Angeles "was one, and by no means the most stylish, of its business districts."[28] Richard Longstreth has likewise argued that "symbolically no less than in function the central district ceased to be of central importance to the experience of many area residents," as developments along Wilshire and Hollywood Boulevards competed for the patronage of Angelenos.[29]

Accompanying the decade's dramatic demographic growth was a substantial increase of theatrical activity, theater construction, and leisure options available in the city. Camille Naomi Rezutko Bokar notes that Los Angeles had only three legitimate houses before World War I. By 1923, however, "it was apparent that Los Angeles was no longer considered a one-week dead-end stop or lay-over for San Francisco engagements," and at least six major theaters were opened between 1926 and 1927 alone.[30] Concurrent with these developments, expansion of shopping and recreation in downtown continued to occur primarily along Broadway, with a flurry of theater, movie palace, and department store construction in the 1920s even more definitively shifting the city's retailing and entertainment center south and west of its previous location along Main and Spring streets. In terms of film exhibition, 1918 alone saw the gala openings of several major movie palaces, including Sid Grauman's Million Dollar Theater and the Rialto on Broadway and Fred A. Miller's California Theater on Main near Ninth. In addition, the construction of movie palaces in outlying neighborhoods in the mid-1920s (including, in Hollywood, Grauman's Chinese and Egyptian Theaters) meant that older exhibition spaces in the downtown area, including the Grand and Mason Opera Houses (on North Broadway), would eventually be converted to Spanish-language venues (see fig. 14).[31]

Because the area near the Plaza retained its significance as a cultural and social center for the Mexican immigrants of the city, new urban development created opportunity for the further growth in the old city center of entertainment venues that catered specifically to the needs of the laboring class, and the

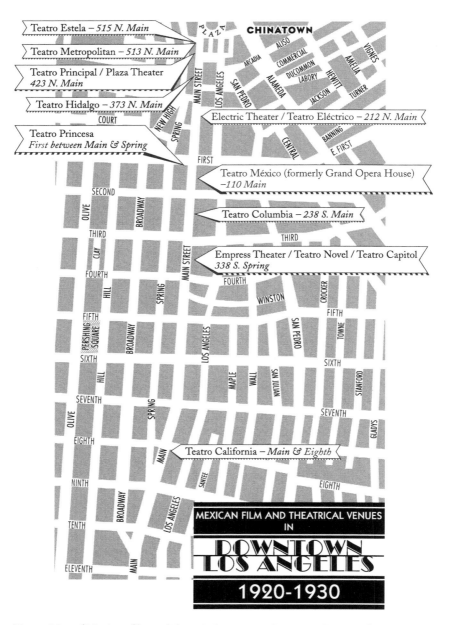

Fig. 14. Map of Mexican film and theatrical venues in downtown Los Angeles, 1920–1930. Designed by Daniel González.

large Mexican immigrant community in particular. The trajectory of what would become the Teatro Novel perhaps constitutes an illustrative case of these broader trends taking shape by 1920. While the venue's history is particularly convoluted, it nonetheless offers a glimpse of the changing entertainment landscape of Los Angeles and key transitions in urban space. Located at Fourth and South Spring (when the area was still a center of business and finance), the building was constructed in 1903 and originally opened as the Casino Theater. Initially promising a museum of attractions (including wax figures), manager Jacob E. Waldeck eventually settled on musical burlesque, while also providing patrons with a billiard room, sidewalk peepshows, and a roof garden.[32] Within the next four years, however, the programming and management would change multiple times.

As the Casino's name changed from the Hotchkiss and then to the Los Angeles, it also experimented with light opera, musical comedy, and vaudeville, often fluctuating between these events. The constant turnover (coupled with a remarkable number of tragic occurrences, including Waldeck's suicide) led some to speculate that the venue suffered from an incurable "hoodoo," while the *Los Angeles Times* commented that the theater "was blessed with a magnificent location and cursed with an endless run of bad luck."[33] The multiple failures attributed to misfortune, however, were more likely the result of a tumultuous, transitional period in theatrical entertainment and urban development. Not only were the major vaudeville houses relocating to Broadway (and abandoning Spring), but local theaters and impresarios struggled to compete or negotiate with the major theatrical exchanges, the offices of which were located in San Francisco when it still functioned as the epicenter of West Coast theatrical activity.

After three years of steady success with vaudeville, the theater's name was changed to the Empress in 1911, and it offered weekly programs of "20th Century Vaudeville" during the early 1910s, presenting a variety of skits, novelty routines, and short films and changing hands between the Marcus Loew and the Sullivan and Considine vaudeville interests on multiple occasions between 1914 and 1915 (see fig. 15).[34] Eventually, the Empress would host boxing matches and other sporting events, with the management installing an "electric scoreboard" that allowed audiences to follow along with baseball games.[35] By 1918 its tenure as a vaudeville theater had come to a definitive end, concurrent with the advent of feature films and the construction of larger, more elegantly appointed movie palaces and vaudeville theaters along Broadway and in the southern end of downtown. The Empress at this point was occupied by the Bible Institute Auditorium and advertised multiple church services on a daily basis. During a transitional period, the theater hosted Spanish-language entertainment, while also occasionally offering sporting events. In fact, the night after a wrestling match between Jim Londos and Angelo "Italian Hercules" Taranasi took place at the Empress, the theater was renamed the Teatro Zendejas, with advertisements promising two daily variety presentations.[36]

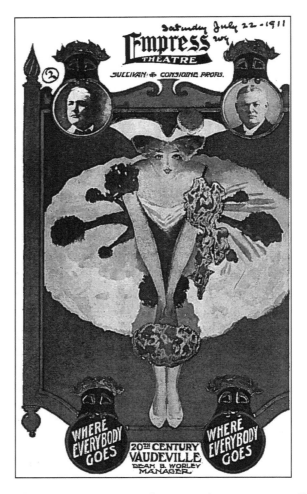

Fig. 15. Program for the Empress Theatre, July 22, 1911. Theater Program Collection, Seaver Center for Western History Research, Los Angeles.

By December 1919 the theater had yet again changed its name to Teatro Novel (after the theatrical company of the same name) and would become one of the more prestigious Spanish-language venues in the city during the next few years (see fig. 16). It was, in fact, one of a number of theaters that emerged along North Broadway, South Spring, or South Main that would aspire to host more "culti-vated" theatrical performances for Mexican audiences by the early 1920s, includ-ing the Teatro Capitol (which itself had once been a playhouse featuring musical comedy, then a movie house). As the history of the Empress suggests, many ven-ues changed management frequently in this area of downtown, with the booming construction of Broadway contributing to conditions in which Spanish-language

Fig. 16. Program for Teatro Novel, November 8, 1920. Theater Program Collection, Seaver Center for Western History Research, Los Angeles.

theater (among other leisure options) found ample opportunity to develop and grow beyond the confines of North Main.

Just as entertainment options expanded dramatically, so did coverage and criticism in local papers like *El Heraldo de México* and *La Opinión* (founded in 1926). Theatrical activity in Los Angeles did provide a source of revenue through advertisements placed by theaters, and entertainment news became a more prominent element of *El Heraldo* until it ceased publication in 1929. Theater and cinema received regular but limited attention in 1920, for instance, with occasional columns noting exceptional events. By 1924 such items had become a daily feature of the paper, often occupying an entire page or more. Not surprisingly, critics and journalists in Spanish-language dailies continued to privilege the-atrical entertainment and venues that participated in the mutually beneficial arrangement between their particular conceptions of Mexican identity and Mexican-owned businesses, the press, and the consulate. In fact, venues that did not adhere to their criteria of respectability and artistry or that lay outside this mutually sustaining network of institutions rarely received mention in the pages of these newspapers, if at all.

While continuing to reinforce connections between consumption, cul-tural retention, political advocacy, and Mexican nationalism, entertainment coverage over the course of the 1920s located the new theatrical convergence along Spring Street in a way that by implication reproduced strains of Main Street discourse. That is, expansion of the Mexican theater district allowed for a perceptible class distinction to emerge within this environment and for Mexican critics to disavow "low-class" entertainment in ways that converged with mainstream representations of the immigrant working class along Main. Several Mexican-oriented venues opened on parts of Spring and Broadway that were indeed equated with the earliest emergence of legitimate theater and opera in the city, somewhat replicating distinctions between taste regimes mapped spatially.

Although continuing to defend Mexico and Mexicans in the light of Hol-lywood's "denigrating" images, Spanish-language journalists often themselves denigrated North Main and its audiences with some regularity. During the 1920s columnists in *La Opinión* and *El Heraldo* did this in part by emphasizing the necessity of theater productions that contributed to the "moral and intellectual elevation of our people," often disparaging less reputable presentations in the process.[37] The attitude of such critics at least partially reflects contemporaneous shifts in the broader cultural sphere, as Lawrence Levine has demonstrated. The early twentieth century, for instance, witnessed a hardened distinction between legitimate and "popular" entertainments, and "the arbiters of culture turned their attention to establishing appropriate means of receiving culture," by "disciplin-ing and training audiences."[38] This phenomenon was also accompanied by the Progressive Era notion that, contrary to the vulgar appeal of mass culture, forms such as opera, symphonic concerts, and legitimate theater held the potential to provide audiences with moral uplift. Mexican critics and playwrights accord-ingly struggled to mark a class-based distinction between proper theater and unruly popular amusements, a distinction that could once again be mapped spatially on the fabric of downtown. This disparagement of North Main, once again, marked an attempt to claim a cultural and moral high ground that would somehow counteract or elevate the low status of Mexicans in the city's racial, economic, and social hierarchies.

In Mexican Los Angeles, however, these emergent hierarchical divisions—between Spring and Main, high and low, elevated and vulgar—proved rather unstable and highly mutable and often yielded to practicality, despite the best efforts of cultural authorities. This instability was undoubtedly the result of the theater environment's utter volatility: venues closed and reopened repeatedly, ownership of theaters changed hands on a regular basis, theatrical performances regularly shared the stage with cinema, troupes disbanded and reformed, and any financial successes relied on the patronage of an economically distressed population. Rather than simply insisting on a clear or rigid demarcation between high and low, therefore, critics and cultural authorities advocated forms of entertainment that bridged class divides in the name of constructing a cohesive Mexican audience and proper national subjects. Just as important, this discursive maneuver attempted to cultivate and harness this unified audience in the name of economic expediency (as with more recent marketing construction of the Latino population); attracting all classes and presenting entertainment suitable for a family audience was essential for the survival of an alternative cultural and economic network *and* the maintenance of a cohesive México de afuera.

This complex relationship between the expatriate elite, theatrical culture, newspapers, the working class, and mass culture was not unique to Mexican Los Angeles. The first decades of the twentieth century witnessed analogous struggles among African American populations, Jewish immigrants in New York, the German American population, and Italian immigrants, among others. With 1900–1930 marking an unprecedented flourishing of immigrant and ethnic theater across the United States (coincident with the rise of mass media, including Hollywood and radio), debates over identity, class, and cultural representation frequently centered on this arena.[39] As a number of scholars have demonstrated, the cultural battles between immigrant newcomers and a native-born cultural elite were also accompanied by a simultaneous struggle internal to many ethnic and immigrant populations. In many of these cases, attempts to produce and promote entertainment across divisions of class constituted a broader effort to construct a "community of consumers" among a heterogeneous ethnic population, as Sabine Haenni has compellingly argued. As she has noted in her analysis of German American theater in particular, "because immigrant cultural entrepreneurs have both a diverse and limited audience, they often actively reshape cultural hierarchies" in a way that encourages national or ethnic affiliations over those of class.[40] This particular effort to forge community differs substantially from the struggles that pitted arbiters of high culture in direct opposition to cinema (and other cheap amusements) in a Euro-American context. In practice, this internal class struggle within heterogeneous ethnic populations often meant that middle-class theater owners and producers made concessions to working-class taste out of financial necessity and ethnic solidarity, while also working to appease the critical sensibilities of their own cultural authorities like journalists and critics (who were often compelled themselves to adopt a negotiated stance).

While commonalities and parallels exist between distinct ethnic contexts, however, it is important when examining such cases to consider precisely what *kind* of community is being constructed or imagined in this reshaping or negotiation. As Nina Warnke has demonstrated, for instance, debates over music halls in New York's Yiddish newspapers occurred between intellectuals who, despite political differences, "regarded themselves as the immigrants' cultural and political educators, as guardians of immigrant immorality, and guides *on the road* to a cautious Americanization" (emphasis mine).[41] Addressing the specificity of the Italian immigrant population in New York, Giorgio Bertellini argues that "moviegoing and theatergoing enhanced an adaptation to pressing ascriptions of vernacular and national identity and leisure-time habits, rather than mere assimilation into the American way of life."[42] Mexican cultural authorities in Los Angeles, by comparison, strove to create a community united in its retention of culture and language against Americanization, fostering the cohesion of a Mexican population that would eventually return to Mexico with its sense of singular national identity intact, if not enhanced. At the same time, advocacy of respectable entertainment on the part of critics would challenge the Euro-American monopoly on the term while implicitly militating against notions of racial or cultural inferiority.

To this extent, it is worth revising accounts of both the Spanish-language theater and the press that assume that either institution provided a facile reflection of a community and its values. Writing about Mexican American theater in Texas, for instance, Elizabeth Ramírez claims that "the theater provided the Mexican American with a type of entertainment that unified the community through language, [and] themes based on familiar experiences and their history, [and] fulfilled their sense of nationalism through identity with the mother country, and through entertainment suitable for the entire family."[43] Instead, theatrical production and criticism produced by the upper classes aspired to formulate a notion of a Mexican audience unified by national identity. Theater marked an attempt to create this "community of consumers" through contesting and constructing representations of Mexican immigrants as textual figures and as an audience. Because this population was fragmented by class, however, the attempts to create entertainment that appealed to *all* Mexicans in Los Angeles, although varied, were often short-lived or limited in their success. As Peter C. Haney has argued about Mexican theater in San Antonio, rather than a straightforward reflection of a community, "the theater offered a space in which ethnic Mexicans symbolically reflected on the contradictions involved in their processes of community formation," a phenomenon that also included cultural criticism, at least in Los Angeles.[44] The identification of tensions within the cultural production that targeted the Mexican population usefully revises assumptions that ethnic theater in general somehow automatically "[brought] together people of widely divergent backgrounds" to share "a common experience."⁴⁵ Instead, the construction of community that occurred through theatrical discourse itself possessed specific attributes, motivated by a class of cultural producers with intertwined cultural and economic investments.

How does this specific conception of community (successful or otherwise) relate to constructions and representations of Mexicanidad produced by cinema? In the broadest sense, Mexican theatrical culture became a staging ground for grappling with the impact and influence of mass culture among an immigrant population. These efforts were multifaceted, inconsistent, and at times even apparently contradictory. Most notably, while "respectable" Mexican theater ostensibly combated the influence of mass culture, it also paradoxically made concessions to elements of working-class appeal (including inspiration drawn from Hollywood film) in the name of crafting community cohesion through consumption. Its producers and playwrights also actively worked to correct unfavorable representations of Mexicans circulating in Hollywood film and other venues. In this respect, initiatives to bridge class divides through entertainment were inextricable from efforts to generate positive images of Mexicans for the benefit of the working class and, at least hypothetically, non-Mexican audiences as well. Consequently, the history of live theater and theatrical criticism became inextricable from the broader history of Mexican film culture, immigrant identity, community formation, and conceptions of Mexicanidad in the context of Los Angeles.

A History of Critical Failures: Cheap Variety and the Pelado

Theatrical and critical efforts to craft a community through this cultural milieu in Los Angeles were troubled by the recurring appearance of a controversial character: the *pelado*. This disheveled, working-class man (not infrequently inebriated) was a staple of cheap variety shows and *revistas* (musical revues) as comic relief (a character type later made famous on film by Cantinflas).⁴⁶ To cultural critics, the pelado's particular mobilization of race and class only reproduced the worst Mexican stereotypes generated by Hollywood. To this extent, it threatened their ongoing efforts to elevate the cultural and racial status of Mexican immigrants in Los Angeles. More than constituting simply another example of the critical policing of the textual representation of Mexicans, the controversy over the pelado instead sheds light on the nature of theatrical criticism produced by the Spanish-language dailies. In particular, it demonstrates how interrelated issues of form (particularly the variety format) and content (stereotypical characters) informed the evaluation of theater in both moral and aesthetic terms. Just as important, this episode provides crucial insight into the kind of formal and textual compromises that critics and playwrights proposed in their efforts to build a respectable, cross-class theatrical culture.

The nature of the pelado controversy in the 1920s was inarguably inextricable from the popularity and prevalence of certain theatrical genres and their reception in Los Angeles. During this flourishing of Mexican theatrical culture, there was a definitive shift away from legitimate theater patronized by the *californio* (descendant of Spanish families living in California before 1848) and Mexican expatriate elite of the nineteenth century and toward genres like the revista and vaudeville offered at "popular prices" and performed in vernacular language and slang, reflecting the tastes of the surrounding working-class population. Indeed, the programs presented by each theater varied widely and changed substantially from week to week and between boundaries of taste and class distinction. As Kanellos notes, "as commercial ventures, the theatrical companies were driven by the tastes and interests of their audiences, and they would perform whatever it was that would please, be it comedy, drama, or variety acts."[47] In the early 1920s a number of resident stock companies (or *cuadros*) generated much of the more prominent Spanish-language theatrical activity in Los Angeles. Probably ranging in size from about ten to thirty members, these troupes were capable of producing a wide range of theatrical offerings, including a repertoire of operettas, plays, and dramas.[48] Cuadro Novel, for instance, reportedly had available more than two hundred works in a range of different genres.[49] For the year 1920 alone, listings for the Teatro Hidalgo included zarzuelas, two-act comedies, translations of Shakespeare plays (including *Othello*), illusionists and magicians, dramas, revistas, concerts, and films. Indeed, the bulk of the productions consisted of what might be considered variety or musicals, and many companies evidently struggled with the demands to consistently present audiences with a fresh variety of acts (see fig. 17).

To some extent, the demands that variety placed on these stock companies were a function of regularly attracting audiences with the promise of novelty by regularly changing bills (sometimes daily), thus encouraging repeat attendance. This strategy was also undoubtedly an attempt on the part of companies and theaters to attract a Mexican audience across class divisions. Perhaps drawing inspiration from the success of English-language vaudeville, theater managers mobilized variety and diversity as a way to offer "something to everyone" in a single program (from condensed operas to slapstick comedy). As M. Alison Kibler has demonstrated in the context of U.S. vaudeville, this involved including forms and entertainment associated with the legitimate stage, while "sanitizing" less reputable forms in a way that would appease middle-class audiences without losing the patronage of the working class. Rather than marking a straightforward rejection or disciplining of low culture, vaudeville instead constitutes a key example of the way in which emergent mass culture simultaneously "uplifted low culture and unraveled high culture," working across social divisions rather than erasing them.[50] Eliminating vulgarity also made theatrical presentations, at least theoretically, suitable for a family audience, with clear economic implications.

TEATROS

Teatro Novel

CALLE SOUTH SPRING, ENTRE 5a. Y 4a.
RESERVE SUS ASIENTOS con Anticipación Tel. 63967

Empresa CUADRO NOVEL en Combinación con
I. P. RIVAS

HOY DOMINGO 25 DE ENERO DE 1920

Por la Tarde a las 2.30

1o.—El Sentimental Drama Mexicano en Seis Actos:

MALDITAS SEAN LAS MUJERES

Por la Noche a las 8 p. m.

1o.—ESTRENO de la Comedia en un Acto, titulado:

"EL MISSISSIPPI"

2o.—La Colosal Zarzuela Española en tres Cuadros:

LOS GUAPOS

MAÑANA LUNES 26 DE ENERO DE 1920
El Célebre Drama Histórico Mexicano en 5 Actos:

JESUS ARRIAGA, CHUCHO EL ROTO
O LA NOBLEZA DE UN BANDIDO

TEATRO HIDALGO

373 N. Main St.—Los Angeles, California

LUNES 26 DE ENERO DE 1920

PRESENTACION DEL CELEBRE

JUSTINIANI

y su Medium EDLANI
——ACTOS SORPRENDENTES DE——

MENTALISMO, PRESTIDIGITACION

E ILUSIONISMO

GRANDIOSAS VISTAS DE CINEMATOGRAFO

CAMBIO DE PROGRAMA TODOS LOS DIAS

PRECIOS : 10 CTS. 20 CTS. Y 30 CTS.

Fig. 17. Listings for the Teatros Novel and Hidalgo. *El Heraldo de México*, January 25, 1920.

The embrace of an analogous variety strategy in Mexican Los Angeles struck a tenuous balance between classes, understandably placing a strain on the companies, while leaving them open to negative assessment. One critic complained in *El Heraldo de México*, for instance, that the Arte Mexicano company "had not at all refreshed its repertoire of songs and dances and what it is offering the public is the same thing from last year's season," noting that its new revue would no doubt be composed of "a series of variety numbers of the sort that are beginning to tire audiences."[51] The paper likewise complained that the Capitol's resident troupe was repeating shows and thus not offering a theatrical experience of true quality. Although it acknowledged that the theater changed bills on a daily basis, it suggested that the troupe instead limit its repertoire and rehearse fewer works more extensively as a way of "satisfying certain tastes of our *colonia* [a term frequently used to refer to the city's Mexican population]" and assuring the regular attendance of the "best families."[52]

While varied programs may have failed to live up to their promise of novelty and technical polish, their blurring of taste distinctions often challenged middle-class and elite conceptions of proper entertainment in which respectability and authentic Mexicanness converged. Journalists (several of them playwrights) writing for local Spanish-language newspapers often expressed lofty disdain for the prevalence of vaudeville and variety acts in Los Angeles, while lamenting the lack of more respectable or legitimate presentations. Of particular concern to these journalists was the emergence and popularity of the revista, a genre of French origin that gained popularity in Mexico during the revolution. As one critic in 1925 commented, revistas were presented in all the local houses and proved very successful regardless of their often vulgar insinuations and double entendres.[53] Journalist and playwright Gabriel Navarro, in an interview with *El Heraldo de México*, complained that playwrights in the city "had gone down the wrong path, motivated by greed, perhaps not realizing that they are producing opportunistic, commercial works, rather than those of pure art." The efforts of others to produce true works of art, he argued, had been hampered by "the inopportune emergence of the revista in our midst." He went on to denounce the genres recently popular with local audiences: "the revista is the degeneration of the zarzuela, as the operetta is the degeneration of lyric theater, and, frankly, I prefer not to occupy myself with absurdities."[54]

Alongside such scathing assessments in defense of theatrical respectability, other critics launched a sustained engagement with stereotypes appearing within Spanish-language theater. Of particular concern to critics was the aforementioned pelado. A great deal of discomfort with the pelado (along with the Mexican marijuana smoker and the degenerate woman, other apparent staples of variety theater) among critics was motivated by the fact that the working class apparently enjoyed character types that resonated with denigrating images generated by Hollywood. In fact, the pelado figure was often insinuated to be of indigenous extraction, a hapless migrant from rural Mexico to the metropolis (whether within Mexico or beyond). The proliferation of this character and its embrace by the working class held the same potential to "denigrate" or "blacken" the racial standing of Mexicans as did Hollywood stereotypes, undermining the efforts of cultural authorities to elevate their status through the production of morally respectable theatrical entertainment.

The working class, in the eyes of these critics, thus constituted the front lines of a battle as textual representations and disobedient audiences. Cultural authorities of the middle class frequently faulted the working classes for embodying stereotypes and for enjoying spectacles that ostensibly degraded Mexico. Francine Medeiros, in her content analysis of *La Opinión* in its first three years of publication (1926–1929), identifies as a subcategory of editorials those articles that included "pleas for Mexicans in the United States not to act in stereotypic manner [that] includes any editorial critical of Mexicans for contributing to the racist views of them by the dominant society."[55] Elevating and sanitizing theatrical culture thus emerged as a corollary to protesting greaser films and swarthy bandidos *and* disciplining the behavior and self-representation of Mexicans in public space. While suggesting that Los Angeles still lacked proper Castilian theater, for instance, one journalist distinguished such theatrical forms from the popular revista, discounting "tacky revues" and "'works' with synthetic Mexican characters like the lazy and poorly dressed pelado and the eccentric '*soldadera*' [woman soldier of the Mexican Revolution] that only serve to make this country see us as 'greasers.'"[56] If these newspapers struggled to promote their own construction of Mexicanidad in response to representations circulating in mainstream media (including Hollywood), the working class and their consumption habits thus figured as a potential impediment to this process.

Easily the period's most extensive engagement with Mexican stereotypes, and the pelado in particular, occurs in Daniel Venegas's novel *Las aventuras de Don Chipote; o, Cuando los pericos mamen* (*The Adventures of Don Chipote; or, When Parrots Breast-Feed*). Originally published in installments in *El Heraldo de México*, this fictional account traces Mexican working-class immigrant experience in Los Angeles through the adventures of its hapless titular character, Don Chipote. Much of the novel concerns itself with the hardships and discrimination faced by the novel's characters and hence functions as a clear condemnation of the exploitation and racism facing Mexican immigrants in the United States Additionally, as Tomás Ybarra-Frausto has pointed out, "*Don Chipote* is a rich compendium of the dialect, customs, and worldview of the Chicano urban working class of the period."[57] Part of this attempted identification with and evocation of the working class, as Rita E. Urquijo-Ruiz has argued, undoubtedly derives from the author's extensive use of the pelado figure popular in cheap theater.[58] Don Chipote and his associates embody the pelado stereotype, along with the narrator of the novel himself, who also employs the slang and attitude characteristic of this type.

The relationship of *Don Chipote* to the Mexican immigrant working class, however, falls short of a complete identification. As a locally based playwright and journalist, author Venegas embodied the multiple affiliations and ideological orientation of this cohort; this status alone provides insight into his representation of Mexican Los Angeles with the pelado. Venegas was the editor of *El Malcriado* newspaper and a noted playwright. His production of *¿Quién es el culpable?* (Who is to blame?) was performed as a benefit for the Union Pro-Mexico at the Capitol, and he was also at one point the president of the Mexican Journalists Association of California. Not only does this imply an education and social standing that casts a dubious light on his historicization as a "working-class writer," but his protective, paternalistic attitude toward the working class is apparent at multiple levels within the novel.[59] Perhaps most obviously, he regularly ridicules and debases Don Chipote and other characters, while the entire narrative serves as a cautionary tale about immigration that ends with the protagonist's inevitable return to Mexico.

Not coincidentally, we might best unravel this ambivalently critical stance toward the working class through the novel's own condemnation of cheap variety theater. One episode in particular allows us to best appreciate the author's mobilization of the pelado and to gauge a broader aesthetic and critical program that hinged precisely on representations of the working class. First, Venegas's fictionalized condemnation of the cheap entertainments offered to Mexican immigrant audiences in the 1920s is consistent with the nationalist orientation of cultural criticism and the broader middle-class and elite cultural and economic network. In short, the author-narrator judges the theatrical scene on its inability to portray Mexico and its inhabitants with dignity. In one chapter, the protagonist, Don Chipote, visits a variety theater on North Main where the acts consists of a woman who "sang and danced while trying to reveal herself all the way up to where her bloomers were fastened," a comedian that entertained the audience by "telling jokes and babbling baloney as dirty or more bawdy than his predecessor's songs and legs," and a performance of the traditional song "Jarabe Tapatío," during which the dancers on stage "started more or less into stomping their heels and kicking their legs to the music," raising enough dust from the floorboards "to build an adobe house."[60]

While Venegas's description of this environment might be sufficient to convey the attitude of local cultural critics toward revistas and variety shows, the author also offers a more explicit and forceful commentary on this genre:

> The horde of Mexican performers who entertain in the United States know that the Chicano community goes crazy when something reminds them of their blessed cactus land. And, naturally, they exploit it all the time. Thus wherever there are theaters or even the humblest stages, whether the performers are good or bad, there will always be a drunken tramp [the pelado] with or without a charro; and if a comic goes to one of these places and doesn't

know how to do the penniless tramp and dance the "Jarabe Tapatío" he will be deprived of a contract.[61]

Thus while *Don Chipote* may at least partially identify with the working class, it does so from a decidedly patronizing perspective clearly aligned (as is the author) with the theatrical criticism published by the major Spanish-language dailies. The constant critique of the pelado in such contexts, however, neglects the critical potential and "anti-establishment stance" of the figure, precisely the capacity of this underdog figure harnessed by Venegas.[62] Wholesale condemnations of the pelado also overlooked the complex function of ethnic humor in the theater of the early twentieth century.[63] To be certain, the novel's attitude proves to be more complex than a straightforward critique or condemnation of the working class. But, as Urquijo-Ruiz argues, "by presenting the situation of the main character—the little pelado Don Chipote—in the form of a parody, the novel offers an ambiguous perspective, as the parody serves as much to ridicule the supposed stupidity of the rural people that immigrate as to lament the labor abuses that they confront in the United States." According to her, this contradiction "emerges from the dialogue between diverse discourses, specifically between elitism, paternalism, and nationalism, discourses that focus on the working class."[64]

What are we to make of this ambiguity, this apparent contradiction evident within and beyond this particular text? More specifically (and as an embodiment of this contradiction), how do we understand Venegas's simultaneous condemnation *and* appropriation of the pelado? On the one hand, imbuing the novel with characters and narration evocative of this figure might be indicative of Venegas's own stereotyping of the working class that resonates with paternalism of his peers. On the other, however, if comic pelados are popular with the working class in the context of variety theater, translating them to the printed page of *El Heraldo* might also be understood as a simultaneous attempt to attract a working-class readership. This appeal would seem particularly pertinent to cultivate in a work designed at least partially with a didactic purpose of dissuading immigration and encouraging a return to Mexico. The source of the ambiguity perceived by Urquijo-Ruiz is thus indicative of a broader attempt to create cross-class entertainment (including a press culture) by simultaneously encouraging identification with *and* against the pelado and hence embedding appeals to multiple audiences within the same text. On another level, *Don Chipote* represents a formal solution to the creation of cultural forms for a Mexican audience across social divisions. Namely, it is crucial to note the stereotype of the pelado is here integrated into a structure modeled on a long tradition of picaresque novels. In this case, working-class appeal is carefully contained by a critical distance from the working class and within a form associated with European literary traditions. *Don Chipote* obviously exemplifies the attitude of cultural authorities toward the consumption habits of the working class. But it also embodies the kinds of textual balances of content and form that would characterize Mexican-oriented theatrical production and press culture in the 1920s and the efforts to construct a cohesive Mexican audience-cum-community.

A History of Momentary Successes: Creating the Mexican Audience

As the 1920s progressed, critics and playwrights alike responded on multiple fronts to the increasing ascendancy of revista and variety presentations to the detriment of dramatic theater. While I have mapped the general contours of this critical backlash, its implications for actual theatrical production bear out a complex series of compromises. Namely, in their critical condemnations of variety and the stereotypes that appeared therein, these journalists and playwrights were not exclusively concerned with the definition and maintenance of cultural distinctions, a condemnation of the low and an exaltation of the high. Instead, these critics sought a balance that would simultaneously attract and elevate the working class while also drawing middle-class audiences, sustaining theatrical venues in the process. Rather than maintain the illusion that working-class audiences would be drawn to high cultural forms, critics and playwrights created and advocated a partial embrace of their ostensible sensibilities (which included enthusiasm for Hollywood), while incorporating an emphasis on cultural standards. In other words, this creative cohort hoped to achieve a delicate compromise between mass culture and locally produced theater. These compromises included a revised conceptual map of the downtown entertainment landscape but would primarily become evident in the form and content of "proper" theater. Ultimately, this cultural elite desired the elimination of negative representations generated by Hollywood and variety theater, aspiring to represent Mexicans as textual figures, to elevate their status through the production of respectable theater, *and* to unite them as a cohesive audience.

While the moral and cultural consequences of representation were often foregrounded within this criticism, it is also apparent that economic factors motivated the orientation of critics and their attempt to imagine and construct a Mexican audience. The persistent complaints about the absence of a "true Mexican theater" held particular stakes for these critics and were linked directly to the sustainability of cross-class, respectable venues rather than the existence of any theatrical presentations per se. The lack of a cross-class balance within theatrical landscape thus facilitated a supposed vacuum where improper representations and problematic consumption habits were likely to emerge. As one critic argued, this void accounted for the fact that Mexicans regularly patronized the Hippodrome (a popular downtown vaudeville venue on South Main), which proved attractive by offering variety and novelty despite its lack of specifically Mexican entertainment. Conversely, this lack of patronage also meant that "quality" Mexican entertainers eschewed Spanish-language venues. The case of Armandita Chirot proved emblematic of artists whose talents were too great for Main and were thus compelled to seek work (as Chirot did) in high-class vaudeville like Loew's. For critics, the lack of true (i.e., respectably national and cross-class) theater thus held multiple, mutually dependent consequences: the moral and cultural corruption of audiences, their concomitant preference for English-language entertainment, the consequent precariousness of Mexican-owned businesses, and (in the completion of this vicious circle) the flight of quality Mexican entertainers that might attract Mexican audiences and thus sustain Spanish-language venues.

The expediency and practicality of a proposed balance also became consistently evident through critics' inability to sustain a distinct conceptual boundary between Main and Spring. That is, if Main was the locus of the basest and least cultivated presentations (and the undisputed home of the pelado), cultural authorities were nonetheless often forced to acknowledge that the Mexican cultural landscape could never completely escape the orbit of this street and its reputation, particularly given the popular appeal of its offerings. The spatial mapping of cultural distinction thus proved a necessarily malleable process, ultimately marked by and indicative of a broader compromise.

Efforts to re-present the Mexican presence downtown through the distinction between Main and Spring or Broadway, although drawing on associations of respectability, was porous, with critics often expressing disappointment that such divisions did not coincide more precisely with cultural distinction. One commentator in 1925 conveyed lofty aspirations for the "respectable" Teatro Capitol on Spring: "all we want is a guarantee to the public that seriousness reigns in all parts in the elegant coliseum on Spring Street, where decent theater is produced and successes happen daily." Because the theater had recently (and unexpectedly) raised its prices, however, this author perceived the tenuousness of this aspiration. Arguing that the Mexican population should have access to quality theater at affordable prices, the author speculated that families surprised by the ticket hike would likely "retire to a ten-cent cinema or go to a theater of lesser quality on Main," thus undermining the very premise of a respectable, unifying Spanish-language theater.[65] Likewise, another critic in 1927 expressed dismay that the only factor ultimately separating Main and Spring were admission prices, with the Capitol charging two dollars more for incomplete repetitions of things already shown on Main (meeting with poor attendance and "indifference").[66] Price might thus act as a (false) guarantor of quality, but it also presented a financial detriment to the theater and hence a potential barrier to the construction of a unified Mexican audience.

Perhaps surprisingly, certain presentations were accused of violating this strategic balance through an excess of elevation. That is, just as vulgarity and shoddy showmanship were derided as too low, ignoring popular taste was likewise regarded as unproductively exclusive. When the Orquesta Típica de Torreblanca visited Los Angeles, it performed at the Philharmonic to a multiethnic audience and at the Capitol, presumably to a more homogenously Mexican public. While

El Heraldo celebrated the orchestra as an example of the kind of entertainment
that would benefit future generations of Mexicans, it was also critical of its performance at the Capitol. In particular, one critic complained that the failure of
the group in this venue could be attributed to "the inclusion of too much classical and opera music." As "Mexicans, and particularly those accustomed to Main
Street, respond more forcefully to the familiar tunes of Mexican music, which
reminds them of their home country," the Orquesta's presentation "should have
been more accessible to the majority of Mexicans in the *colonia*." By attracting a
general audience, the group may have represented "another artist that dignifies
Mexico in the eyes of foreigners," but it served as a negative example in the creation of a broader Mexican audience.[67]

What kind of presentations, then, did Mexican critics advocate? How did
journalists and playwrights imagine and construct an expedient brand of Mexicanidad through theatrical production and criticism? How precisely was a
cross-class balance imagined or executed on a textual level? For the most part,
playwrights proposed reaching this tenuous balance through a necessary compromise of either form or content (but rarely both at once). More specifically, if
critics framed variety shows and revistas as particularly problematic, it was often
through the adjustment of their very conventions that an acceptable balance was
achieved. On the one hand, many of the very critics that condemned revistas
adapted a more negotiated stance toward them during the course of the 1920s,
even composing works in this genre. The elevation of this particular form, however, required a modification of content: songs and routines expressed acceptable forms of nationalism, while narrative trajectories emphasized an inevitable
return to Mexico (and cultural maintenance in the United States). On the other
hand, it was not only that variety and revistas supposedly fostered repetition,
but that their modular form and improvisational quality too easily allowed for
unpredictable digressions into the popular and vulgar. Through more formally
centered solutions, playwrights thus aspired to displace and avoid problematic
spontaneity through reliance on a legitimate form like scripted drama, while
drawing on and sanitizing cultural forms popular with the working class (Hollywood film, revistas, sensational current events, etc.). On both counts, local
playwrights and critics strove to promote live theater that acknowledged and
harnessed popular appeal while expunging its more objectionable qualities.

Even the reviled revista form itself, for instance, could be recuperated as part
of the broader strategy of balance and cross-class compromise if properly executed. Despite the avowed distaste for musical revues among this group of critics, the arrival of Mexican playwright Guz Aguila in 1924 was widely celebrated
and his oeuvre distinguished from local fare described by Venegas and others:
"When Guz Aguila came, the revista had fallen from prestige. With the exception of two or three exemplary works, the overwhelming majority of revistas
have been copies, sketches, simulated reproductions, and modified repetitions
presented as premiers. And we were already fed up with these vulgar, tedious,

incoherent, and worn out revistas." This and other reviews made apparent that what made Aguila's pieces worthy of attendance were their "nationalist and political themes" and the way the revues "sing of the past, the hearty ancestry of our people, which is enough of a calling card for a public that likes to breathe in the ambience of Glory and Nation."[68] Aguila himself made the underlying logic of such praise apparent: it hinged precisely on the elimination of the vulgarity and stereotypes associated with the working class. Introducing his work at Teatro Hidalgo, he explained "his constant efforts to dignify our scenic art, to remove from it immoral mystifications, the nauseating and repulsive pelado, and the ignoble, dirty and degenerate woman presented by authors without conscience." The purpose of eliminating such elements, as one critic explained, would be "to show that we have theater and that it can be presented abroad without contempt for our prestige."[69] This aspiration toward prestige also involved strategically creating distance for Mexicans from the racialization implied by stereotypes like the pelado, with their lowness linked as it was to indigenous or mixed-race heritage.

The emphasis on prestige coincided directly with aforementioned discourses of nationalism emerging in postrevolutionary Mexico. Within the cultural component of Mexico's nation-building project, regional musical forms (mariachi, for instance), certain cultural types (the charro and his female counterpart, the *china poblana*, a national type associated with traditional femininity), and a certain visual vocabulary (a celebration of a romanticized indigenous past) would eventually be elevated to the status of an essential national expression. Not surprisingly, these cultural types and forms became central to this effort because they attempted to correct disparaging images of Mexico circulating abroad in Hollywood and the yellow press; countered the notion of Mexico as a war-torn, impoverished, and racially "mongrel" republic; and capitalized on specific aspects of the growing fascination with the country in the United States. For the Mexican population of Los Angeles, stereotypes of Mexico held by North Americans also justified discrimination and inequality on multiple levels. The stakes of representation would thus take on a distinct meaning in this context, where transnational Mexicanidad aspired toward forming a national community across classes (and borders) *and* toward elevating the social and racial status of Mexicans in Los Angeles. In particular, it was Aguila's expulsion of the working-class pelado and the so-called degenerate woman from this genre that ultimately made it an acceptable form of national entertainment and a strategic elevation of Mexicans. Not surprisingly, the much-heralded Aguila revues in question featured a number of folkloric elements that would soon become the undisputed hallmarks of cultural nationalism (in cinema and otherwise), a quality that theater critics in Los Angeles would value relative to presentations that supposedly conveyed an unfavorable image of Mexico and Mexicans.

Naturally, this emergent brand of nationalism figured prominently and regularly in theatrical productions of the cohort of playwrights and critics working in Mexican Los Angeles, coinciding with their broader ideological impetus. In fact, despite the initially vitriolic condemnations of variety and revistas as vulgar and base, many of the prominent playwrights (including critics like Gabriel Navarro) would themselves eventually pen revistas produced in Los Angeles. Although working within generic conventions, these individuals typically distanced their works from supposedly more vulgar examples of this genre. Most significant, despite the lack of extant theatrical texts, plot summaries in local newspapers and elsewhere indicate a consistent narrative trope, regardless of form: the resistance to Americanization and the return to Mexico. Examples of this trope abound, as it functioned to sanitize and elevate the revista genre while at least implicitly claiming the moral superiority of Mexican culture over U.S. mass culture. A 1927 musical titled *El maldito jazz* (Damned jazz) staged at Teatro Capitol, for instance, chronicled the descent of a Mexican girl through her love of U.S. culture while simultaneously trading on the popularity of jazz music as an Americanizing influence.[70] This play coincided with the aforementioned anxiety about de-Mexicanization of a second generation, and of young Mexican girls in particular.[71] While commentators in the Spanish-language press consistently posited jazz as the antithesis to elevated Mexican music, the implications of this perspective (while never explicitly stated) suggest that they advocated for an interrelated moral and racial elevation by again distancing proper Mexicanidad from blackness. By positing American popular culture as attractive yet immoral, such a play self-reflexively validates itself as an antidote to a brand of cultural consumption that presents a threat on multiple fronts.

Several of Navarro's own revistas likewise embodied this tendency while somewhat paradoxically embracing and critiquing the allure of Hollywood. The 1927 adaptation of his serialized novel *La ciudad de irás y no volverás* (The city of you go and never come back) chronicled the journey of an aspiring Mexican actress who arrives in Hollywood to find only disappointment and anonymity (simultaneously appropriating and critiquing the appeal of Hollywood). As did *Maldito jazz*, this novel proposed a gendered nationalism that exhibited anxieties about the impact of mass culture on young Mexican women. The protagonist's migration to Hollywood and quest for stardom requires her to repeatedly violate accepted standards of Mexican womanhood (including the loss of her virginity). Both this production and his *La ciudad de los extras* also include encounters between the protagonist and assimilated Mexicans, the latter held up for critical scrutiny and ridicule.[72] Some of the cultural production of this group might easily be characterized as morality tales about immigration, acculturation, and cultural consumption, as was the case with *Don Chipote*. As such, they provide us at least a partial glimpse of how these critics imagined cultural distinctions and their potential transformation and Mexican theater as a bulwark against assimilation despite its incorporation of mass culture. Navarro's revistas in particular, not surprisingly, harness the popularity of Hollywood and Mexicanize it through theatrical adaptation, a dynamic reminiscent of his ambivalent coverage of Hollywood stars during this period.[73]

If content and message remained a consistent concern of critics, formal conceits also provided their own solutions to the conception of proper Mexican theater. To some degree, the theaters and critics equated cultural elevation and respectability with European theatrical genres and properties. One of the more prevalent staples during the 1920s was the zarzuela, and theaters featured them consistently as part of a variety program, along with comedies, dramas, and other light operas. In addition, many of the dramas performed were penned by Spanish playwrights, while Spanish-language adaptations of Shakespeare were also programmed with regular frequency. Not coincidentally, critics consistently equated true theater with works performed in academic Castilian Spanish, the language of legitimate drama (and analogous in some respects to British English).

To some degree, the valuation of such theater apparently corresponded to racial constructions of Mexicans during the period, an effort to sanitize and whiten a group that was often represented as mongrels (the half-breeds of the greaser films), hence discursively distancing them from the racial taints of indigenous heritage and working-class sensibility. In fact, the critics and playwrights often lauded and promoted the development of "Hispano-American" theater, thus emphasizing European cultural heritage to the exclusion of the indigenous, with the attendant notions of cultural elevation. Plans to construct the Teatro Latino in 1927 coincided with such an emphasis, by aligning its proposed programming with European high culture through the presentation of French, Italian, and Spanish theater, including the formation of an opera company. According to *La Opinión*, this effort would remedy the lack of a "'true' theater: amply sized, comfortable, decent, and worthy of the 200,000 Mexicans and other thousands of Spaniards and Hispano-Americans that live in this city."[74] Furthermore, though the revista was often singled out for criticism, newspaper critics acknowledged its derivation from French genres. The problem resided not in the genre per se, then, only that "revistas in Mexico have not reached the level of accomplishment of those in Europe," establishing French precedent as a standard against which to measure local theater.[75]

While a reliance on traditional forms constituted one component of a strategy of elevation, the logic of this approach at least partially hinged on the actors' adherence to a fixed script, eliminating the risks of improvisation (and hence vulgarity). When *El Heraldo* announced the formation of the Sociedad de Actores Latinos (Society of Latino Actors), it explained the purpose of the organization thusly: "to encourage the production of true theater and true Mexican culture, to possibly improve the well-being of the artists, and to advocate for the public," an aspiration consistent with the orientation of Mexican press I have thus far outlined. To achieve these aims, Carlos J. Vargas argued that the theater should be monitored and regulated as it was in Mexico, because "it is prostituted here more than anywhere else on the continent." If the Mexican theater often resorted to the use of culturally recognizable types, it did so "tastefully and in a way that places them in correct context and light, not using them endlessly and irresponsibly as an expression of national culture." Following the "Mexican example" would entail restraint on the part of theatrical troupes, the monitoring of theater by "authorities," and the production of theater in "respectable theaters [that] *respect the letter of the work*" (emphasis mine).[76]

Within this embrace of scripted works, perhaps the most notable examples of theatrical compromise were the original dramatic works penned by local authors. As Kanellos indicates, such works were part of a larger trend: "1922 to 1933 saw the emergence and box-office success of a group of playwrights in Los Angeles that was made up mainly of Mexican theatrical expatriates and newspapermen" who produced works dealing with social and political issues, current events, and recent crimes.[77] As in Texas, the production of locally authored plays may have emerged as a response to audience demand for new works that would remedy the repeated appearance of established productions or classic works.[78] In addition to Adalberto González, this cohort consisted of Eduardo Carrillo, Esteban V. Escalante, Brígido Caro, and Gabriel Navarro, some of whom also wrote for both *El Heraldo de México* and *La Opinión*. As John Koegel has likewise pointed out, such works continued and updated conventions of Mexican theater where "social and political commentary was prominent . . . and working-class sensibilities were addressed to a greater extent," fulfilling a demand for topical productions throughout the Southwest.[79] These plays were often written for contests sponsored by local theaters, again reinforcing the mutual dependence of newspapers, playwrights, and theatrical venues. Apparently many of these plays were indeed successful in Los Angeles, and several of them were performed by troupes touring other cities in the Southwest.

Perhaps most curiously, however, the plays written by the theatrical critics seem to belie their own emphasis on legitimate or Castilian theater and evince a ready concession to popular culture and a working-class sensibility through either sensational subject matter or recourse to melodrama. Two of González's plays performed at the Teatro Hidalgo in 1923 are typical of this trend: *La muerte de Francisco Villa* (The death of Francisco Villa), which dramatized the events leading up to the assassination of revolutionary leader Pancho Villa, and *La defensa; o, El asesino del martillo* (The defense; or, The hammer murderer), a production based on a sensational murder case in Los Angeles.[80] Others, including González's *Los amores de Ramona* (The loves of Ramona, 1927) and Esteban V. Escalante's *La vida de amor de Rodolfo Valentino* (The love life of Rudolf Valentino, 1928) were designed to coincide with major film releases (in the case of the González play, the feature film *Ramona*, Edwin Carewe, 1928, starring Dolores del Rio) or capitalize on the popularity of certain stars or of Hollywood film in general.

What apparently emerges through these works is the awareness (despite critical admonitions) that Mexican audiences were indeed fans of Hollywood and engaged with mainstream media and popular culture on a regular basis. Here, the construction of a cross-class audience was potentially facilitated by another canny compromise between form and content. That is, although the subject matter of such plays might have been inconsistent with notions of legitimate drama and high culture, it is elaborated within the form of a scripted dramatic play. Playwrights thus purposefully avoided the modularity and inconsistency of variety or musical revues, relying instead on a closed text that prevented the potential intrusion of vulgar language or denigrating stereotypes. Novelty was preserved through the emphasis on current events, while formal conventions prevented an unexpected foray into ribald humor or sexually suggestive presentations, trading on formal associations of legitimate theater.

These varied attempts to create and sustain a cultural form that would unite all Mexicans, however, were tenuous and often short-lived precisely because their continued success relied on a number of factors: differing tastes among segments of the Mexican population, the financial complications of operating theaters (eventually exacerbated by the Depression), and competition from radio and film, among others. The situation in Mexican Los Angeles thus resonated with concurrent developments in Mexico itself, despite critics' advocacy for an emulation of the "Mexican example." As Willis Knapp Jones has pointed out, "the attempt at a theater for the masses was a failure. The trouble was that what most Mexicans preferred was not serious drama in regular theaters, but the kind of near-burlesque turns that had been entertaining them for years in barnlike tents in small towns and public fairs."[81] By 1930 the dire situation of Spanish-language theater in the United States would also be exacerbated by the obstacles confronting touring troupes from Mexico, including the required acquisition of visas, a fee of one dollar per person, documentation of citizenship, and a letter of guarantee from a theater manager in the United States.[82]

By the 1926–1927 season, with the recent closings of the Teatro Novel and Teatro Capitol, critics frequently complained that no viable venue remained in which to host touring companies from Mexico, much less an appropriate space for locally produced dramatic works. Despite the much-heralded openings of the larger-capacity México (1927) and California (1928) Theaters (both were formerly English-language venues, with the Mexico occupying the former Grand Opera House), theater critic and playwright Gabriel Navarro already sensed the impending decline of live theater in Spanish, apparently linked directly to class divisions and the failure to unite a fragmented population. More affluent members of the Mexican-descent population, according to Navarro, lived on the west side of Los Angeles and preferred theater spoken in English, traveling to downtown only for major touring productions. Conversely, the poorer classes residing near downtown and in East Los Angeles continued to "prefer suggestive puns and colorful spectacles over the legitimate emotions of the theater," so local engagements now only rarely facilitated the mixing of the "families from the West" with "those of the popular masses."[83]

In fact, while even many of the reviled venues on North Main in the 1910s and 1920s alternated between straight film exhibition and variety presentation interspersed with short films, even this practice seemed plagued by instability by the late 1920s. In September 1926, for instance, listings for three Spanish-language venues (the Hidalgo, the Principal, and the Estela) all offered *cine y variedades* (film and variety).[84] The subsequent plight of the Estela Theater foreshadowed a broader trend developing by 1928 by which even the less reputable musical revues and vaudeville shows were threatened. In a context where such venues were regularly closing, changing formats, or only sporadically offering live performance, the theater managed by Frank Fouce was forced to "defend itself" with film showings, thus "momentarily suspending variety, in order to preserve the low prices of the show."[85]

This last development seems to affirm the fragmentation and divisions among the Mexican population and divergent consumption habits informed by class status. It also apparently confirms the truism that cinema replaced theater or can be blamed for its decline. But the reason theater waned, as we have seen, is decidedly more complex. More important, however, this examination of theatrical culture in Mexican Los Angeles reveals the multifaceted relationship between theatrical production and cinema in this context. Theater was situated as a defense against the Americanizing effects of mass culture and also conceived of as a means of countering disparaging images produced by the mainstream media, and Hollywood in particular. These factors, along with its mobilization as a tool of national community formation, lent it more than a passing affinity with concurrent national cinemas emerging in the shadow of Hollywood. The inability of Mexicans (in Los Angeles and beyond) to create a stable transnational cinema that would provide an alternative to Hollywood actually fueled the brief renaissance of theatrical culture. Rather than simple antagonism, however, theatrical production in Los Angeles paradoxically drew on mass culture to attract audiences in a convoluted attempt to protect them from these very influences. Perhaps most important, the multifaceted nature of this relationship demonstrates the centrality of theatrical culture to ongoing debates about cinematic representation, the construction of Mexicanidad, and the formation of community.

CODA: THE VOICES OF THE INVISIBLE

Theater as a multimedia institution represented a vision of Mexican Los Angeles through a reconception of urban space, an idealized construction of local audiences, and a reworking of theatrical genres. But the traces of these practices (however scant) overwhelmingly reflect the perspective of a particular class, a class with the means to produce theatrical and press culture. For instance, not only do we lack direct access to the pelado as a theatrical figure during this period, but we may also never have any true understanding of his appeal or significance to working-class audiences attending cheap theaters. Instead, our analysis of such a figure is necessarily based on evidence already colored by the moral, aesthetic, and political agenda of the Mexican expatriate elite (like Venegas and his novel). Thus despite our best efforts to gauge the experience or tastes of a working-class audience in this context, we are consistently confronted with a lack of archival traces. Any retrospective reconstruction or representation of this environment, however useful, remains speculative. Theorizing the critical or subversive potential of the pelado for such audiences is equally speculative, particularly given the dearth of extant texts, recorded performances, or any accounts of actual audience reception.

However inconclusive and partial they may be, fissures and inconsistencies remain apparent within the upper-class construction of Mexican identity and community. There are moments within the historical record, in fact, when working-class subjects seem to defy and even resist complicity with the agenda of their more privileged compatriots. Rather than the more cohesive conception promoted by the elite's notion of theatrical culture, it is instead a certain degree of ongoing working-class incoherence that ultimately proves most troubling for the construction of a unified Mexican community (and by proxy, a nation unified as Mexico). Thus, it is not a necessarily a matter of reconstructing a working-class counterrepresentation that is more accurate or necessarily subversive but rather of remaining attuned to the heterogeneity and multiplicity silenced by expedient constructions of nation, ethnicity, and community (past or present).

During the period in question, this multiplicity is perhaps most glaringly apparent through another sort of representational practice: the ethnographic works of Mexican anthropologist Manuel Gamio. Over the course of two years in the late 1920s, Gamio and his researchers conducted a binational study of Mexican immigration notable for its ambitious scope and innovative methodology (including the analysis of money transfers to gauge population shifts). Conducting interviews and gathering information in multiple cities across the United States, Gamio ultimately published two works from this research: the more sociologically conventional *Mexican Immigration to the United States* and the more impressionistic *The Life Story of the Mexican Immigrant*. The latter is based on interviews with hundreds of immigrants across the United States and, as its title suggests, seems intended to construct a biography of the "typical" immigrant through collective accounts of experience. What emerges, however, is a decidedly complex and rich set of representations of immigrant life that ultimately challenges any pretense toward a monolithic notion of the Mexican immigrant.

As Arturo J. Aldama argues in his insightful analysis of *The Life Story*, the final text in which these interviews are embedded reflects Gamio's own class standing and attitudes toward race.[86] As the author of the foundational *Forjando patria* (Forging a nation), Gamio was a key voice of postrevolutionary Mexican nationalism and instrumental to the conceptualization of *indigenismo*, a philosophy by which Mexico's indigenous population were discursively (but not materially) incorporated into the nation. Despite this apparent elevation of the indigenous, his brand of indigenismo (as was the case with José Vasconcelos's conception of *la raza cósmica*) acknowledged the indispensable contribution of these populations to Mexico's character and heritage, while continuing to frame them as inferior and ultimately advocating for their assimilation or racial elevation through intermarriage and eventual elimination. Of course, this brand of essentializing nationalism clearly resonates with the class- and race-based notions of Mexicanidad promoted by Mexican elites in Los Angeles, including their rejection of the racially problematic, working-class pelado.

Not surprisingly, Gamio explicitly aligns himself with this group in the pages of *Life Story*. Aldama notes that in addition to identifying the apparent racial makeup of his informants (e.g., "mestizo, markedly Indian"), Gamio also places them within a familiar hierarchy that privileges whiteness. Referring specifically to the cultural elite (in a section titled "The Leader and the Intellectual"), Gamio argues that "the following section assembles the accounts of immigrants with greater sophistication and education. These persons are in most cases, of white blood. It is not surprising to find them giving fuller expression to their race consciousness and . . . to hear from them a fairly objective and realistic statement as to race relations."[87] From such statements and other editorial commentary, it would seem that Gamio's ethnographic account is indeed aligned with the Mexican elite in Los Angeles and their own effort to "forge a nation" abroad through racial and cultural "elevation."

While such a conclusion may seem unsurprising given Gamio's own level of formal education and class standing, *Life Story* proves a much more complex and multivocal text than Gamio's "editorial violations" might initially suggest.[88] Namely, the interviews reproduced in the text seem to undermine or at least complicate the construction of a singular Mexican immigrant implied by the text's title. Just as important, the book challenges the notion of a unified Mexican audience or community proposed by journalists working in Los Angeles. For instance, interviewees, although characterized by racial type, identify themselves with different regions of Mexico and reveal diverse political views, religious beliefs, and life experiences. While the varied life experiences of these immigrants pose one kind of challenge to the construction of a monolithic Mexican, their habits and entertainment preferences evince an evasion of or resistance to build a national community through cultural production, consumption, and criticism. The accounts of leisure activities gathered by Gamio and his researchers, in fact, reveals a diverse and inconsistent array of attitudes and practices relative to leisure.

In 2002 the complete interviews conducted by Gamio and his researchers between 1926 and 1927 were published, evincing even more varied attitudes and consumption habits among Mexican immigrants than were already present in the original *Life Story*. In one account, interviewee Arturo Morales provides perhaps a typical yet vague portrait of his Sunday routine: "We go to the pool hall or to some movie theater. I like cinema very much. At night we go to some dance hall or a little party, then we return home to keep working for another day. One doesn't have as much fun here as in Mexico, but that's what we like to do." Other interviews reveal divergent moviegoing preferences among immigrants.

Santiago Rivera, who also expressed particular concern about instilling Mexican pride in his children, "goes only to Mexican theaters and has never gone to the elegant American theaters, nor to American restaurants." José Rocha's leisure habits, however, contrasted sharply with Rivera's: "The cinemas and theaters here are not fun to me, but I go to take my wife. She especially likes the American cinemas."[89] These accounts and others suggest the heterogeneous tastes of Mexican immigrants; they also affirm the obstacles to the creation of a unified Mexican audience (or a "community of consumers"), perhaps partially accounting for the financial failures and instability of the Spanish-language theatrical scene.

Gamio's research also reveals that the relationship of immigrants to the press was decidedly mixed and inconsistent, calling into question the influence of elite institutions and their vision of nationalism. So while the writing of middle-class journalists may suggest a sense of the discursive horizons shaping the reception of entertainment by actual audiences, it is also undoubtedly true that these audiences may have been resistant to, unaware of, or apathetic toward the writing of these critics and the types of theater they produced or promoted. Some immigrants interviewed expressed enthusiasm for the Spanish-language press and participated in the kind of civic activities it frequently promoted. A researcher described Fortino V. Tenorio in the following terms: "He knows how to read the Mexican and American paper and buys the Mexican newspapers every day. He has always been the member of a Mexican society of the mutualist sort."[90]

Other accounts recorded by Gamio and his researchers, however, suggest a negotiated or even antagonistic relationship with the Spanish-language press. Miguel Alonso's attitude, for instance, approximates a perspective expressed by many interviewees, particularly of the working class: "I read the newspapers, but they almost always tell lies. In addition, one is so tired after work that you don't even feel like reading newspapers of any kind."[91] Informant Pablo Mares's response demonstrates a similar sentiment, while revealing another obstacle to the influence of the press: "I hardly ever read the papers for I know they tell nothing but lies. They exaggerate everything, and besides, I hardly know how to read, for my parents didn't have the means with which to send me to school."[92] Other interviewees, like Felipe Orozco, seemed to avoid the major dailies altogether, opting instead to read more radical or labor-oriented publications like the communist *El Machete*. Assimilation, language acquisition, and length of stay in the United States also seems to have affected reading habits, embodying Mexican journalists' worst fears. Ruhe López explained, for instance, that "we always buy the daily, the *Los Angeles Examiner*, and we read the principal items. I don't read the Mexican newspapers, because I am hardly at all interested in Mexico anymore, for my family is almost all here."[93]

Given this range of attitudes toward the Spanish-language press among its constituency, therefore, it is exceedingly difficult to assess the impact of its entertainment coverage or to assume that its views coincided with those of the larger, working-class population. It could certainly not claim to represent them as a coherent community without substantial elisions and exclusions. Ultimately, it is the inconsistency and heterogeneity of the interviews (and Gamio's work on immigration in general) rather than any singular counterrepresentation that disrupts the homogenizing impulse of cultural nationalism and uniform conceptions of identity promoted by cultural authorities during the period. This heterogeneity further points to the fragmentation and stratification of the Mexican immigrant cultural sphere, including theatrical entertainment. Indeed, this chapter points to at least two distinct yet overlapping Mexican theater and cinema cultures in Los Angeles: one constituted by the actual practices and habits of the working class and the other an aspirational ideal crafted by the middle class and elite. It is thus crucial when speaking of these alternative cultural spheres to not mistake one for the other, particularly as the power to produce theater and generate discourse generally did not reside with the working class. In this case, the representational power of the cultural authorities of the 1920s, including the ability to leave perhaps the only historical records of theatrical culture, has the continuing potential to shape and distort our understanding of cultural life and the terms of Mexicanidad in Mexican Los Angeles.

CHAPTER 3

THE AUDIBLE AND
THE INVISIBLE

THE TRANSITION TO SOUND AND THE
DE-MEXICANIZATION OF HOLLYWOOD

Through the 1920s the Mexican press in Los Angeles imagined the implications of cinematic representation as multiple yet interrelated effects: the vilification of Mexicans, the ways this influenced the treatment of Mexicans, the relation of these to conceptions of Los Angeles, the creation of a cohesive and elevated national consciousness among Mexican audiences, and the prevention of the de-Mexicanization (or assimilation) of this population. With the addition of dialogue to motion pictures in the late 1920s, the stakes of cinematic representation and Hollywood's constructions of Mexicanidad were amplified. To be certain, stereotypes did not disappear, nor did the counterrepresentations constructed by the Mexican upper classes. The arrival of sound, however, brought with it a new set of concerns that shifted the terms of these debates. Namely, the linguistic barriers confronting the international distribution of films prompted Hollywood explicitly to target a cohesive Latin American market ostensibly unified by the use of the Spanish language. Although the specific textual solutions varied over time (from dubbing to foreign-language production and subtitles), their emphasis on continental appeal and linguistic unity gave new meaning to the concept of de-Mexicanization. If journalists and other authorities remained concerned about the Americanizing potential of Hollywood film, the transition to sound also generated anxiety about the elision of Mexican specificity within a homogenized conception of the Latin American audience. In other words, struggles to define the terms of Mexicanidad, particularly in the cultural realm, would increasingly unfold in relation to various, overarching notions of an all-encompassing Latinidad. Whether as industry labor, working-class immigrants, or textual figures, Mexicans faced erasure and invisibility; journalists fought against this supposed de-Mexicanization by struggling for visibility and presence on-screen, in the film industry, and within the fabric of the city itself.

According to many histories, the rise and fall of Spanish-language Hollywood was part and parcel of the experimentation that typified the early years of sound, an anomaly that evaporated once production practices stabilized and alternative lines of development were abandoned in favor of classical narrative structure.[1] Taking issue with this perspective, Malte Hagener has usefully argued that "multi-language versions can be adequately assessed only when viewed within a context of the various forms that cinema has tried out in order to cross and overcome national borders."[2] By situating Spanish-language film within the broader history of Hollywood's international distribution, we can thus understand this period of production as marking a key moment in the construction of a transnational Latin American audience by the culture industries. Crucially, it also marks a key instance of resistance to this construction on the part of elements within the Mexican audience. As other scholars have noted, the critical debates around Hollywood's attempt (and ultimate failure) to retain its Latin American market through the production of foreign-language versions hinged most emphatically on supposed misuses of language. While this assessment is certainly true, a number of underlying issues converged within discussions more explicitly addressing accent and vocabulary in Los Angeles: representations that evacuated cultural specificity, allegations of discrimination against Mexican labor in Hollywood, the struggle to maintain Mexican-oriented venues during the Depression, and a lack of film production from Latin American countries.

Ultimately, this transitional period marks important changes in the broader representation of Mexicans and Latinos in Hollywood. First of all, Hollywood shifted from embracing cosmopolitan sophistication and exoticism in the 1920s toward a reassertion of a racially coded all-Americanism in the 1930s that increasingly marginalized Latinos as actors and characters. Although a complex process, many have attributed this shift to the intertwined phenomena of the Depression and the transition to sound. That is, if stars like Ramón Novarro and Dolores del Rio once constituted exotic, sensual embodiments of the Latin lover, Hollywood by the 1930s witnessed a backlash against silent-era trends in favor of "all-American" casting. While sociohistorical context may at least partially explain this shift, sound technology contributed to this dynamic by making the "un-American" (i.e., nonwhite, non-European) accents of such stars unavoidably apparent.[3] Along with the anti-Mexican sentiment that fueled deportations, these factors led to a decrease in the quality and quantity of roles available to Latino actors.

Furthermore, the Studio Relations Committee of the Motion Picture Producers and Distributors of America (MPPDA) enacted measures to avoid offenses to foreign nations in an effort to retain international markets. Hollywood responded by setting films in nondescript or fictional Latin American locales—the "mythical kingdoms" described by Ruth Vasey.[4] The effect of all these changes presented the threat of representational erasure, a de-Mexicanizing of Hollywood. For Mexican journalists in Los Angeles, the cautious optimism occasioned by a generation of Mexican silent actors and the corrective potential of a Spanish-language cinema dissipated in the face of Hollywood's generalized (and not always flattering) notion of the general Latin American as a screen presence *and* as an audience. This chapter thus works to correct the notion that "discussion of race and spectatorship . . . was largely absent from the industry's classification and construction of its audience," demonstrating instead precisely how such considerations greatly shaped on-screen representations of Latinos (and by implication, other racial and ethnic groups).[5]

Significantly, these textual trends coincided with threats to the viability of Mexican-oriented entertainment venues in downtown Los Angeles, which were drastically impacted by the decline of live theater and the Depression (along with the fate of Spanish-language Hollywood). Most notably, concerted efforts to remove Mexican immigrants from the city through repatriation and deportation made their public presence a risky prospect and imperiled the sustainability of Mexican-oriented entertainment. Paradoxically, this attempted erasure of actual Mexicans from public space coincided exactly with their highly visible representation through a widely publicized repurposing of space downtown. Precisely at this moment, the transformation of the Plaza area into the Olvera Street tourist attraction in the early 1930s reframed the city's Mexican heritage in mythic and romanticized terms. As Mary C. Beltrán has noted, "an argument can be made that the same thing was happening in the film industry and in Hollywood films themselves in these years."[6] As we shall see, both Spanish-language Hollywood and urban revitalization constructed respective notions of Latinidad and Mexicanidad from which the immigrant working class and their experiences were largely absent. By the 1930s, however, Mexican theatrical culture could no longer be sustained as an alternative cultural sphere from which to launch competing constructions of Mexicanidad. For critics writing for the Mexican immigrant press, the solution to these overlapping representational erasures resided in Hollywood acknowledging (and valuing) its Mexican audience by adopting more inclusive hiring practices that placed Mexicans (whether as consultants or talent) in a position to shape the industry's projection of Mexicanidad from within.

THE INVASION OF THE TOQUIS: SOUND CINEMA AND LINGUISTIC DE-MEXICANIZATION

Before Hollywood's Spanish-language films provoked debate about the intertwined matters of on-screen representation and industry labor, the very advent of spoken dialogue emerged to intensify existing debates about the impact of Hollywood on the Mexican immigrant population (and youth in particular). More specifically, the first controversy occasioned by the transition to sound in Los Angeles centered on the fact that Hollywood's earliest efforts were spoken entirely in English at a moment when Latin American countries had yet to initiate sound production. Resonant with the international reception of early sound

film, critics in Mexican Los Angeles regarded such productions as a palpable
threat. This was due in no small part to the fact that Americanization efforts
within and beyond the city's public schools hinged on the teaching of English
and that many Mexicans thus regarded speaking English as a betrayal of Mexico,
"as tantamount to acceptance of Anglo mores and society."[7] If in Europe, Hollywood presented a challenge to "bourgeois cultural nationalism," it presented an
analogous challenge in Los Angeles, one that converged with a particular history
of cultural representation and local power dynamics.[8] That is, while this line of
criticism hinged less precisely on actual images on-screen, it positioned early
talkies as an aggressive and blatant Americanization of the movies that exerted
a de-Mexicanizing effect on individuals and the entertainment landscape of Los
Angeles.

Of course, the reaction to these films in Mexican Los Angeles was indicative
of the broader obstacles facing Hollywood during the early years of sound. More
specifically, among the other upheavals wrought by the transitional moment
of the late 1920s were the adjustments that Hollywood studios had to make to
secure their international markets. Over the course of the previous decade, the
consolidation and vertical integration of the studios, aided by a large domestic
market, provided Hollywood the structural and financial advantage necessary to
dominate foreign territories. If these factors, along with aggressive distribution
and marketing efforts (coupled with the frequent intervention of the U.S. government), can be ultimately credited with securing Hollywood's globalization,
this was also greatly facilitated by the "chameleonlike nature of the silent film
cinema."[9] Most notably, the lack of spoken dialogue allowed cinema to traverse
international borders with relative ease. For the most part, tailoring a silent film
to a particular linguistic market required a studio or its distributor to translate
and replace printed intertitles. In many cases even this measure was deemed
unnecessary as the clarity of visual storytelling and silent performance styles
often made narratives legible without recourse to explanatory text or dialogue.
Adjustments to the text for censorship purposes (or to accommodate a particular cultural sensibility) were likewise largely uncomplicated and did not seriously impede international distribution. Furthermore, Hollywood consistently
recruited talent from around the globe simultaneously to secure international
appeal and weaken competing industries.

The addition of spoken dialogue to motion pictures irrevocably altered this
situation. The language barrier suddenly became a central concern of Hollywood
and other film industries reliant on foreign revenue. As Andrew Higson puts it,
"motion pictures could no longer be understood so carelessly as the outpourings
of an international language; they were now, precisely, 'talkies,' and they talked
in many different languages."[10] Because other film industries found themselves
competing at a disadvantage relative to Hollywood, however, the obstacle of language to exportation was compounded by concerns over Hollywood's imposition of English on a global audience. If during this period in Europe "bourgeois

commentators frequently worried over the displacement of indigenous cultural, and especially national, identities" occasioned by Hollywood's popularity, this concern was exacerbated by the question of language.[11] In addition to other protective measures like quotas and tariffs, a number of governments (both national and local) attempted to regulate or restrict the importation and exhibition of English-language cinema. The international excitement that initially greeted the novelty of Hollywood's first talkies thus quickly gave way to anxiety and defensiveness on a global scale. As Ginette Vincendeau has noted, "despite the instant success of *The Jazz Singer* and other early Hollywood sound productions, the news of hostile reactions—sometimes going as far as riots—started flooding in from all over Europe and South America."[12]

These anxieties about the imposition of English by Hollywood resonated with the cultural protectionism and nationalism of Mexican cultural authorities in Los Angeles. Accordingly, *La Opinión* chronicled international reactions to this "crisis," charting the various responses and solutions to the advent of English-language talking pictures. Journalists writing for the paper most frequently quoted essays and editorials that first appeared in Mexican papers, which would echo much of the discourse generated concurrently in Los Angeles. The Mexico City newspaper *El Universal* conducted perhaps the most vocal campaign against English-language films. Luis Reyes de la Maza has summarized the anxieties driving this campaign: critics believed that "if all movies were going to be made in the English language, the Latin American public would be forced to learn this language if it wanted to be entertained, and within a few years Spanish would be forgotten and pass into the category of dead languages."[13] Some predicted the Americanization of cinema would hence be complete and total; the dominance of English would provoke an exodus of all foreign actors and any pretense of incorporating international appeal.[14] For critics participating in this campaign, English dialogue solidified the status of Hollywood films as "American propaganda," particularly as language figured for some as "one of the pillars that sustain the magnificent chapel of nationalism."[15] The transition to sound was denounced by one critic as a "peaceful and sonorous conquest," a turn of phrase that borrowed from terminology historically used to describe the "peaceful conquest" of U.S. economic imperialism in Mexico.[16]

In Mexican Los Angeles, critics couched this supposed usurpation of nationalism in terms of assimilation and acculturation, with English-language dialogue poised to accelerate the apparent de-Mexicanization already under way among second-generation youth, many of whom had become avid moviegoers. Much of this controversy, as Douglas Monroy has pointed out, focused on young women, whose increasing independence from parents and access to expendable income generated considerable anxiety, with film situated as a potential corrupting factor that inspired behavior and fashion trends that departed from the values espoused by their parents.[17] Beyond the projected impact of Hollywood's films and their content, there was also a substantial concern about young Mexican women's desire to participate in or migrate to Hollywood. This anxiety was in no way unique to Mexicans in the United States, yet the Mexican immigrant press in Los Angeles and beyond framed Hollywood's moral danger as one that undermined cultural standards of behavior, and of femininity in particular.[18] The allure of Hollywood—as both a body of production and a place—was seen as facilitating the process of *desmexicanización* (de-Mexicanization) by which a second generation was apparently assimilating the norms and customs of the United States. Within these debates, the Spanish language was situated as a crucial point of cultural cohesion, and its maintenance by Mexicans in the United States was often regarded as a barometer of cultural integrity and as a central element of the struggle against assimilation. Accordingly, talking pictures (initially called *toquis* in the Spanish-language press) were greeted by *La Opinión* with a degree of anxiety: the ubiquity and popularity of English-language features appeared to threaten the very survival of the Spanish language among the Mexican population, a central facet of Mexicanidad.

Just as significant, if Hollywood sound films threatened to undermine cultural continuity on a textual level, critics often blamed their popularity for the instability (and eventual decline) of a Mexican-oriented theatrical sphere. This de-Mexicanization would thus occur not only as a function of an individual's reception of cinema but also as a supposed threat to the sustenance of a Mexican audience and community through theatrical entertainment downtown. This in turn threatened the intertwined cultural and economic interests of the Mexican middle class and elite. Although Mexican Los Angeles may not have had a national cinema to protect, cultural authorities there framed the cultural and economic function of the theatrical scene in an analogous sense, as I demonstrate in the previous chapter. The threat of Americanization, as perceived by critics in Los Angeles and elsewhere, was thus multifaceted and operated at the level of both production and exhibition. As theaters downtown closed or transitioned to the programming of cinema, an alternative sphere of self-representation and transnational community formation (no matter how uneven its efforts) found itself endangered. Critics accused Hollywood of contributing greatly to the fragmentation and cultural assimilation of the Mexican audience. It was the ongoing response to these developments that greatly shaped subsequent battles over representation and language in the early 1930s.

"Monstrous Amplifications": Spanish-Language Cinema Arrives in Los Angeles

The obstacles presented by the language barrier, including the backlash against English-dialogue films, sent Hollywood studios in search of solutions to retain their global markets. As Martine Danan argues, for example, "nationalistic feelings aroused by sound films proved to be a much more formidable challenge to Hollywood's international hegemony than the projected union of the main

European film industries in the late 1920s."[19] Because dubbing and subtitling technology were insufficiently developed and not widely accepted by audiences, Hollywood began exploring the production of multiple-language versions of their films for different language markets, including Spanish-speaking nations. Given the attitude toward English-language cinema among Mexican journalists in Los Angeles, the possibility of a culturally specific Spanish-language cinema generated momentary optimism about a medium that might approach the cultural value of live dramatic theater (and perhaps employ theatrical talent adversely affected by its local decline).

But Hollywood's Spanish-language versions, while apparently imbuing cinema with a central element of cultural retention, produced their own critical backlash connected to the fear of de-Mexicanization distinct from, but related to, the anxieties provoked by English-language films. Most notably, within *La Opinión*'s entertainment coverage, the issue of spoken Spanish (pronunciation, regional vocabulary, and diction) assumed a central position, whereby issues of class, generational conflict, nationality, and cultural integrity were collapsed into a discussion of cinematic dialogue and the proper use of Spanish. While the issue of insulting or inaccurate images persisted, such concerns were overshadowed by the apparent invisibility of Mexicans within Hollywood's attempt to reach a broad Latin American audience. Hollywood's conceptions of this audience, along with the lack of Mexicans in studio supervisory positions or leading roles, meant that Mexicans in Los Angeles found themselves struggling to be represented at all.

Once the alteration and production of films designed specifically for the Spanish-language market began, *La Opinión* offered extensive treatment of these early efforts and their suitability for local audiences. Independents and studios alike experimented with a variety of strategies and genres to capitalize on the novelty of talking pictures in Spanish, during a highly speculative and competitive period of production that one journalist characterized as a "gold rush."[20] Unsatisfied demand for Spanish-language films (and backlash against those spoken in English) domestically and abroad compelled investment and production by a diverse array of independent interests, all of which scrambled to either establish a position or make a quick profit in an emerging market.[21]

By the last half of 1929, in fact, several independent companies in Los Angeles were rushing to complete the first Spanish-language feature film. Producers at Sono-Art prepared a Spanish version of their film *Blaze O' Glory* (George Hoffman and Renaud Hoffman, 1929) titled *Sombras de gloria* (Shadows of glory, Andrew L. Stone and Fernando C. Tamayo, 1929), starring Argentine José Bohr, while Hollywood Spanish Pictures Company produced the musical revue *Charros, gauchos y manolas* (1930), directed by bandleader Xavier Cugat.[22] Beating their competitors into theaters by over a month, Hispania Talking Film (formerly Cuban Pictures International), cofounded by René Cardona and Rodolfo Montes, premiered *Sombras habaneras* (Shadows in Havana), the first all-Spanish feature produced and exhibited in the United States, on December

4, 1929, at the Teatro México in downtown Los Angeles.[23] The initial Spanish-language productions, however, were hardly regarded as presenting a viable solution to the problem of spoken dialogue, particularly as many early films (including *Sombras habaneras*) met with the ridicule or indifference of both local and foreign audiences.[24] The obstacles of expense and technical experience made independent production even riskier and more volatile than it had during the silent period; most of these independent companies made only one film before permanently disbanding.

For the next two years, subsequent Spanish-language films exhibited in Los Angeles and elsewhere would primarily consist of those produced or distributed by the major studios. By 1930 all of them were producing films in foreign languages, either by importing talent from abroad or by establishing or funding production facilities in Europe. For the most part, these films (often referred to as "direct versions") were made as separate productions with alternative casts performing dialogue for each language. Paramount's Joinville Studios outside of Paris, where films were produced in up to fourteen separate languages, was perhaps the most elaborate and prolific of these efforts (with an estimated output of eighty-two features in 1930 alone).[25] Studios initially regarded the solution of foreign-language versions as the most viable one, particularly as international audiences responded negatively to the interruption of intertitles in sound films, dubbing technology was not sufficiently advanced, and subtitles posed a problem for countries with low rates of literacy.[26]

In addition to the French and German markets, Hollywood studios regarded Latin America as one of their most lucrative markets by the time the transition to sound occurred, particularly as European nations began implementing protective legislation and Spanish-speaking nations were slower to initiate sound production. In addition, U.S. films constituted anywhere from 80 to 95 percent of films screened in Latin American nations.[27] Given this state of affairs, Hollywood prioritized the production of Spanish-language features as a way to retain these markets and to forestall the development of national cinemas in the region. Subsequent Spanish-language features would thus be produced as alternate versions of Hollywood films with entirely different casts performing roles in Spanish, or with the original actors (including, most curiously, Laurel and Hardy, Buster Keaton, Harry Langdon, and Our Gang) speaking phonetic Spanish. Eventually, several studios would also produce a limited number of original Spanish-language films produced from scripts written expressly for this market (see fig. 18).

Although originally conceived of as an inevitable, necessary fixture of the sound era, this production strategy was almost entirely abandoned within three years, as the films failed to generate the kind of earnings that would justify the investment they entailed. Even for Spanish-language production (once regarded as a surefire prospect) the "gold rush" was over by late 1931. Extending this metaphor, *Variety* declared that studio efforts in this arena had left the

Fig. 18. Print advertisement for Universal's *Dracula*, perhaps the best known of the Hollywood Spanish-language versions. *La Opinión*, May 7, 1931. Reproduced courtesy of *La Opinión*.

landscape "littered with banana peels instead of gold dust."[28] Film historians have suggested a number of factors that contributed to the abrupt decline of these productions. Perhaps most obviously, international audiences consistently criticized the films for their neglect and misunderstanding of culturally specific subject matter, ridiculed their linguistic blunders, and typically demonstrated a preference for recognizable Hollywood stars over the less popular or even unknown actors performing in foreign-language versions.

For Spanish-speaking films, the latter factor apparently proved to be a substantial obstacle. As Clarence J. North and Nathan D. Golden of the Department of Commerce's Motion Picture Section noted, audiences in Mexico "know all the American stars and they go to see them play in English, as against a picture in Spanish where the actors are comparatively unknown."[29] Mary Lanigan, in a 1932 sociological study of second-generation Mexican youth in Belvedere (a neighborhood in East Los Angeles) also noted this preference among her informants. Aside from issues of language ("I don't like to go to Spanish pictures, they sound queer"), she documented a marked preference for Hollywood stars or for the Fox films featuring renowned Mexican tenor José Mojica.[30] The studios also identified star appeal and a dearth of qualified talent as a factor shaping these films' poor performance. Henry Blanke, head of the Warner Bros. Foreign Department, acknowledged that performances in these films were "amateurish," lamenting that "the local talent in Hollywood that we are forced to use, is the only one available and the only one which speaks perfect Spanish. Most of them have never been actors but all we tried to do is make them act." Frustrated by budget limitations for these versions (set at $50,000), he summarized the studio's options thusly: "there is only one thing left to do, and that is stop production, or to import a good stock company."[31] Indeed, Warner Bros. opted for the former, and its Spanish-language production during this period was restricted to four feature films.[32] Blanke's comments aptly epitomize the central dilemma studios faced in producing direct versions, as Ruth Vasey has explained, "high capitalization was impossible, since the movies' intended markets were too small to recoup large investments, but less expensive productions did not have sufficient drawing power to justify their relatively modest costs."[33]

Blanke's comments also indicated the extent to which production in each language followed a slightly distinct trajectory and was shaped by the particular nature of national markets and localized audience reception. Spanish-language films, for instance, presented their own unique obstacles and challenges in addition to those it shared with other foreign-language versions. Most notably, because of the large territory and multiple nationalities encompassed by this market, language usage became a major point of contention for Spanish versions, perhaps to an extent unparalleled by productions in other languages. As *La Opinión* theater and film critic Rafael M. Saavedra complained, these early

U.S.-made Spanish-language films exhibited "an absolute ignorance of our customs, our clothing, and our lexicon," reducing characters and setting to the level of caricature while employing a Spanish he describes as "horribly mutilated, full of mystifications; and in addition to the terrible defects of pronunciation, a strange accent."[34] Another article, referring to the cultural and linguistic oversights of Hollywood sound film as "denaturalizations of sound and monstrous amplifications," suggests that the industry's Spanish-language films represented no improvement: "after hearing the sound films that ruin our language, I would declare free entry to English-talking pictures. Listening to the latter, the audience gets bored by not understanding the dialogue, but hearing the others would mean the danger of corruption."[35]

Part of this controversy undoubtedly arose from the ambitions of producers to release films that would appeal simultaneously to all Spanish-speaking territories in an attempt to construct "a homogenized regional community of cultural consumers."[36] The recruitment of actors from theater and opera companies throughout Latin America and Spain attested to this strategy and coincides with Hollywood's long-standing practice of importing international talent to secure international appeal. This initial approach met with immediate criticism and even ridicule, however, as a multitude of regional accents left producers struggling to concoct textual solutions capable of reconciling this bewildering linguistic diversity with notions of cinematic realism. Furthermore, while ideas of realism and textual logic would seem to demand a coincidence between language usage and geographic setting, producing films with this narrow a focus ostensibly threatened to limit their appeal to a specific, corresponding market (Argentina or Mexico, for instance) and might restrict the manner in which studios used its recently imported talent. This, according to Hagener, was the primary tension confronting such productions on the international market: "films produced with the intention to be exported have to try to be as specific and culturally grounded as possible (language, milieu, stars, setting, style) in order to address a specific audience, yet they are also made with the intention to cross borders in linguistic, political, and cultural respect as easily as possible."[37]

The debates over language thus confronted producers with a considerable obstacle, and Hollywood studios even temporarily postponed Spanish-language production until they were able to better gauge public opinion and a permanent linguistic solution could be agreed upon.[38] La Opinión and its writers intervened frequently in this debate, publishing commentary and opinion from critics, intellectuals, public officials, and movie stars. Every film review during this period invariably contributed to this discussion, and almost every entertainment item during this period at least implicitly referenced this ongoing "war of the accents."[39] While a multiplicity of positions became apparent, most fell along a continuum between those advocating the adoption of theatrical

Castilian Spanish and those proposing the use of "Hispano-American" accents
and vocabulary. In many instances, the controversy centered on the difference in
pronunciation of three consonants: *c*, *z*, and *ll* (the double *l*, pronounced as the
consonant *y*). While commentators often conceded that any variation on these
positions, given the complexity of the situation, would not necessarily represent a complete or permanent resolution, there was general agreement that the
industry should adapt some standards or guidelines.

Hollywood studios, having imported talent from multiple countries, were
understandably stumped and frustrated by this controversy, and they strove to
arrive at a linguistic solution that would somehow ensure "the approval of the
average theater-goer in Spain, Mexico, [and] Central and South American countries."[40] Several studios had devised piecemeal or tentative, region-specific measures, but the investment entailed by these productions made the prospect of an
industry-wide standard desirable (if ultimately untenable). The resolution finally
agreed upon represented somewhat of a compromise and was achieved at least
partially through the intervention of organizations like the Spanish-American
Cultural Association and the Spanish Latin-American Film Bureau in their lob-
bying of the MPPDA.[41] This process culminated in early 1930 when the Foreign
Department of the MPPDA formed a Committee on Foreign Production composed of foreign-language supervisors from each major studio, with the intent of
developing standards of production and settling linguistic controversies.[42] The
guidelines eventually released suggested an adherence to the Spanish customar-
ily used in theater productions but also made provisions to vary accents according to character and setting.[43] More specifically, they advised that "every film
whose action does not take place in any country in which definite idioms and
accents predominate will be produced in the language used in the Spanish theater, and when certain characters represent persons who in real life would use the
accents and idioms of a specific country, the idioms, accents and pronunciation
peculiar to that country will be used."[44]

Aside from matters of language, the guidelines established by the committee also covered issues of costuming, casting, cultural customs, music and setting, for which the Cultural Association offered its future services as consultant.
Embedded in and overlapping with the concerns over linguistic accuracy and
realism were issues of cultural specificity and respectful and precise representations of cultural elements. But the implications of language usage for culturally accurate representation proved more complex than the committee and the
studios perhaps anticipated. More specifically, the national pride and cultural
retention that Mexican critics in Los Angeles initially associated with the proper
use of Spanish language were undermined by the wide-ranging implications of
a linguistic unity and a concomitant representational logic that folded Mexicans
into a generalized, continental Latinidad.

SPANISH CONQUISTADORS AND MEXICAN LABOR:
THE STAKES OF THE LINGUISTIC DEBATES

Perhaps the most surprising dimension of the Spanish-language versions was not their cultural inaccuracies or offensive nature (which were regularly commented on in the press). To be certain, as Lisa Jarvinen has argued, "even when the transition to sound led Hollywood studios to develop new strategies for making and selling movies to international audiences, this concern did not produce a dramatic change in attitude toward the people, customs, and cultures of foreign countries."[45] Just as significant, however, Hollywood's mistaken supposition that a common linguistic solution would satisfy all "Latins" had its parallel in the representational politics of the films. Namely, regional specificity was generally either evacuated from such films or subjected to a befuddling amalgamation that carried across accent, visualization, narrative, and casting. Commenting on the confusing array of mise-en-scène and dialogue in *La rosa de fuego* (The fiery rose, W. L. Griffith, 1930), for instance, critic Gabriel Navarro complained that the film's "action unfolds neither in Mexico, nor in Spain, nor in any other of the Latin American republics, judging by the costuming and lexicon used."[46] In some respects, violations of accuracy and the constant mystification of cultural markers and language served to confirm the talking picture as a cultural threat that might contribute to the deterioration and loss of established cultural norms. Perhaps paradoxically, these texts, as solutions to the problem of appealing to a Latin American audience (and incorporating multinational casts), once again shifted concerns over representation from the denigration or vilification of Mexicans to the de-Mexicanization of Hollywood. It is during these debates, furthermore, that critics linked representational politics to labor practices, aspiring to change industry practice as a way of altering Hollywood's constructions (or erasures) of Mexicanidad.

Directly related to this representational issue was the direct translation of Hollywood scripts whose narratives were not tailored for a Latin American or Mexican audience. Indeed, as Jarvinen has pointed out, aside from allowing for more suggestive material and racier costuming, the films selected for adaptation (including *Dracula*, Tod Browning, 1931; *The Benson Murder Case*, Frank Tuttle, 1930; *Min and Bill*, George W. Hill, 1930; and *Madame X*, Lionel Barrymore, 1929) would seem to hold no culturally specific appeal. This practice appears to be generally consistent with the border crossing aspirations of multilanguage versions, including those produced by European nations.[47] Robert G. Dickson has suggested the implications of this strategy for Mexican Los Angeles: "Given the proximity of California and Mexico, one would think that Hispanic cinema would have had plenty of films with Mexican themes, but in reality there were few."[48] As a consequence, Mexican immigrants didn't see their culture or experiences reflected on-screen, nor was there a high demand for their labor as performers. For critics, newfound Latino visibility on-screen (as talent) was thus mitigated by a nearly complete evacuation of cultural specificity and even an apparent bias against Mexicans in the industry.

Given this projection of nonspecific Latinidad, the very presence of Latinos on-screen seemed to generate a representational dissonance in this context. A review of First National's *La llama sagrada* (The sacred flame, William C. McGann, 1930), for instance, illustrates the dilemma these films represented for critics. While praising the film as "intensely human," Gabriel Navarro nonetheless regards the film a failure because "its thesis is based on a cold, cruel morality; in a word, an Anglo-Saxon morality. For this reason, I'm afraid that the public in our countries won't receive it well." Based on the studio's English-language adaptation of the W. Somerset Maugham story "The Sacred Flame," the film involves a mother who poisons her paralyzed son Mauricio, so that his young wife Estela might find happiness with his younger brother. As this particular review demonstrates, issues of cultural difference and translation often hinged on the acceptable behavior of Mexican women: "The film's resolution, which English and American critics will probably applaud, will possibly not go over as well with our critics, who write and think for the world in which they live. In this environment—Spanish and Hispano-American in general—we are sure that there is not one single mother, as progressive as she may be, who would dare to commit an act of this nature."[49] In subsequent articles, Navarro consistently expands on this line of criticism, emphasizing the inadequacy of faithfully translating Hollywood scripts for Latino talent in a way that does not account for differences of cultural sensibility. In one instance, he complained that Spanish-speaking characters that exhibit the "exoticism of Menjou, dance to the music of Paul Whiteman, [and] abandon *bizcochos* [traditional sugar cookies] for 'hot cakes'" do not coincide with the "racial sensibility" of the masses that are "devoted to tradition and old-fashioned sentimentality."[50]

Although direct versions may have produced cultural dissonance, their nondescript locales and avoidance of national or regional specificity were part and parcel of the studios' efforts to target a broad Latin American audience. This dynamic becomes particularly apparent in the case of Warner Bros.'s *El hombre malo* (a Spanish-language version of First National's *The Bad Man* [Clarence G. Badger, 1930], directed by Robert E. Guzmán and William C. McGann). As one of the few Spanish-language films to feature explicitly Mexican subject matter and characters, it provides an apt example of the complexity of cultural specificity within this mode of production, the controversies that erupted over representation, and how these debates involved marketing, labor, exhibition, and the text itself. Adapted from a 1920 play by Porter Emerson Browne and previously produced by First National in 1923, the film follows the exploits of Pancho López (Antonio Moreno), a Robin Hood figure who possesses a rather uncomfortable resemblance to the recurring stereotype of the bandido. In fact, the silent version had actually generated critical backlash in Mexico, prompting the government to ban all of First National's productions for a period.

In producing the film again, Warner Bros. itself seemed mindful of the delicate position it had to navigate to avoid international controversy and negative reviews, as the studio consulted with Mexican officials from an early stage of the project's development. On the one hand, this property demonstrated a national and regional specificity that other Spanish-language versions of the period typically avoided. On the other, it was precisely this specificity (and stereotypes in particular) that had generated controversy and boycotts over the course of previous decades. As a way of negotiating these tensions, the studio was careful to hire Mexicans in supporting roles, continued to court Mexican officials and representatives of the Mexican press, and employed the services of multiple consultants, including the Mexican vice consul Joel Quiñones—facts the studio consistently emphasized in its public relations campaign. The studio also did its best to court the favor of the local Spanish-language press, holding a sold-out, late-night premier of the film at which 30 percent of ticket sales were donated to the Damas Católicas charity organization.[51] The film was also aggressively marketed in Mexican neighborhoods in Los Angeles and publicized in local Spanish-language publications and radio.

While these tactics produced a relatively positive review of the film in *La Opinión*, and the film apparently met with audience approval in Los Angeles, it did little to quell the broader dissatisfaction with Hollywood Spanish-language production's troubled relationship to cultural specificity.[52] In fact, much of the commentary on the film in the Mexican press centered on Quiñones's resignation as consultant in protest over matters of accent, costuming, and stereotypical characters, predicting the negative reception the film would eventually receive in his home country. Perhaps most notably (and as critics were quick to point out), although it was one of the few Spanish-language versions actually set in Mexico, the lead actor, Antonio Moreno, was Spanish and several other members of the cast spoke with Castilian accents.[53] Details from the script suggest even more bewildering linguistic contortions linked directly with targeting a general Latin American market. While Moreno, in the film's trailer, promises a film featuring "typical Spanish-speaking characters" and assures viewers that the film's director was "a great admirer of all Latin America," his dialogue features verb conjugations more common to Spain or Argentina than to Mexico. And despite speaking with an apparent Castilian accent in his portrayal of Pancho López, Moreno's dialogue in the film is peppered with Mexican colloquialisms and pronunciations (e.g., *pos* instead of *pues*, *guena* instead of *buena*).[54] These are clearly examples of the inconsistent treatments of language that so infuriated critics and at least partially contributed to the unpopularity of Spanish-language Hollywood.

The negative publicity and uneven reception of the film only convinced First National and Warner Bros. of the risks and limitations of producing films that focused on a specific nation or population while attempting to negotiate a broader appeal. Commenting on the Quiñones incident (and the publicity it generated), an unsigned letter to Jack Warner hinted at the obstacles the studios faced as they navigated pressure from multiple groups, attempting to appease Latin American and Spanish audiences on textual terms and relative to hiring practices: "the concern of the Consul and Vice Consul was only for Mexico, whereas we hope to release the picture in a great number of Spanish-speaking countries throughout the world."[55] Likewise, supervisor Baltasar Fernández Cué affirmed that the adaptation "has not been written for Mexico or any other particular country or audience, but for the whole Spanish speaking world. Consequently, I avoided every word or idiom that might not be understood outside of Mexico."[56] It was, however, this approach to making Spanish-language versions, and the solutions and practices it generated, which ensured ongoing advocacy and criticism on the part of what one studio official referred to as "a bunch of disgruntled Mexicans in Los Angeles," which undoubtedly included the critics of La Opinión.[57] Despite the efforts of Warner Bros. and other studios, these individuals saw the representation of Mexico and Mexicans distorted by this process and objected to the supposed second-class status of Mexicans within the film industry. The dilemmas occasioned by this incident also perhaps suggest the economic factors motivating studios to sustain the relative invisibility of Mexicans within foreign-language production as a way to avoid controversies over culturally specific representation.

Despite predictions that, according to one article title, "The Problem of Spanish-Speaking Films Is About to Disappear Here," in the wake of the MPPDA language agreement, controversies over language usage and cultural representation thus continued to shape the reception of Hollywood Spanish-language production in the pages of La Opinión and elsewhere.[58] Furthermore, after the language agreement, the studios also came under attack by La Opinión for supposedly engaging in discriminatory hiring practices, allegedly favoring Spanish talent over Mexican. As many individuals of Mexican descent participated in the film industry during this period, these claims might be (and were) disputed. Nonetheless, the connections proposed between representational invisibility and labor discrimination became a central critical framework whereby journalists responded to Hollywood's construction of a generic Latin American audience at the expense of Mexican specificity.

In this light, the standards agreed to by the Foreign Department, for instance, were interpreted less as an equitable compromise than a de facto advocacy of Castilian Spanish and thus met with immediate disapproval by some, foreshadowing conflicts and debates that would emerge more forcefully over the next two years. A letter printed in the trade journal Hollywood Filmograph (which featured extensive coverage of Spanish-language production and even briefly published a section in Spanish) and addressed to "the motion picture producers" denounced the agreement as discriminatory against Latin Americans, both as the most lucrative market for Spanish-language films and as potential

industry labor.⁵⁹ Significantly, the letter was signed by Mexico's previous minis-
ter of education José Vasconcelos; faculty members of Occidental College, the
University of Southern California, and the University of California, Los Angeles;
La Opinión editor José Rodríguez; and the consuls of Peru, Guatemala, Colom-
bia, Cuba, Costa Rica, Venezuela, and Nicaragua. Countering this position, T.
Navarro Tomás, in his 1930 book *El idioma español en el cine parlante* (The Spanish language in talking cinema) explicitly addresses the letter printed in *Hollywood Filmograph*, listing it among "a number of articles, written by Spanish
Americans, which contain the most violent and partisan attacks against the use
of normal Spanish pronunciation in the talkies." Such attacks, he argues, give the
erroneous impression "that the purity and propriety of the Spanish language are
now synonymous with the complete exclusion of all Spanish Americans from
speaking films." Agreeing with the guidelines issued by the MPPDA, Navarro
Tomás (echoing similar positions reprinted in *La Opinión*) asserts the necessity
of the uniform use of a standard, literary Spanish, as "every Spanish talkie must
be suitable for exhibition in every Spanish-speaking country."⁶⁰

As these debates make apparent, the issue of language usage was increasingly linked to employment opportunities and discrimination within the
industry, which was in turn directly linked to representational practices *and*
Hollywood's conception of its audience. With the simultaneous emergence
of Spanish-language production in Hollywood and the decline of local theatrical activity, a number of actors in Los Angeles sensed renewed opportunities with the transition to sound and aspired again to "invade the cinema
studios."⁶¹ The importation of actors from Broadway during the years of transition seemed to bode well for participants in the nation's most vibrant center
of Spanish-language theater. From the perspective of journalists, the casting
of local Mexican actors would solve their employment woes, with the potential to imbue Hollywood features with an unprecedented cultural specificity
and sensitivity, correcting decades of unfavorable representations. That is, if
theater presentations (and the venues sustaining them) proved exceedingly
scarce at the onset of the Depression, and Mexican cinema was slow to begin
sound production, observers hoped that this element of mass culture (and
foreign-language versions in particular) would fill this void on multiple counts.
Instead, what Mexican-descent journalists encountered was another kind of
de-Mexicanization that occurred both on-screen and off.

For critics writing for *La Opinión*, Hollywood's failure to capture the moral
and cultural sensibility of "Hispano-Americans" not only could be attributed
to literal translations of Hollywood scripts and linguistic blunders but was also
intimately linked to the employment of Euro-American directors and supposed
hiring of unqualified (and non-Mexican) actors. Accordingly, Warner Bros.'s
La llama sagrada was condemned for its unimaginative direction oblivious to
cultural nuance, while one of the actors, Guillermo del Rincón, was called "a
Spanish actor, speaking in a Spanish movie with a disagreeable English accent!"

Because issues of language held such central importance as guarantors of cultural integrity, the translators and dialogue coaches for these productions often received particular consideration in film reviews. In the case of *La llama sagrada*, Navarro devoted a section to the efforts of Guillermo Prieto Yeme, a Mexican writer who adapted the Spanish-language script from the original version. This once again signaled dedicated attention to linguistic matters, as it exemplified *La Opinión*'s ongoing analysis of production conditions that emphasized the limited agency of Mexicans and Latin Americans within the studio system. In the case of Prieto Yeme, Navarro tempers his complaints about the movie with a concession to these limitations: "the dialogue suffers from lengthy duration, but, we repeat, this could be because Mr. Prieto Yeme did not have complete control over the dramatization."[62] As in this case, such personnel were often situated as well-intentioned intermediaries that struggled with varying degrees of success against a culturally insensitive mode of production.

Perhaps the most heated controversy in this regard concerned the studios supposed hiring of Spanish actors, writers, and consultants, to the exclusion of Mexican or other Hispano-American talent, an arrangement allegedly facilitated by the MPPDA agreement. The industry's informal adoption of academic Castilian Spanish as a uniform standard, its supposed deference to the theatrical tradition of Spain, and the production of films set in often nondescript, cosmopolitan locales further corroborated claims that such films were culturally insensitive or irrelevant and would fail to resonate with Latin American audiences, much less those in Los Angeles. Beyond the case of *El hombre malo*, specific accusations made by these aforementioned "disgruntled Mexicans" within the broader controversy over labor centered particularly on four Spaniards working as supervisors or studio consultants—Manuel Paris, Andrés de Segurola, Salvador Alberich, and Baltasar Fernández Cué—whose alleged exclusionary hiring practices favored their fellow countrymen.

This controversy culminated with a meeting in 1930 of the Union of Mexican Film Exhibitors in El Paso that issued a statement advocating the employment of more Mexican actors in Spanish-language film. Subsequently, a group of Latin American actors in Hollywood proposed a continent-wide boycott of Spanish-language film, arguing that "films for these republics should reflect the life of these peoples."[63] The supervisors and consultants in question were eventually allowed to defend themselves in the pages of *La Opinión*, and several Latin American actors denied any anti-Mexican bias in hiring. Even the aforementioned Guillermo Prieto Yeme dismissed the controversy as an "economic war waged for personal reasons," the product of fierce competition over employment by individuals who "have forgotten the sacred interest common to the Spanish-speaking world," a clear reference to the notion of a cohesive Latin American market somehow united by cultural sensibility.[64] Ironically, when Prieto Yeme himself attempted to establish a Spanish Academy in Hollywood and offered his services to the MPPDA as a consultant, John V. Wilson perhaps accurately gauged part of the underlying motivation of the language controversy: "If we should endorse [the academy] and the studios should depend on it for advice, pictures produced under the arrangement would be no more acceptable than heretofore to those that are criticizing our effort. It is all a matter of 'who is employed' and not at all one of language."[65]

For many, the issues of language and "who is employed" were directly linked to the visibility of Mexicans on-screen. Despite the explanations of Spanish supervisors, frequent news items continued to appear in the pages of *La Opinión*, corroborating accounts of apparent ongoing discrimination on the part of the studios and fanning the flames of the controversy. Mexican actor Alfonso Tirado, for instance, recounted his unsuccessful audition for MGM, during which Alberich forced him to sing in a Castilian accent and then criticized his pronunciation. Needless to say, he was denied the part. An interview with legendary Mexican stage actress Virginia Fábregas (who performed Marie Dressler's role in MGM's Spanish-language version of *Min and Bill* [George W. Hill, 1930], titled *La fruta amarga* [Bitter fruit, Arthur Gregor and José López Rubio, 1931]) exemplifies the accusations leveled at Hollywood. Characterizing Spanish supervisors as "conquistadors," she affirms that "Mexicans in Hollywood . . . have to struggle against the prejudice that they don't speak Spanish, but a 'Mexican' dialect" and are forced to work for "directors of Spanish talking films that only know how to speak English."[66] Such comments suggest that prejudice against Mexicans in Hollywood—both on-screen and off—paralleled and perhaps even perpetuated the discrimination they faced more broadly in the United States (see fig. 19).

Critics' accusations of discrimination were also motivated by economic concerns, in addition to cultural concerns, specific to Mexican Los Angeles. Most notably, a supposed preference for Spanish talent further disrupted a mutually beneficial relationship between the Los Angeles–based theatrical producers, venues, talent, and critics that had previously exercised greater control over Spanish-language entertainment in the city. Despite early attempts by the Foreign Department of the MPPDA to create a registry of local Spanish-speaking theater actors, for instance, most major talent was recruited from abroad, ostensibly returning to their countries of origin when production at the studios was eventually suspended. When Spaniard Miguel de Zárraga (who would also become an occasional contributor to *La Opinión*) was brought from New York by MGM for its adaptation of *Olimpia* (Chester M. Franklin and Juan de Homs, 1930; a remake of *His Glorious Night*, Lionel Barrymore, 1929), Navarro expressed his frustration at the situation: "Aren't there individuals here who are familiar with both languages and with the machinations of the studios, individuals who have practically lived at the studios and Spanish-language newspapers and who could have done the adaptation of *Olimpia*? There are those who have seen cinema from the inside more than don Miguel and who have on occasion written for theater and cinema."[67]

That Navarro, a playwright, was one of these individuals certainly clarifies the motivation behind his frequent criticism of Hollywood practice. The abundance

Fig. 19. Print advertisement for *La fruta amarga*. *La Opinión*, March 22, 1931. Reproduced courtesy of *La Opinión*.

of negative film criticism in *La Opinión*, while acting in the name of cultural defense, also betrays elite anxiety regarding this transformation and constitutes an attempt to shape consumption and reception in an arena in which Mexican cultural authorities retained little control over the production of cultural content. To this extent, the decline of theatrical culture as an alternative cultural sphere through which transnational Mexicanidad might be constructed prompted a strategic shift whereby critics and talents aspired to alter the cinematic representation of Mexicans from within the film industry.

To be certain, one might be tempted to dismiss these controversies over labor discrimination as the product of self-interested parties, as the comments of studio executives seem to suggest. Indeed, one Mexican journalist summarized the situation thusly: "this disagreeable and absurd matter has been sustained neither by Spaniards nor by Mexicans; it has been a small, ignorant group of different nationalities: Spaniards, Argentines, Mexicans who have woven this web with economic motivations," ultimately undermining their common interests.[68] And despite the evidence presented by actors and journalists at the time, the contemporary historian has no way of accurately gauging the existence or extent of this discrimination.[69] Neither of these concerns, however, describes the retrospective significance of this particular episode. Rather, these debates reveal the manner in which screen images, language usage, audience composition, hiring practices, and press culture constituted interrelated components of a battle over cinematic representation. Regardless of the motivation of the parties involved (or the veracity of their claims), this case indeed demonstrates the complexity of such struggles, as they occur at multiple registers and across multiple media, including conceptions of urban space.

De-Mexicanizing Downtown: A Parallel Struggle for Visibility

As one of the most celebrated Mexican theater actors of the previous decades, Virginia Fábregas and her company toured frequently to Los Angeles in the 1920s and were regarded by local theater critics as the epitome and last remaining vestige of Mexican legitimate theater. Her comments and subsequent withdrawal from Hollywood film production perhaps suggest another motivation underlying the reception of Spanish-language film in *La Opinión* and the perceived effect of this production on the cultural and social environment of Mexican Los Angeles. In particular, critics posited a clear causality between the popularity of Hollywood films and the final decline of Mexican theatrical culture. From their perspective, the Spanish-language versions never facilitated any meaningful improvement in the representation or employment of Mexicans in U.S. mass culture, and they also failed to present the kind of culturally specific, cross-class leisure alternative privileged by elite and middle-class journalists over the course of previous decades.

Despite early predictions printed in the newspaper (in this case, quoting legendary Spanish playwright Jacinto Benavente) that "theater has absolutely nothing to fear from cinema" because the two "are perfectly compatible" and share mutual influence, by 1931 major venues for live Spanish-language theater in Los Angeles had indeed either closed or converted almost entirely to cinema.[70] This seemed to validate fears about the transition to sound eliminating locally produced, culturally specific forms of entertainment and (at least on the surface) corroborated notions of an incipient homogenization or standardization that in this context was often equated with Americanization. Invisibility on-screen, for these cultural critics, found its corollary in the dissipation of theatrical entertainment and the disappearance of true Mexican culture from the downtown entertainment landscape. Thus at the levels of filmic content, exhibition and theatrical space, and audience composition, multiple circumstances endangered their conception and construction of Mexicanidad through cultural consumption.

If Mexicans faced a particular kind of representational invisibility in the Spanish-language versions of Hollywood, this particular "Mexican problem," as in previous decades, also corresponded to their actual presence in downtown Los Angeles. Perhaps most obviously, the massive repatriations and forced deportations of Mexicans during this period not only substantially reduced the Mexican population of Los Angeles but made their presence in public a risky prospect. While the presence of Mexicans in the United States had remained a contested issue throughout the 1920s, a strong group of interests (from agricultural associations to the *Los Angeles Times*) publicly argued for the necessity of their presence as labor.[71] This rhetoric hinged on racial qualities that supposedly made Mexicans highly adaptable to hard labor and on the characterization of them as "birds of passage," temporary sojourners who would eventually return to their homeland.[72] As the effects of the Depression intensified, however, Mexicans were increasingly considered an unwelcome source of labor competition for unemployed Euro-Americans, a drain on public services, and perhaps even responsible for the economic downturn. While all these claims were either exaggerations or blatant falsehoods (Los Angeles County misrepresented statistics of Mexicans receiving public relief, for instance), Mexicans were increasingly unwelcome in the United States. Voluntary repatriation campaigns were initiated as a series of collaborative ventures among local authorities, the U.S and Mexican governments, and regional consulate offices. In addition to these efforts, immigration raids—and there were a number conducted in and around the Plaza area—resulted in the deportation of Mexicans, regardless of their citizenship status. As Monroy explains, the year "1931 was a fearful one for la raza in Los Angeles: the racial thinking that motivated the dragnets meant that anyone could be snared, regardless of his or her rootedness in the north."[73]

These attempts to eliminate or reduce the Mexican population of Los Angeles on the part of agitators, charity organizations, and city officials exerted a predictably direct impact on the viability of Mexican-oriented venues in downtown. According to Francisco E. Balderrama and Raymond Rodríguez, approximately one-third of the Mexican descent population of Los Angeles departed the city under these circumstances during a five-month period in 1931, and "many struggling Mexican entrepreneurs faced economic disaster and had to liquidate their properties," while many immigrants avoided public spaces for fear of being detained.[74] As Nicolás Kanellos explains, these circumstances exerted a direct impact on Mexican actors, whose most viable options were to return to Mexico, perform for church or community charities, or travel to New York, where a recent Puerto Rican influx could sustain Spanish-language theater.[75] As most studios halted Spanish production by late 1931, even this source of potential, sporadic employment for local actors dried up almost permanently. Either through physical removal, economic hardship, or reluctance to occupy public space, the circumstances facing Mexican immigrants (including theatrical talent) forced many of these venues to either close or show Hollywood features almost exclusively.

The challenge to Mexican visibility thus describes on-screen representation, along with a corresponding process under way in the conception of urban space and exhibition practices. All these circumstances threatened to disrupt the upper-class economic and cultural networks established in previous decades and sustained by the Spanish-language press. This class no longer held the power to control or influence the cultural construction of Mexicanidad in this environment (where Hollywood film increasingly held sway), while the Depression threatened other elements of this arrangement. As Navarro explained, the effects of the financial hardship, the apathy of the public, and the predominance of cinema at "popular prices" created unfavorable conditions for sustained theatrical activity.[76] Broader changes in the exhibition landscape also exerted an effect on Mexican-oriented theaters. Most notably, many downtown theaters experienced declining patronage during the Depression, as the city expanded and neighborhood theaters (often with lower prices and free parking) were increasingly constructed beyond the city center, including in East Los Angeles. Although his prediction was slightly premature, the situation downtown led one exhibitor to lament in 1931 that the "downtown section of the city is washed up as an amusement center" and that theaters there would soon be demoted to second-run venues, at best.[77] All these factors seemed to endanger the existence and visibility of a Mexican audience as national community.

Indicative of these transitions for Mexican-oriented theaters was the trajectory of the California Theater as a venue dedicated exclusively to the screening of Spanish-language films. Originally built in 1918 and operated by Fred A. Miller, the California was one of the theaters, along with Sid Grauman's Million Dollar, that initiated a trend of movie palace construction downtown (see fig. 20). Goldwyn Pictures Corporation then managed the theater beginning in 1919, and Miller (along with his brother Roy) began concentrating their efforts on the construction and operation of the Carthay Circle Theater near Beverly Hills (which opened in 1926). As Robert G. Dickson notes, Goldwyn ceased operation of the California in 1925, "after which it remained dark for most of the remainder of the

Fig. 20. The California Theater shortly after its opening in 1918. Los Angeles Public
Library Photograph Collection.

decade."[78] Bruce W. LaLanne has attributed this closure directly to the construction of newer and more spacious theaters elsewhere in the city.[79] Significantly,
however, following the precedent established by Virginia Fábregas's company
in 1927, the California soon began hosting Spanish-language theatrical performances, at least on an occasional basis.

By 1930, a theater manager named Tom White, capitalizing on a possible local
interest in Hollywood Spanish-language films (and the theater's reputation with
Mexican audiences), announced his intention to lease the California, inaugurating it with "the first all Spanish program in America," which began with the
premier of *La rosa de fuego*. According to White, this exhibition practice would
also provide an important function for Hollywood: "It will not only serve as a
'try-out' for a purely Spanish reaction to Hollywood product made in the Spanish language, but will serve as well as a laboratory in which the Latin mind may
be observed at first hand and its likes and dislikes carefully noted for future productions."[80] After White's plan apparently floundered, Miller once again assumed
management of the California, which would henceforth be known as the International California Theater and feature "the presentation of all-talking films in
every language but English."[81] As a unique marketing ploy, Miller even converted
part of the mezzanine floor into an art gallery that would feature works resonating with the film being screened.[82] Notably, this effort was recognized by the

Hoover administration as an effort of much significance to the transition-era film industry and a gesture of international cooperation (not to mention public relations). The president's secretary, Lawrence Richey, praised the California in the following terms:

> [a] place for review of the work of our producers of foreign language motion pictures should stimulate and assist our producers in meeting the change in American pictures now required to meet the revolution brought about by the spoken word. The spread of effectively produced pictures in foreign languages can be made a further instrument of international understanding and good will.[83]

Paramount's first Spanish-language version, *El cuerpo del delito* (Cyril Gardener and A. Washington Pezet, 1930; a remake of *The Benson Murder Case*) marked the opening of the theater as the International California (advertised in the Spanish-language press as the Teatro Internacional California), with the venue dedicating its programming to foreign versions just as the major studios began releasing a regular supply of them (see fig. 21). Soon after its inauguration in August, Miller discovered that Spanish-language films attracted bigger audiences than others and subsequently converted almost entirely to the exhibition of features and shorts in this language.[84] As a large movie palace of more recent construction than other Mexican-oriented venues, the California would provide a visible showcase for the studios' constant output and soon "would become the Los Angeles first-run theater for these films," fulfilling a demand for cinema in the Spanish language and serving as the physical epicenter of Mexican film culture.[85]

As the first theater dedicated (however briefly) to the exhibition of films in Spanish, the Teatro California (as it was referred to in the Spanish-language press) thus exerted a transformative impact on the landscape of Spanish-language entertainment in Los Angeles. Nevertheless, it would soon suffer from the same hardships afflicting other venues serving the Mexican population. The Teatro México, for instance, soon found itself imperiled by the confluence of challenges facing other theaters. Originally constructed in 1884 as Child's Opera House (and subsequently operated as the Grand Opera House), the theater was located on 110 South Main. Although it managed to stay in business through early 1931 with a combination of variety and second-run Spanish-language versions, for instance, it soon converted to a burlesque house (a form that enjoyed a resurgence during the Depression), with only the California and Hidalgo now offering regular programming in Spanish.

In an effort inextricable from battles over cinematic representation and industry labor, critics rallied to preserve the existence of specifically Mexican entertainment within the fabric downtown. *La Opinión's* ongoing advocacy for Los Angeles–based talent and local venues, for instance, at least partially explains a surprisingly abrupt shift in its reception of Hollywood Spanish-language film during 1931. Although most studios had suspended or reduced Spanish-language

Fig. 21. Print advertisement for the grand opening of the Teatro Internacional California. *La Opinión*, August 26, 1930. Reproduced courtesy of *La Opinión*.

production by the spring of 1931, the Teatro California was able to premier a new film every week through the fall (with second runs at Teatro Hidalgo), relying on a backlog of Hollywood films. At this point, reviews of these productions in *La Opinión* become almost uniformly positive, departing from the caustic critiques that typified the paper's earlier coverage. Navarro's review of *La mujer X* (1931) (a Spanish-language version of *Madame X*) praises the work of director Carlos F. Borcosque, for instance, as somehow possessing "an individual touch, which approaches the particular sensibility we have as Latinos."[86] Assessments of these films also become suddenly and unabashedly superlative. Discussing *Su noche de bodas* (Louis Mercanton and Florián Rey, 1931; from *Her Wedding Night*, Frank Tuttle, 1930), a reviewer declared that "it seems to us the most serious, complete, and luminous work of cinema in Spanish thus far," a distinction suddenly bestowed on such films on almost a weekly basis during this period.[87]

This effort to recover the critical reputation of Spanish-language Hollywood films was also accompanied by Navarro's insistent advocacy for continued production. His frequent (and lengthy) assessments of studio activity in this regard shift from a litany of complaints to become increasingly prescriptive, suggesting reasons for the failure of these films to attract audiences while also conducting interviews with studio personnel. Lamenting Hollywood's impending transition to dubbed films, for instance, Navarro explained to an anonymous production supervisor that misguided casting, lower budgets, and shorter shooting schedules placed Spanish-language films at a disadvantage, with studios not allowing star personas and audience allegiance to develop over time.[88] Despite his critical interventions and the occasional promise of renewed production, studios like Fox and MGM were rapidly terminating the contracts of Spanish-language actors and reducing output to a limited number of vehicles for established stars like José Mojica and Spanish comedian Ernesto Vilches. Critics like Navarro thus adopted at this point a pragmatic ambivalence, acknowledging (and at times clearly exaggerating) the improvement of Hollywood films in Spanish while simultaneously pointing out their continued deficiencies, ultimately advocating their ongoing production as the only extant Spanish-language entertainment upon which Mexican-oriented venues had become almost entirely dependent.

The downturn in production, for instance, predictably exerted a direct and immediate effect on the Mexican entertainment landscape, when the Teatro California was forced to suspend Spanish-language exhibition and transition to the screening of films in German, Yiddish, and Japanese by November 1931. Although owner Fred Miller reinstituted Spanish-language screenings in early 1932, he was again forced to suspend this practice by March of the same year, due to a lack of available product. The theater then closed, with subsequent (and multiple) changes of management and sporadic bookings through 1932. With the disappearance of the only first-run theater for Spanish-language film, the Teatro Hidalgo remained the sole option for regular entertainment in Spanish, offering second-run films and variety shows geared toward working-class Mexicans. Thus the supposed colonization of Spanish-language entertainment in Los Angeles hinged less exclusively on the imposition or appropriation of particular textual forms or technology, as Curtis Marez has argued, than on a complex shift involving *multiple* factors including competing regimes of taste, economic circumstance, urban development, press culture, studio policy, industrial labor practices, and the broader exhibition landscape.[89]

Not surprisingly, Spanish-language theater and film exhibition during the subsequent year continued to prove unsustainable without a steady supply of films from the studios. Contrary to journalist Fidel Murillo's prediction that the lack of product would spur a theatrical renaissance throughout Latin America (with acting styles greatly improved by the influence of cinema), this period was marked by theater closures and financial failures in Los Angeles.[90] Perhaps the most notable attempt to rejuvenate Spanish-language entertainment in Los Angeles was the return of the Teatro México, which had been operating as a burlesque house called the Grand. Opening with a screening of the independently produced travelogue *Pro-patria* (Guillermo Calles, 1931), the theater was decorated with the colors of the Mexican flag, and motifs of eagles and Aztec calendars graced the lobby. This constituted an unabashed reclamation of the theater and its offerings as a repository of nationalism. Navarro celebrated the venue's replacement of American popular music like jazz by "the languid songs of Mexico, by artful and sentimental entertainment, by Hispanic culture that survives against all odds in this corner of the United States."[91] Because of poor attendance, however, the México reverted to burlesque within two weeks, although it would occasionally host theater performances or screenings of independent productions. For the remainder of 1932, film premiers were held at the Hidalgo, and while sporadic performances were held at the California and México Theaters, these trends would continue until a more regular supply of Spanish-language feature films could be imported from abroad.

Given all these circumstances, the final fate of Mexican theatrical culture, at least as it had been practiced since the 1920s, was a foregone conclusion. In 1934 Murillo conducted a lengthy analysis of its precipitous decline and the consequent fragmentation of the Mexican audience and community. Noting that the remaining theaters opened only on weekends, privileging cinema and occasionally featuring touring companies, the columnist reminded potential impresarios of the wealth of available local talent. Despite such pleas however, Murillo also acknowledged the formidable obstacles facing any attempt to mount live performance, summarizing the central issue succinctly: "there is no more audience for our theaters." Reminiscing about (and clearly romanticizing) the days in which "any miniscule incentive was enough to drag the multitudes to the theater," he lamented that "unless it involves [a movie starring] José Mojica, Dolores del Rio, or Lupe Velez—one cannot fill a theater." He continued by listing the multiple factors that had contributed to this situation: the summer heat, the economics of the Depression, and the repatriations that have left only "the families that haven't been able to abandon the city, or those who refused to." While most of these individuals "think more about resolving the problem at hand than about having fun," the younger generation preferred to attend the first-run English-language cinemas downtown that provided a level of entertainment unattainable by Spanish-language venues. These conditions led Murillo to a rather bleak and pessimistic conclusion: "The worst, most disparaging part is that theater is dying little by little, just like an old man, without resistance, without hope and with no remedy. It would be best to kill it off with one blow and forget about it."[92]

One particular 1934 stage production proves emblematic of the declining Spanish-language theatrical environment, although it also hints at a nascent shift in the nature of live performance. In December, the Cine Club of Los Angeles presented a staging at the Wilshire Ebell Theatre of Gregorio Martínez Sierra's play *Canción de cuna* (Cradle song), about an infant abandoned at a convent. Intended to raise money to purchase Christmas gifts for local Mexican children, the play received a relatively disappointing attendance that "although not very numerous, was extraordinarily distinguished."[93] Despite its lackluster reception, the Cine Club's production also marked the emergence of a practice that would be deployed more effectively and pervasively in the coming years. Namely, the play was designed as a tribute to Argentine actress Catalina Bárcena and playwright Martínez Sierra, both "prominent elements of Hispanic cinema" involved in the 1934 Fox production *Ciudad de cartón* (City of cardboard, Louis King, 1934), as was the play's director, José Crespo, and another featured actress, Luz Alba.[94] The play's production was clearly designed, at least in part, as promotion for the film and, more broadly speaking, for Fox Film Corporation (one of the only studios that continued to produce Spanish-language films). Furthermore, the production marked an attempt to attract a theatrical audience through the pretense of a film club, included a finale directed by former MGM translator and *La Opinión* contributor Miguel de Zárraga, and featured a play that had recently been adapted as the Paramount film *The Cradle Song* (Mitchell Leisen, 1933). Quite obviously, the Cine Club was mobilizing an intriguing array of intermedial connections. Its relative lack of success, however, suggests that it perhaps relied too heavily on increasingly outmoded (or less popular) cultural forms and frames of reference, namely Spanish-language Hollywood and legitimate theater.

More indicative of future trends, however, were the Hollywood films starring José Mojica (at Fox) and Carlos Gardel (at Paramount). Produced largely between 1934 and 1935, these were among the handful of Spanish-language films made beyond 1932, and they reportedly enjoyed critical and financial success. In Mojica and Gardel, the studios seemed to finally have found the stars that eluded them only several years earlier. Crucially, both men were familiar to international audiences from radio programs, recorded music, and live performances, and their films might justifiably be categorized as musicals. As Rielle Navitski has argued, Gardel's "career is inextricable from economic and technological developments in the cultural sphere—the availability of affordable phonographs and records, the rise of radio broadcasting, and the transition to sound film."[95] By capitalizing on such intermedial connections, Hollywood had perhaps belatedly stumbled on a successful Spanish-language formula and, as Navitski argues, a basis on which Latin American film industries would soon model their own national productions. In fact, as Marvin D'Lugo further argues, the transnational circulation of music through radio and film "contribute[d] to the forging of a

Hispanic 'transnation' of listeners," encouraging the formation of the sort of continental audience and community that Hollywood had aspired to construct with its earlier Spanish-language versions.[96] The fact that Gardel's films were identifiably Argentine in terms of their settings, dialogue, and music also demonstrated the viability of an accessible cultural specificity, as opposed to Hollywood's generic (and often confusing) construction of a continental Latinidad.

Not surprisingly, downtown theaters in Los Angeles also began capitalizing on this synergy by incorporating radio personalities and other local talent into variety prologues, particularly in the context of film premiers. The retirement of Mojica (who would subsequently become a priest) and the premature death of Gardel, among other factors, likely forestalled continued production along these lines within Hollywood, although these trends in exhibition would only expand as intermedial cultural production grew in Mexico. To some extent, this practice would represent the refinement of the "'horizontal' linkage of film companies with other entertainment businesses, including radio, phonograph recording, illustrated magazines, sheet-music publishing, and the popular stage" that emerged after the transition to sound.[97] Of course, these connections were forged differently in various national and regional contexts, but it also became apparent that Latin American audiences responded precisely to this kind of specificity. By developing an identifiably Mexican-oriented intermedial model to capitalize on the cross-promotional synergy of radio, cinema, and live performance, exhibitors in Mexican Los Angeles would, within the next few years, perfect practices that fostered the resurgence and survival of Spanish-language movie houses. If Gardel's transnational stardom through Hollywood inspired Argentine national cinema, the development of Mexican national cinema would provide the basis of a transnational, intermedial construction of Mexicanidad, one that altered the terms and stakes of cinematic representation in Mexican Los Angeles at multiple levels.

CODA: TEATRO LEO CARRILLO

By positing the transition to sound in Los Angeles as a struggle over representational visibility both on-screen and within the fabric of the city, I must also acknowledge that another construction of Mexicanidad achieved dominance at this very moment. That is, reconstructing this pivotal moment in Mexican film culture requires distinguishing the terms of visibility as defined by the Mexican press from other apparent manifestations of Mexican culture. More specifically, the repeated closures (and overall precariousness) of Mexican-oriented venues in the early 1930s coincided with another theatrical opening, one highly indicative of intermedial representations of Mexicans in Los Angeles. It was at this very juncture that the historical Plaza area was repackaged and re-presented by Christine Sterling and her supporters as Olvera Street, a tourist attraction that reconfigured the Mexican presence in Los Angeles as a sanitized fantasy, with a particular emphasis on "Old California's" Spanish legacy.

With the help of boosters, including real estate developers and the *Los Angeles Times*, Sterling would transform an area in supposed decline (and associated with vice, disease, and racial heterogeneity) into a romantic celebration of the city's Mexican past, complete with souvenir shops, restaurants, and "authentically" dressed vendors. As immigrant workers faced deportation and journalists struggled against the threat of cultural invisibility, this other representational complex emerged as a rather forceful erasure of the contemporary Mexican experience. As part of this renovation, the Leo Carrillo Theater at 21 Olvera Street was inaugurated on June 12, 1932. This venture was significant for a number of reasons. Perhaps most obviously, as William Estrada has argued, if Sterling's designs for Olvera Street were influenced by cinematic and artistic renderings of Mexico, the establishment of a theater sponsored by and named after a Hollywood actor of Mexican descent once again underlines the coincidence, overlap, and dialogue between representations in the spheres of cinema, the mainstream media, and urban space.[98]

As it had in previous decades, for instance, the conception of Mexicanness undergirding Olvera Street manifested itself in mainstream journalistic accounts of the Plaza area. Again, these representations remain inextricable from the economic interests of dailies like the *Times* and other civic boosters that had supported Sterling and her efforts. Although adopting the touristic address of earlier and more salacious accounts of the area (as detailed in chapter 1), such articles, when focused on Olvera Street, departed from these by replacing conceptions of dangerous and unsanitary Mexicans with stereotypes of a romantic, harmless populace. Strolling down Olvera Street, for instance, reporter Philip K. Scheuer declared, "Old Mexico is upon me." Aside from floridly describing the general atmosphere of the street and the wares of its vendors, Scheuer took note of two of its denizens: "an indolent Mexican flat-palms a guitar, paying no attention" and "an old, gnarled Mexican—part Indian, he looked to be—sound asleep behind his tamale stand."[99] Such images deny the actual existence and conditions of contemporary Mexican labor through the stereotype of the lazy Mexican, but they also situate Mexicans as something to be visually consumed by Euro-American tourists, a crucial part of the experiential package of Olvera Street. Despite the claims of other accounts that Olvera Street's apparent authenticity somehow distanced it from the falsity of cinematic Mexico, the tourist attraction (along with its promotion and reception) clearly drew on long-standing conceptions of Mexico and Mexicans that circulated through multiple media.[100]

This convergence and dialogue between different modes of representation becomes even more apparent considering Carrillo's persona as public figure: although often portraying versions of a bandido or Mexican "bad man" in the early sound period, his image offscreen emphasized the fact that he was a descendant of the *californio* elite of Spanish descent that predated even the state's Mexican period. In this way, his public image is clearly analogous to the nostalgic, Spanish-inflected version of Mexico constructed through Olvera Street. As an earlier profile on the actor claimed, he was a descendant of "the old Spanish family of Carrillo, which settled on the Coast about two hundred years ago."[101] In Carrillo's own family history–cum-autobiography, *The California I Love* (written nearly thirty years later), he described his family as "those of us of Spanish blood whose veins carry the red fire pumped from the hot fountains of medieval Castile." This book recounts tales of Mexican California from the colonial period to the late nineteenth century, with his ancestors (and "Spanish-Mexican culture" in general) as protagonists.[102]

Aptly enough, however, the Mexican presence of the twentieth century (including, most notably, the massive influx of recent immigrants) remains a complete textual absence until his chapter of tribute to Olvera Street. His frequent participation in civic festivities dressed as a Spanish *don* further distanced him from a recent, immigrant working-class population and conveniently elided the indigenous component of Mexican history and identity in the process. If, as a 1932 promotional brochure about the theater claimed, "the aim of Olvera St. is to keep *Spanish* culture alive" (my emphasis), the theater's name honors the Carrillo family, who "played an important part in building the city."[103] This framing of the actor and his family history aptly epitomizes Olvera Street's conception of the city's Mexican presence through a distortion and Europeanizing of its history, its mobilization of the "Spanish fantasy heritage."[104]

Beyond this, in the context of Olvera Street, the assumed status of the Carrillo Theater as a Mexican venue belies its disconnection from networks of Mexican cultural nationalism and community formation in Los Angeles. At first glance, its programming would seem consistent with the concerns and tastes of Mexican cultural authorities. The theater did promise to "encourage the development of Latin-American drama by discovering new playwrights," announced intentions to program "the best of Spanish and Mexican plays and dancing," and had an opening that marked a "revival of the pomp once common in California in the days of Spanish and Mexican dominion" (what one newspaper article characterized as an "early Spanish ritual").[105] The subsequent presentations there were decidedly eclectic, including (quite curiously), a revival of the controversial play *The Bad Man*, starring Carrillo himself in a reprisal of his earlier stage role.[106]

Although many of the shows indeed featured Spanish, Mexican, or (in one rather peculiar case) "Aztec" elements, the venue never functioned as a component of Mexican-oriented cultural nationalism in Los Angeles.[107] There are a number of likely reasons for this. Perhaps most obviously, this theater was not designed for a Mexican audience, or at least not for those of the working class that frequented other venues around the Plaza. The 1932 brochure (written in English) encouraged city residents to "bring your Olympic guests to the theater," suggesting that it was indeed pitched toward non-Mexican, tourist audiences. Furthermore, the admission prices of $1.00 to $1.50 were considerably higher than concurrent prices at Mexican-oriented venues and would likely have excluded an immigrant audience, particularly during the Depression. The working-class audience of the Teatro Hidalgo, for instance, would have paid an admission of between fifteen and twenty cents in 1932. And although performances may have been of Spanish or Mexican origins, they were typically performed in English (including a staging of Jacinto Benavente's 1913 *La malquerida* [*Passion Flower*]).[108] Furthermore, the theater was operated by the Olvera Street Theater Association, whose board was made up entirely of Euro-American theater boosters to the exclusion of local Mexican cultural authorities.[109]

Despite extensive coverage of other theater openings and closings, and the general crisis of Mexican entertainment in the early 1930s, *La Opinión* rarely mentioned the Carrillo during its brief existence, much less reviewed its offerings (although it did receive extensive coverage in the *Times* as part of its enthusiasm and support for Olvera Street). Not only did the Carrillo Theater coincide with a representational regime that promoted a romanticizing tourist gaze across urban space and cinema, but it also operated outside the circuits of Mexican community formation in Los Angeles. Indeed, its mobilization of Spanish-Mexican culture seemed instead to operate as a function of the broader power structure of Los Angeles, in conjunction with the very forces that pushed working-class residents out of the Plaza to replace them with a picturesque fantasy of Old Mexico in the name of civic improvement. This is an apt example of Monroy's observation that within Los Angeles, "Mexicans were simultaneously manifest and concealed upon the landscape."[110] Again, the status of Mexicans in Los Angeles held strong correlations to cinematic representation and its relation to transformations of the entertainment landscape downtown—in this case an ostensible presence that masked some significant erasures at multiple levels.

CHAPTER 4

FASHIONABLE CHARROS AND CHINAS POBLANAS

MEXICAN CINEMA AND THE DILEMMA OF THE COMEDIA RANCHERA

The decline of Spanish-language Hollywood coincided with and even contributed to the development of the Mexican film industry. While the late 1920s and early 1930s witnessed only sporadic feature production in Mexico, the nation's newfound social and political stability soon facilitated more concerted efforts to establish the regular production of films and an industrial infrastructure. As Aurelio de los Reyes argues, "The years 1932 and 1933 were characterized by the return of Mexican actors who had played secondary roles in Hollywood . . . by talk of fabulous film projects and the arrival of directors, actors, and technicians from other nations ready to collaborate with the emergence of an industry that some regarded as national, and others simply saw as Spanish speaking."[1] From this perspective, the acquisition of technical training and expertise compensated for the financial failures and representational erasures of Spanish-language Hollywood. Typifying the optimism that these developments generated, Baltasar Fernández Cué argued in the pages of Mexico City's *El Universal* that "this is the opportune moment to begin film production in Mexico. There is no country more appropriate. Its proximity to Hollywood makes it privileged. Furthermore, a significant majority of foreigners in Hollywood are Mexican, and they could bring their knowledge and experience to Mexican production."[2] The production of the first Mexican sound feature, *Santa* (Antonio Moreno, 1931), predicted this broader shift, as it relied heavily on Hollywood-trained talent including silent-star-turned-director Antonio Moreno, actress Lupita Tovar, and sound technicians José and Roberto Rodríguez (see fig. 22).

As Mexico began steadily producing and distributing feature films by the mid-1930s, critical discourse in Los Angeles (as in Mexico) continued to focus squarely on issue of cultural nationalism and representational authenticity in a

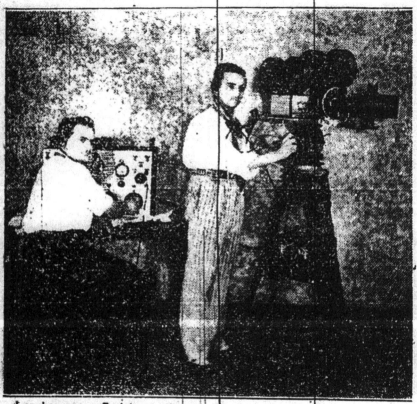

Los hermanos Rodríguez y su invento que ha sido recibido con admiración

Los hermanos Rodríguez, José y Roberto, inventores de un aparato para grabar sonidos simultáneamente con la impresión de películas, aparecen en esta fotografía. José está en el "mixer" y Roberto operando en la cámara.

Nótese cuan pequeño y por consiguiente cómodo es el aparato, que está adicionado a la cámara y registra el sonido con igual fidelidad que los grandes y costosos usados en la producción cinefónica de los grandes estudios.

Fig. 22. While working in Hollywood, the Rodríguez brothers (José and Roberto) developed motion picture sound technology. They would subsequently employ this technology on Mexican productions, including *Santa*. *La Opinión*, November 30, 1930. Reproduced courtesy of *La Opinión*.

way that resonated with yet departed from earlier criticisms leveled at Hollywood. In particular, substantial debate circulated about the development of a cinema that, following both cultural and economic dictates, would be a proper reflection of the nation while simultaneously securing foreign markets necessary for its sustenance, consistent with the impetus of other national cinemas during the period.[3] As had been the case in previous decades, these debates about cinema proved inextricable from its circulation within a multimedia landscape that now included the expansion of Mexican mass media in conjunction with official strains of cultural nationalism.

All the manifestations of nationalism in Los Angeles, from theater publicity and decor to cinematic texts, framed national cinema as authentic in its liberation from dependence on Hollywood. But these instantiations of "authentic" Mexicanidad across media often masked the contested nature of national cultural expression and the utterly transnational foundations of cultural production in Mexico. As Nataša Ďurovičová has pointed out, industries engaging in sound production around the globe found themselves connected to the national on the basis of language or cultural traditions *and* working to maximize international revenue, a tension that "formed the baseline condition of cinema as ever more reflective of, and enmeshed in, a transnational scale of space—a scale characterized by a simultaneous dependence on and transcendence of the nation-state."[4] Once again, Mexican film culture in Los Angeles proves a fertile site from which to gauge these apparently paradoxical intersections that attended the emergence of national cinemas. Although the confluence of multiple venues and a supposedly more authentic cinema indeed inaugurated a renaissance of Spanish-language exhibition in Los Angeles, its transnational origins and operation also implicitly served as a source of ongoing critical controversy.

To gauge the changing nature and stakes of cultural representation and the ongoing construction of transnational Mexicanidad in the mid-1930s, there is perhaps no more appropriate text than the landmark *Allá en el Rancho Grande*. Largely regarded as "the film that saved the industry from imminent ruin" on both a cultural and economic level, this film secured the *comedia ranchera* genre (the Mexican equivalent of Hollywood's singing cowboy films) as a staple of Mexican cinema for decades to come.[5] With its roots in theater, its reliance on popular music like mariachi, and its evocation of Mexican types such as the singing charro (Mexican cowboy), the genre aptly epitomized the intermedial synergy that accounts for the success of Mexican cinema through the Golden Age and beyond. While incredibly popular with international audiences, *Rancho Grande* reflected and exacerbated debate in Los Angeles about the terms of an emergent national identity through cinema, its value to Mexico's reputation, and its relation to the city's Mexican presence.

Once again, transnational Mexicanidad in Los Angeles operated as a force oriented toward the formation of a national community *and* toward elevating the status of Mexicans in the city. It was the latter aspect of this dynamic upon which critical controversy largely fixated. On the one hand, the film's mobilization of a folkloric visual and aural vocabulary resonated with forms of cultural nationalism promoted by the Mexican state with its emphasis on international public relations. It thus facilitated not only the expansion of a patently Mexican-oriented exhibition practice, but one that also aspired to attract a non-Mexican audience in the name of changing local perceptions of Mexico. On the other hand, a number of critics decried the similarity between the Mexico of the comedia ranchera films and stereotypes that circulated through U.S. mass culture, tourist promotion, and the city's embrace of a mythical, romanticized version of its Mexican heritage (at sites like Olvera Street). That is, if, for such critics, these films presented a version of transnational Mexicanidad that combined elements of modernization (through the mastery of Hollywood technology) with cultural specificity (through the evocation of a folkloric past), they did so by resonating with established stereotypes. Thus while multiple scholars have condemned *Rancho Grande* and the ranchera genre as simply ideologically suspect or conservative, its reception in Los Angeles reveals it instead as a rich site of contestation over the very terms and stakes of transnational Mexicanidad.

EXHIBITING PATRIOTISM: THE STRUGGLE TO DEFINE MEXICAN CINEMA

To properly understand the multifaceted impact and significance of the comedia ranchera in Los Angeles (and beyond), it is first necessary to survey the contested formulations of Mexican cinema that preceded the genre's emergence and their relation to the sustenance of a Mexican exhibition practice in the city. For journalists, issues of production and exhibition were inextricably linked. They regarded the variable Mexicanness of both as indicative of the vitality of Mexican identity and community formation. Crucial to these debates, however, was the undeniable fact of Hollywood's global domination and influence. The central dilemma here consisted of how Mexican cinema might simultaneously establish itself as a national cultural expression and a viable industry in the face of such a formidable obstacle. Perhaps paradoxically, this required conceiving of its relation to Hollywood as both competition and an indispensable resource. The transnational dimensions of films like *Allá en el Rancho Grande* thus have their origins in early attempts to locate a technological, generic, and textual compromise that would ensure the international success of Mexican cinema and the sustenance of local theaters. Even in the early years of sound production, critics pragmatically proposed a range of strategic engagements with Hollywood, rather than a complete rejection, solutions that strove to locate a balance between technological mastery and cultural specificity. Here, even in its earliest stages, Mexican sound cinema was conceived of as an inevitably transnational enterprise. A close examination of these discursive maneuvers illuminates the motivation behind the critical success and controversies accompanying the reception of the comedia ranchera.

Initially, early sound film production in Mexico seemed posed to fulfill the predictions and proposals of journalists in Mexico and Los Angeles who were dissatisfied by Spanish production in Hollywood and its supposed bias against Mexicans. As the city's Spanish-language theater and film venues closed and reopened during 1931 and 1932, for instance, the possibility of Mexican cinema generated considerable optimism, promising the conjoined potential of culturally specific productions and the related sustainability of regular exhibition. Not coincidentally, the sporadic screening of films produced in Mexico, as I demonstrated in the last chapter, was often connected with the reopening of a particular venue. The 1931 landmark film *Santa* again proves indicative of broader trends. Not only was the film regarded as evidence that Mexican films would provide a welcome and timely replacement of problematic Hollywood productions, but its star-studded premier (with Lupita Tovar and Antonio Moreno in attendance), as a highly symbolic gesture, would also mark the reopening of the Teatro California, regarded as a central fixture of the community's cultural vitality since 1927.

This confluence of factors undoubtedly accounts for *La Opinión*'s enthusiastic coverage of the film, which adopted a patently nationalistic tone. In one interview, the film's distributor, Rafael Calderón, affirmed, "It seems to me that [*Santa*] is more than just a movie, but a part of the very life of Mexico; something so intimately national, like an artistic flag. And the reason is because it is the first evidence of Mexico as a producer of Spanish-language films, probably the beginning of a brilliant future."[6] For *La Opinión* critic Gabriel Navarro, this film positioned Mexico as an emerging competitor with Hollywood and signaled the potential impact of cinema on cultural preservation: "This is what we want, at the very least, for the benefit of our language and customs, threatened more now than ever by those of the United States, which, as good as they may be, do not derive from our own unique sensibility."[7]

During the early 1930s Mexican cinema was thus consistently situated by critics as crucial to the maintenance of cultural integrity and directly linked to the ongoing viability of Spanish-language exhibition and, as an extension, community formation through cultural consumption. The effects of the Depression and the repatriation of Mexican immigrants, as I have mentioned, significantly diminished the audience for these entertainments, further limiting the success of theatrical venues. Although *Santa* initially generated enthusiasm, for instance, the Teatro California quickly returned to showing Hollywood films. Another gala reopening of the Teatro México in 1932 likewise proved only temporary, despite overdetermined efforts to emphasize the event as an unadulterated expression of national pride. Scheduled in conjunction with Mexican Independence Day (September 16), the México screened the independent feature *Contrabando* (Frank Wells and Alberto Méndez Bernal, 1932), produced in Baja California, assuring the readers of *La Opinión* that the film was "spoken entirely in Spanish, made in Mexico, with Mexican capital and with Mexican actors and direction as well" (this perhaps in distinction to *Santa*, with its extensive reliance on talent trained in Hollywood). The theater's interior was also renovated and decorated with Mexican flags, "to erase from this center of Mexican culture any remaining detail of the kind of entertainment that our people have always rejected" (a probable reference to the venue's previous incarnation as a burlesque house).[8] As these comments suggest, patriotic theater display served the interrelated functions of niche marketing, an expression of imagined community, and cultural elevation through distance from U.S. popular culture.

Both the unpredictable nature of Mexican production in the early 1930s (*Santa* was one of only two features produced in 1931) and the concomitant instability of local theaters initially prevented the consistent convergence of nationally specific content exhibited in decidedly Mexican spaces. If these circumstances promised to forestall the creation of a broader Mexican film culture, the undeniable influence of Hollywood threatened to thwart the cultural specificity necessary for the creation of a national cinema at the very site of production. Initial enthusiasm to the contrary, the early sound film *Santa* and the subsequent *Aguilas frente al sol* (Eagles before the sun, Antonio Moreno, 1932) were regarded as somewhat deficient, albeit well-intentioned efforts, with one editorial declaring that "they are almost as bad as the Spanish films made in Hollywood."[9] Mexican sound cinema, at least in its earliest years, did not represent the straightforward solution initially predicted by critics, either in terms of textual content or the transformation of exhibition practice. The early struggle to develop a culturally and economically viable cinema consequently produced its own set of debates about what would constitute an authentic and successful expression of Mexicanidad that would support the industry at every level.

Central to these critical debates about Mexican cinema was the representation of the nation and its residents, along with the cinematic articulation of the national character that would distinguish its films from Hollywood productions, in turn allowing local theaters to mark their offerings as distinctly Mexican. But the nature of cinema as a medium (along with the global dominance of Hollywood) prompted a conception of national cinematic identity that mapped the combination of artistry and technology in fundamentally transnational terms. As countless excerpts from *La Opinión* readily demonstrate, journalists in Los Angeles consistently aligned Mexican (or, in a broader sense, Latin American) culture and the Spanish language with sentimentality, spirituality, and traditional morality, while U.S. culture was often characterized by technical expertise, modernization, and a lack of emotion. As Helen Delpar explains, this attitude became prevalent during the first two decades of the twentieth century: "intellectuals in Mexico as elsewhere in Latin America usually regarded Americans as vulgar materialists who were interested only in amassing wealth and lacked the desire and the ability to distinguish themselves in artistic creation or appreciation. The corollary, whether stated or not, was that Mexicans, like other Latin Americans and Latin peoples in general, were endowed with superior aesthetic and spiritual sensibilities."[10] Cultural criticism in Los Angeles, as I demonstrated in the first chapter, often evoked this notion of cultural superiority as a reversal of discourses that insisted on Mexican racial inferiority. They recognized however that cinema, as art and industry, required the successful combination of both sensibilities.

During this transitional moment in the early 1930s, when journalists acknowledged that Hollywood would no longer serve as the epicenter of Spanish-language cinema, this logic also (and perhaps paradoxically) supported the contentions that Mexico, rather than Spain or Argentina, should fulfill this function. In other words, the proximity of Mexico to Southern California would guarantee the availability of equipment and technical expertise, while producing within Mexico would ensure a level of cultural authenticity that had evaded Hollywood productions. Consequently, as *La Opinión* tracked the growth of other national cinemas and reported on Hollywood studios' latest attempts to foster Spanish-language production abroad, Mexico consistently emerged as the most logical supplier of cinema to the rest of the Spanish-speaking world. Ironically, it was the simultaneous proximity to *and* difference from Hollywood that was conceived of as one of the foundational conditions for the proper formation of a national cinema.

In fact, before Mexico City became the unequivocal center of the Mexican industry, the viability of regional production was proposed precisely on the basis of this transnational division of cultural and technological labor. The case of Mexican National Films, a production company announcing its inception in 1934, proves instructive in this regard. Headed by Roberto Farfán Jr., the company intended to establish studios in Rosarito, Baja California (south of the border city of Tijuana), while maintaining an office in Los Angeles to "contract only the technical elements necessary." As Farfán explained, "it seems that Baja California is the most logical place for the production of photo-dramas and photo-comedies in Spanish. They are produced in Mexican territory, and at the same time, the appropriate materials can be brought from Hollywood in only a matter of hours, when necessary."[11] Despite these ambitions, however, it appears that the studio's production of *El retorno del gaucho* (The return of the gaucho), which apparently drew on Argentine cultural references, never progressed beyond the planning stages.

Beyond the location of production, observers consistently expressed concern about exactly how these apparently divergent cultural tendencies would combine to influence the actual content of a national cinema. Film critics obviously rejected the wholesale adoption of U.S. values in the name of cultural retention but also acknowledged the benefit of selectively integrating certain of these elements into the nascent Mexican industry. Reviewers, for instance, consistently evaluated the technical qualities (including editing, sound, and photography) of both Spanish-language Hollywood and Mexican films in relation to the polish of regular Hollywood productions. To be certain, critics like Gabriel Navarro avowed an initial willingness to overlook certain shortcomings of the fledging industry, since "Mexican cinematic production, deficient in technical execution, lacking true and significant artistic value, is still superior on an ideological level to Hollywood offerings adorned with the luxuries afforded by money and nearing perfection in sound and photography."[12] Nonetheless, most also linked the ultimate success of Mexican cinema to the ability of producers to overcome technical obstacles, to "Americanize" to a limited extent. In an article on the Mexican industry, for instance, Navarro admitted that "the cinema is essentially a Saxon art" and concluded that "Hispano cinema needs to Saxonize, not in terms of ideological tendencies, but in its technical aspects."[13] Referring to the negative reception of Chano Urueta's *Profanación* (1933), one critic likewise lamented an overall lack of training and preparedness on the part of Mexican producers, offering the apparently counterintuitive proposal that foreign expertise would be necessary to create an industry capable of evading foreign ownership and intervention in the future.[14]

Critics writing for *La Opinión* insisted, however, that this American influence (especially at the level of content) remain limited to certain arenas. Due in part to the influx of Hollywood-trained talent, these journalists regularly expressed skepticism regarding the ability of Mexican film to effectively resist "North American influence, before it absorbs the spiritual quality of the Latin Race."[15] They often expressed dismay at the overwhelming amount of foreign talent in the Mexican industry, suggesting that the same agents of technical expertise, as necessary as they may be, could exert a potentially deleterious effect on the cinema's cultural value. Roberto Cantú Robert (who would go on to found the Mexican trade journal *Cinema Reporter*) complained that by 1933 only two Mexican films featured male leads from Mexico.[16] In a similar vein, journalists often linked foreign producers and directors to labor exploitation. In one case, Luis F. Bustamante recounted rumors circulating about Hollywood-trained Argentine José Bohr, including accusations that he underpaid actors while directing a film in Mexico and that he referred to someone on set as a "wretched Mexican," ostensibly extending Hollywood's discriminatory labor practices to its own emergent film industry.[17]

As was the case during the height of Hollywood Spanish productions, these concerns about labor practices were also inextricable from issues of cinematic representation, with foreign talent and influence threatening to undermine Mexican cinema's distinction from Hollywood. Correspondent X. Campos Ponce observed that producers in Mexico too often reproduced the aristocratic environments of Spanish Hollywood productions or merely imitated Hollywood films: "We see American period films and we make period films; China was in vogue and we made a film about Shanghai; we saw 'gangster' films and we made gangster films, too." As he further argued, this dynamic prevented the development of a cinema that corresponded to a national sensibility and constituted an ineffective strategy for an industry struggling to capture international markets.

Echoing the sentiments of other critics, he maintained that "we have committed a series of barbarities, nonsense, and poor imitations, trying to place ourselves on the same level as North American producers, without remembering that we do not have at our disposal sufficient money, technicians, the marvelous machinery, and, above all, the experience that the North Americans have achieved through years of production."[18]

If the direct emulation of Hollywood could undermine the cultural integrity and economic viability of Mexican cinema, other critics feared an *excess* of national expression. That is, if national cinema could be achieved through a necessary balance between art and technology or between U.S. expertise and Mexican cultural heritage, this negotiation of the transnational could apparently be compromised in either direction. While most critics, like Campos Ponce, agreed that the integration of specifically Mexican content would distinguish national productions in the international marketplace, others initially expressed doubts about the potentially limited appeal of such material. A. Patiño Gómez argued, for instance, that films emphasizing Mexican history, customs, and regionalisms had routinely earned disappointing revenue in foreign markets. Instead, he proposed that films with universal appeal be produced and that those with a nondescript setting (he offered no specific examples) had already proven successful in Latin America.[19] Likewise, Fidel Murillo argued that "regional themes cannot garner attention beyond borders, and their success at the box office will be nil. It is necessary to treat general themes that can be understood in all of Latin America."[20] But because this emphasis on universal appeal and representational ambiguity was precisely the quality to which many attributed the failure of Spanish-language Hollywood, such prescriptions would eventually be dismissed as unfeasible solutions.

The inclusion of specifically Mexican content, at least in the context of Los Angeles, would indeed facilitate the transformation of Mexican cinema culture, and exhibition in particular. If theatrical advertisements, decor, and publicity hailed potential audiences as Mexican nationals, the content of films and their status as products of Mexican origin allowed exhibitors to further extend this appeal. In many cases, for instance, print advertisements adopted rhetoric about the films that capitalized on a nostalgic longing for Mexico. As Murillo claimed regarding the travelogue *Pro-patria* in 1932, "For Mexicans living abroad, *Pro-patria* offers a strong attraction, reminding us of the landscapes we have seen, and those we would like to see just one more time before our final days."[21] Likewise, the Teatro México advertised the 1935 film *El tesoro de Pancho Villa* (The treasure of Pancho Villa, Arcady Boytler) as "the most sensational national picture that with its impetuous story will make you remember with overwhelming force the final stage of the Mexican Revolution," an obvious effort to appeal to the life experiences of many Mexican immigrants.[22] In an apt example of overdetermined nationalism, advertisements for the simultaneous opening of Miguel Contreras Torres's *Juárez y Maximiliano* in all three of the downtown theaters managed by Frank Fouce in 1935 declared the film "the crowning work of national cinema" and "the glory and pride of Mexico," further emphasizing that it was filmed in actual historical locations and used authentic artifacts and furniture borrowed from national museums.[23]

If critical discourse and theater publicity collectively emphasized the necessary inclusion of Mexican content in films, ongoing discussions arose about how precisely Mexicanness might be defined or quantified in light of its need for foreign markets and Hollywood expertise. As the previous examples indicate, both the treatment of particularly Mexican social and historical events and an emphasis on landscape were regarded as a means of effectively differentiating Mexican productions from those produced elsewhere, for the interrelated purposes of promoting a specific film and the venues in which it screened. Films that foregrounded these elements were often praised by critics for being inherently more national than many of the cosmopolitan social melodramas prevalent during the early 1930s (like *Woman of the Port* [Arcady Boytler, 1934]), and theater owners in Los Angeles promoted them along these lines. According to columnist Hortensia Elizondo, such culturally specific productions appeared to make sound economic sense for the fledging industry. In particular, films about the revolution combined both elements and thus constituted a potential economizing strategy by maximizing exterior shooting and obviating set construction in favor of "free 'sets' like haciendas, streets, the countryside, and farm fields." From a strictly financial perspective, it was also natural for the emerging industry to target a domestic audience, and in this respect there was "nothing more rational than giving them something familiar, Revolutionary topics that would sell to the predominant mass of the population."[24]

But while films like *Janitzio* (Carlos Navarro, 1935), *El compadre Mendoza* (Fernando de Fuentes, 1934), and *Vámonos con Pancho Villa* (Let's go with Pancho Villa, Fernando de Fuentes, 1936) and the productions of Miguel Contreras Torres, including *La sombra de Pancho Villa* (The shadow of Pancho Villa, aka *Revolución*, 1933) and *Juárez y Maximiliano* (1934) garnered recognition for engaging Mexican history and culture, journalists ultimately remained skeptical about using these films as a model for subsequent national production. First, strictly economic arguments militated against a reliance on revolutionary subject matter. Despite the apparent benefits of producing such historical films, Elizondo (in an increasingly common line of argumentation) pointed out that "Mexican pictures already go abroad to other countries" where "purely regional themes without international transcendence, like Zapatista revolutions, etc., do not meet with understanding or interest." Even the domestic attraction to such films is dubious, she explains, since Mexico "has lived in a

revolutionary atmosphere for more than twenty years, and the public is looking more for an oasis that removes it from this reality, and not a reminder of
the frightful bloodshed of the Revolution."[25]

The unsuitability of establishing the revolution as the generic foundation of
the industry was also opposed on the basis of its dubious value as international
public relations. For some observers, films about the revolution only served as
a reminder of fragmentation and upheaval and were often seen as being coun-
terproductive to the nation-building project, regardless of their resonance with
the Mexican public, at home and abroad. If imitating Hollywood promised the
same representational invisibility or ambiguous Latinidad as Spanish-language
Hollywood, revolutionary films (and other historical epics) too closely recalled
the excessive visibility of problematic, denigrating images generated by Hollywood in previous decades. Thus, while they may have drawn on specifically
Mexican cultural sensibilities and historical references, they often recalled the
stereotypes of the greaser and the bandido that were staples of the U.S. obsession
with the revolution and explicitly tied to notions of racial inferiority (the discursive "blackening" suggested by the term "denigrating"). As Elizondo complained
in another one of her reviews, "We disapprove of films like *El tigre de Yuantepec*
[Fernando de Fuentes, 1933] and other Revolutionary stories, not only because
repetition always brings monotony, but because they dishonor Mexico in the
eyes of other countries and because they are guilty of doing the same thing for
which American films were criticized and that even led to boycotts: denigrating
the nation."[26] Echoing her sentiments, a subsequent editorial urged producers to
"make other nations talk about Mexico, not as a country of permanent revolt, but
as a progressive nation whose people have a profound artistic sensibility and a
dedicated love of the arts."[27]

By 1936 producers would embrace a solution that proved economically promising and also effectively balanced a "positive" brand of cultural specificity with
international appeal: the comedia ranchera. One editorial exemplifies the growing impetus for such a shift: "send to other countries a portrait of our vernacular customs, the echo of our heartfelt music, the image of our landscapes, and
the beauty of our women."[28] Appropriately, this textual solution drew extensively
from theatrical and musical traditions like mariachi; these diverse sources in turn
shaped a multimedia exhibition practice inextricable from the flourishing of cinema production. On its surface, the comedia ranchera genre seemed to finally
fulfill the promises and predictions of a Mexican cinema that was economically
viable and culturally valuable. It would indeed foster a multifaceted Mexican
experience of cinema through the expansion and stability of Mexican-oriented
theaters in Los Angeles and elsewhere. Its successes at multiple levels, however,
did not exempt the genre from the controversies and debates that had accompanied the earliest Mexican sound productions. In fact, the comedia ranchera
would bring these tensions to the fore.

MASS CULTURE AS MEXICAN CULTURE: THE COMEDIA
RANCHERA AND CULTURAL NATIONALISM

If the viability of the comedia ranchera resided at least partially in its ability to achieve an effective transnational balance that eluded earlier Mexican sound production, the ultimate success of the genre also hinged on a number of inextricable factors: its canny negotiation of cultural and commercial concerns, its synthesis of modern technology with nostalgic renderings of the national past, its particular mobilization of multimedia synergy, and its ability to harness the zeitgeist of Mexican cultural nationalism. To understand the nature of representations that circulated through the multiple elements of Mexican film culture and the intertexts of the comedia ranchera in particular, it is also thus necessary to briefly trace how these coincided with official efforts to create a national culture across media. Rather than positing a national cultural expression in opposition to mass media, this moment marks the convergence of the two in the Mexican context. At the same time, this apparent nationalism was itself fundamentally transnational in its operation, a dynamic that will become patently apparent in the development of the ranchera genre.

The visual and aural elements of cultural nationalism central to the comedia ranchera and framed retrospectively as authentically Mexican were constructed and actively promoted through official nation-building programs in postrevolutionary Mexico. The government elevated regional dances and music genres, particularly those from Jalisco, to the level of a genuinely national expression, disseminating this transformation through institutions like the Secretaria de Educación Pública and the Ballet Folklórico and through public relations campaigns intended to nationalize a diverse populace. The genre indeed drew on a number of sources promoted by state organs as inherently Mexican, embodying the impetus of official cultural nationalism: mariachi and ranchera music, the all-important archetype of the charro and his female counterpart the china poblana, and a structure and character types derived from popular theater. Although charro culture itself had been widely disseminated throughout Mexico since the nineteenth century in the form of lithographs, paintings, song, poetry, and dime novels, in the postrevolutionary period it was "elevated to the level of cultural iconography in which the *charro* became a symbol of the emerging nationhood through performance of a time-honored tradition in the public arena," with *charrería* (the Mexican equivalent of rodeo) even declared the national sport in 1932.[29] Olga Nájera Ramírez also points out that the Mexican government further consolidated an important set of associations by "requiring mariachis performing for official functions to wear *charro* outfits."[30]

The visual dimensions of this official nationalism have their origins in nineteenth-century *costumbrismo*, "a genre of imagery and literature that focused on traditional customs and dress" and that heavily influenced the "nationalist imaginary."[31] Appropriately, *costumbrista* imagery was generated primarily through the Mexican press of that period, "which was concerned with constituting and entitling an autochthonous identity, and visualizing a national order," in the face of ethnic and regional diversity.[32] In the broader context of Latin America, Thomas Turino has described this brand of cultural nationalism as "using expressive practices and forms to fashion the concrete emblems that stand for and create the 'nation,' that distinguish one nation from another, and most importantly, that serve as the basis for socializing citizens to inculcate national sentiment."[33] Such a cultural emphasis by the postrevolutionary state constituted an attempt to consolidate legitimacy by unifying a heterogeneous population under a cohesive Mexican national identity, which coincided with its efforts to manage the image of Mexico abroad to secure its "entry into the cosmopolitan club of nations, overcoming or at least counteracting prevailing images of Mexican bellicosity, savagery, and backwardness," in the interest of stimulating investment and tourism.[34]

As the case of the comedia ranchera suggests, the involvement of the emergent culture industries in Mexico contributed substantially to this process. While analogous government campaigns at the turn of the century included photo postcards, tourist guides, and displays at international expositions, media including cinema, radio, and theater had become more central to the construction of cultural nationalism by the mid-1930s.[35] Although not directly aligned with or entirely supported by the state, commercial interests facilitated the dissemination of this national culture and secured its mass popularity, serving the dual purpose of interpellating a national audience and stimulating the kind of consumption necessary for postrevolutionary economic development. As the culture industries became increasingly centralized in Mexico City, the state attempted to more effectively integrate these media into the nation-building project. In the case of cinema, the Cárdenas administration struggled unsuccessfully to protect the nascent industry by establishing quotas that required theaters to dedicate a percentage of their programming to Mexican films, a strategy that culminated in Hollywood's debilitating boycott of the nation's exhibitors. In the context of radio, as Joy Elizabeth Hayes explains, the passage of the 1936 Radio Law "increased the amount of government programming that all stations were required to carry and demanded that all stations include at least 25 percent 'typical Mexican music' [*música típica*] in each radio program," accompanying other efforts to promote a particular brand of musical nationalism.[36]

Significantly, the relationship between mass media and national culture exhibited a substantial degree of synergy and cross-pollenization. The commercialization and professionalization of ranchera music in the form of mariachi ensembles, as Daniel Sheehy points out, is emblematic of this process, not least of all because of the genre's reputation as the most authentically national musical expression.[37] Predicting the circulation of music that would standardize in the decades to come, the mariachi ensemble Cuarteto Coculense would become the first to perform in a legitimate theater and to record their music commercially. With the birth of Mexican sound cinema in 1931, the Cuarteto's appearance in *Santa* also marked an important precedent, hinting at the manner in which musical nationalism would soon become inextricable from the development of the film industry.[38] Significantly, the same film also featured the songs of crooner Agustín Lara, establishing a "relationship between cinema and radio that would remain very productive, contributing to each other's growth."[39] While indicating the central role that media of mass communications occupied in the official construction of national identity, this dynamic would also contribute considerably to exhibition practices in Los Angeles. In fact, with the consulate's partial retreat from Mexican public life in the mid-1930s, the emergence and exchange between Mexican culture industries would assume a more central place in the cultural life of Mexican Los Angeles and shape the way expatriates interfaced with constructs of national identity.[40]

In keeping with this emphasis on cultural nationalism, live theatrical performance in Mexico and the United States underwent a substantial shift during this period as well. Most notably, while dramatic theater and revistas suffered as a result of cinema's popularity and the economic hardships of the Depression, working-class audiences in Mexico began patronizing performances referred to as *carpas*. Named after the large and often mobile tentlike structures in which they occurred, they revived the practice of variety and vaudeville presentations. If they differed from revistas on a formal level by not adhering to a narrative or thematic unity, carpas also typically dispensed with the political satire and topicality associated with this earlier genre as a particular brand of cultural nationalism took shape and the government increased its surveillance of these theaters. By 1930, as Socorro Merlín points out, even revistas had attenuated their incisive commentary as

> the Revolutionary symbols began to be assimilated and rarified by power, which was then echoed by producers of revistas. Critical dialogue disappears to give priority to folkloric songs and dances, taking as a flag the nationalism of these years that stimulates the representation of symbols that are plastic, physical, musical, and even expressed in fashion, referring to indigenous habits, customs, and trades, emerging from the interest of the state in consolidating as a nation.

Carpa performances followed suit, particularly with the onset of the reformist Cárdenas administration in 1934. In addition to adopting the forms and aesthetics of cultural nationalism, the carpas also sustained important connections across media and themselves became an important pool of talent for radio and cinema. According to Merlín, radio in Mexico City "assimilated its artists and its genres and gave [the carpas] the opportunity to organize its spectacular material in another way, through the imposition of tastes and styles."[41] This dynamic also typified its relationship to cinema, as producers frequently attended the carpas to scout new talent. At the same time, carpa performances were often adapted to incorporate film screenings, and companies were regularly hired by cinemas to perform between showings. This theatrical form would also extend to the United States, Los Angeles included, as Mexican groups associated with the carpas regularly toured the Southwest, with the companies of Roberto Soto and Paco Miller among the most prominent of these.

The gradual adoption of these cultural nationalist forms in Mexican cinema aptly illustrates the ways in which the national was frequently constructed through a process of transnational exchange. As the cultural nationalist initiatives proposed by the Cárdenas administration suggest, the development of the Mexican film industry itself, particular content aside, was regarded as an important element of public relations and an indicator of industrial and cultural sophistication at an international level. In a review of the Arcady Boytler film *Celos* (Jealousy, 1936), for instance, A. Padilla Mellado reminded producers that "the film they produce is destined not only for Mexico but for the entire world and that we are judged abroad through our films."[42] When El Paso exhibitor and distributor Rubén A. Calderón opened a Los Angeles office of Azteca Films in 1935, soon to become the primary distributor of Mexican films in the United States for nearly a decade, he likewise linked the aspirations of his company to those of producers: "a group of daring men that through effort and sacrifice, and the quixotic nature of our race, have tried to show the world that their country is not behind others in terms of cinema."[43] As this last comment suggests, many regarded Mexican cinema as possessing the ability to solidify identification with nationalist versions of Mexicanidad and thus elevate the status (racial and otherwise) of Mexicans in the United States.

As a particular brand of cultural nationalism was increasingly exploited by the culture industries, however, the value of cinema as public relations became increasingly connected to specific textual features. When the Banco de Crédito Popular began financing Mexican films (beginning with its support of the Cinematográfica Latino Americana, S.A. [CLASA] studio in 1935), the Mexican government stressed the production of short documentaries and features, some of which were to be produced in English. *Motion Picture Herald* characterized these as potential "tourist-attracting pictures depicting Mexico's scenic beauties, folklore, regional singing, music and dancing and ruins . . . showing public works that have been accomplished by the Revolutionary governments which have functioned during the past quarter of a century."[44] In the pages of *La Opinión*, Campos Ponce noted the institution's "preference for films of a national character, with Mexican ambience, not only for the benefit of success in the international market, but to maintain the originality of our customs, our music, our dances, and our costumes."[45] This statement effectively encapsulates the dialectic nature of Mexican nationalism during the period as it strove to reconcile the cosmopolitan with the national. This dynamic, not coincidentally, corresponded to the internal and external motivations informing the construction of transnational Mexicanidad in Los Angeles.

For many critics, if technology entailed reliance on American expertise, an identifiably Mexican cinema would thus necessarily have to rely on several undeniably Mexican cultural elements that had forcefully emerged as national expressions: music, folklore, and landscape. A. Patiño Gómez, noting the popularity of Spanish costumbrista films (and deviating from his earlier position on the subject), complained that "if instead of the 'costumbrista' films that foreign markets want to see, our cinema sends them films that have no connection whatsoever to our people and their idiosyncrasies, they will feel defrauded and even doubt that these pictures were produced in Mexico." More extensive use of exterior shooting and a reliance on Mexico's landscapes, he argued, would prove "the salvation of our national cinema."[46] In another article, he proposed that the use of landscape be combined with authentic regional legends and folklore, noting that Mexican attempts at costumbrista films had heretofore amounted to little more than superficial displays of "sandaled Indians, theatrical charros, cactus, and maguey." More effectively mobilizing these elements, he speculated, would thus contribute to a more internationally competitive Mexican cinema, since the nation possessed "natural scenes and a rich variety of regional stories that Hollywood does not have, and is even unaware of."[47] Another anonymous critic, adopting the same position, even proposed a cinematic formula that seemed to predict the structural logic of the ranchera genre: "Seventy percent panoramas and music. The other thirty percent, dialogue and action."[48] Although this formula was perhaps slightly exaggerated, *Allá en el Rancho Grande* and the films that followed in its footsteps harnessed multiple elements of cultural nationalism, placing a heavy emphasis on musical performance and folkloric visual spectacle. Both elements secured the popularity of the genre across media, greatly shaping Spanish-language exhibition practices in Los Angeles and the rest of Latin America.

THE PRODUCTION AND EXHIBITION OF TRANSNATIONAL MEXICAN CINEMA: THE CASE OF *ALLÁ EN EL RANCHO GRANDE*

With an emphasis on the rural and folkloric, the landmark film *Allá en el Rancho Grande* epitomizes the rather complex impetus of cultural nationalism and itself served as important model for the combination of its constitutive elements within a cinematic text. The film's incredible popularity with domestic and foreign audiences also stimulated unprecedented growth and stability within the Mexican film industry. It is largely due to the film's international success that scholars and critics alike have credited it with establishing a solid economic and cultural foundation for a national cinema that had been plagued by experimentation, low budgets, and lack of infrastructure. Writing ten years after its initial release, one Mexican critic, referring to the early 1930s as a period of "uncertainty and isolated experiments," situates the film as a watershed: "Then came the movie that saved the industry from imminent ruin and proved that in Mexico we are capable of producing quality cinema."[49] Ana M. López credits the film with developing a formula that "combined an appealing exoticism with a comforting familiarity that easily won over Latin American audiences looking for points of cinematic identification," solidifying the position of Mexican cinema in markets across the continent.[50] While the ranchera genre has thus been conventionally and justifiably associated with a particular type of Mexican cultural nationalism that looked toward a romanticized past, however, its contested value as a national expression at the time of its release hinged precisely on factors of its transnational, intermedial dimensions. In Los Angeles, the comedia ranchera would indeed become part of a larger debate about the cultural expression of Mexicanidad and its implications for the city's Mexican residents.

Based on the popular song of the same name, *Allá en el Rancho Grande* takes place on a rural hacienda, where Felipe, the ranch's owner (René Cardona), and his lifelong friend and ranch manager, José Francisco (Tito Guízar), find themselves in love with the same woman: Cruz (Esther Fernández). A number of misunderstandings ensue, punctuated by a series of contests in which the men attempt to best each other in feats of masculine bravado (cockfights, horse races, guitar duels, etc.). Despite the fact that Felipe attempts to rape Cruz in an exercise of his authority, harmony is eventually reestablished on the ranch and order restored (four separate couples are also united in a marriage ceremony that ends the film). Significantly, *Rancho Grande* firmly established the quintessential formula for the comedia ranchera genre. As Eduardo de la Vega Alfaro notes, these films drew from a number of extant sources, including "popular genre theater, *costumbrista* novels, and painting and especially from popular music and radio programs."[51] Typically taking place on rural haciendas, the narratives of ranchera films tend to hinge on a love triangle or some romantic misunderstanding and are uniformly characterized by multiple musical interludes. López has succinctly summarized the key features of the genre as evident in *Rancho Grande*: "popular music in the form of *rancheras*, here sung by Tito Guízar and Lorenzo Barcelata; a loose and episodic narrative structure derived from variety theater, with songs often taking the place of dialogue; and the introduction of familiar yet picturesque character types (*charros*, innocent *señoritas* with long-braided hair, and peppery old housekeepers) and situations (cockfights, *fiestas*, and *jarabes tapatío* [a regional dance from Jalisco])."[52]

The preponderance of scholarly work on the film, while acknowledging its undeniable centrality to the industrial history of Mexican cinema, also criticizes the film for its supposed nostalgia for the prerevolutionary era of Porfirio Díaz's dictatorship, as an indirect backlash against the reforms of the Cárdenas administration, for its disingenuous claims to folkloric authenticity and its apparently conservative bent. Analyses of the film (and comedia rancheras in general) have largely placed emphasis on its narrative conventions through

which prerevolutionary gender and class hierarchies are recuperated and idealized. In a typical passage, López argues that "the film posits the possibility of a
perfectly harmonious relationship between the rich *hacendado* [ranch owner]
and his employee . . . and promotes the maintenance of the socio-political status
quo through an unbridled nostalgia for an imaginary past where such relationships could be conceived."[53] Emilio García Riera likewise points out that the film
"professed openly reactionary sentiments" and that its producers had inadver-
tently "stumbled upon a public that yearned for idyllic, utopian ranches."[54] Even
more forcefully, Nájera Ramírez argues that the film

> came to represent the onset of a conservative mood in Mexico which appealed
> to an earlier idealized, romanticized social structure where everyone knew
> their place, where certain privileged men ruled. Harsh and abusive behavior by
> men seemed acceptable and even necessary to control and rule the "ignorant
> masses." By appealing to an idealized past, such films made critical comment
> on the social ills of their day and legitimized ironfisted tyrannical rule.[55]

Reliant largely on textual analyses that place the film in conversation with
major social and political developments within Mexico, such readings represent
only one possible interpretation of the film and its appeal. In particular, while
the steadfastly national influences on the genre have been widely recognized
and documented by scholars, the less frequently documented transnational origins of this genre were nonetheless central to its conception and reception. If
the comedia ranchera relied on a complex web of intermedial and transnational
convergences that included yet extended beyond the cinematic text, it is only by
considering these factors that we may understand its historical significance. Such
an analytical approach challenges the conclusions of most scholarly analyses that
emphasize the cinematic text to the exclusion of others, thereby opening up the
film (and others of the genre) to a multiplicity of local or site-specific readings.
In Los Angeles, the popularity of the genre would finally consolidate the viability of Mexican-oriented film exhibition in the city that momentarily restored a
nationalist circuit of textual content, cultural criticism, live performance, music,
and local commercial enterprise. It consequently promised the formation of a
national audience in Los Angeles, one united by a completely Mexican experience of cinema across media. At the same time, however, this genre's transnational origins and global aspirations were at the center of its representation and
projections of Mexicanidad. It is only by accounting for the inextricable nature
of its transnational *and* intermedial dimensions—within and beyond the film
itself—that its impact and reception can be more fully apprehended.

While often contextualized by critics and scholars as an expression of national
character and identity (however misguided), the origins and history of *Rancho
Grande* place it in dialogue with a number of transnational cultural currents that
informed its production and critical reception. Perhaps most obviously, *Rancho
Grande* and the genre it inspired owe a substantial debt to the singing cowboy

films of Hollywood, which began production by the mid-1930s.[56] Notably, both genres capitalized on nostalgia for the traditional and rural as bastions of national culture, a romanticizing of the past that ironically occurred through the expansion of modern technology and mass culture (radio and cinema in particular), perhaps assuaging fears about the impact of these developments. Both emerged almost simultaneously, and if the ranchera was at all indebted to the singing cowboy genre, the latter also drew on the former; in 1940 Gene Autry appeared in a Western titled *Rancho Grande* (Frank McDonald), in addition to making other Mexican-themed films like *In Old Monterrey* (Joseph Kane, 1939) and *South of the Border* (George Sherman, 1939).[57]

Furthermore, critics often predicted the appeal of the comedia ranchera to audiences in the United States, based on the popularity of Mexican music on U.S. radio. In fact, *Rancho Grande* lead Tito Guízar first rose to international stardom through broadcasts on New York City radio station WABC and performances with the Chicago Metropolitan Opera. In this respect, Guízar was hardly an exception, as a number of prominent Mexican singers soon associated with the genre were either performing or recording in the United States during the period, including Lorenzo Barcelata, Ernesto Cortázar, and Jorge Negrete. As Donald Andrew Henriques points out, this arrangement was facilitated by media mogul Emilio Azcárraga (owner of the XEW radio station in Mexico City), who negotiated a strategic position between multiple U.S. companies (like NBC and RCA Victor) and the Mexican culture industry. Reportedly, Azcárraga would often send emerging talent to New York for professional training, a practice that would also, in many cases, contribute to their international celebrity.[58] Aside from the career of individual musicians, Mexican songs circulated widely within the United States as recordings and sheet music.

Not surprisingly, the circulation and growing popularity of Mexican music within the United States had already begun influencing trends in film production by the mid-1930s, as Guízar's presence on the radio attests. When Mexico proposed to institute a quota that would require studios to produce one film in Mexico (with Mexican talent) for each Hollywood film distributed there, Universal announced plans to coproduce a film titled *Adelita*, based on a *corrido* (narrative folk song) made popular during the Mexican Revolution.[59] Perhaps most notably, in 1934 Pioneer Pictures Corporation (later purchased by RKO) produced the Technicolor short *La Cucaracha* (Lloyd Corrigan), based on the song of the same title that had gained substantial popularity in the United States. Distributed widely, the short film was produced at a cost of about $65,000 and grossed a remarkable $500,000, and its success (at least partially attributed to the novelty of the three-color process) instigated reaction from the Mexican industry.[60] By early 1936 Mexican producer and painter Juan José Segura planned to produce a series of shorts based on Mexican songs, beginning with "La chapparrita" and "La cucaracha," a direct response to the Pioneer film, an effort he "considers necessary to rectify its presentation by North American producers."[61]

By the mid-1930s producers like Segura became increasingly convinced that a combination of culturally specific music and character types would prove a viable formula for international success. Beyond the influence of exchange between the United States and Mexico, Mexican producers were apparently also influenced by the success of the Spanish film *Nobleza baturra* (*Aragonese Virtue*, Florián Rey, 1935), a costumbrista film popular with audiences across Latin America that was often referenced as a model worthy of emulation. Jorge Luis Bueno, the producer of *Cielito lindo* (Robert Quigley, 1936), perhaps the first Mexican feature based on a popular song, cited this film and others like it as important precedents, particularly in relation to international appeal: "In the United States 'Cielito Lindo' means Mexico, and it is among four of our songs that North Americans know by heart."[62] Likewise, director Fernando de Fuentes claimed that the Spanish film compelled him to develop a cinematic equivalent for Mexico, ultimately inspiring him to produce *Allá en el Rancho Grande*.[63] If this film is indebted to cultural nationalism and international influences, these generative factors also suggest the range of its intended audiences. Not coincidentally, the film's distributor, United Artists, selected the film as one of the first Mexican features to be subtitled in English, and *Rancho Grande* enjoyed an incredible international success that included, most notably, an award for cinematographer Gabriel Figueroa at the Venice Film Festival.

The ranchera genre and its impact on exhibition in Los Angeles coincided with and reinforced the combination of multimedia programming practices and nationalist rhetoric that increasingly accompanied the growth of the Mexican film industry. As downtown venues repeatedly reopened and closed during the early 1930s, Frank Fouce eventually leased the California Theater in 1933, declaring that the new venue would provide the "Hispano" public "a center worthy of its culture and social refinement." Indicative of a transition between conventions of exhibition practice, Fouce organized a gala premiere reminiscent of those prevalent during the heyday of Spanish-language Hollywood, complete with special appearances by tenor José Mojica and comedians Laurel and Hardy. Consistent with publicity practices that reinforced national sentiment, however, the theater owner also timed the opening to coincide with Mexican Independence Day. Inaugurating the theater with an engagement of *La llorona* (The weeping woman, Ramón Peón, 1933), he emphasized the "popularity of the legend among our people," declaring that "the company that produced it is Mexican, as are the screenwriter and the two lead actresses."[64]

Likewise, the print advertisement for the theater described the California as a "theater worthy of our race," urging the public to "Protect the National Industry."[65] For one anonymous critic, the significance of the enterprise overshadowed the value of any particular film: "But the most important thing about this event is not the premier of the aforementioned national production. It is instead the reopening of the California as the meeting place of a '*colonia*' that hopes that this reopening is the last and that wants the definitive establishment of a theater for the exclusive exhibition of our films."[66] Both *La Opinión* and Fouce himself linked the success of the theater to the quality of social and cultural life in Mexican Los Angeles, situating the theater as a significant component of community building. The newspaper thus featured frequent and explicit appeals to the public, emphasizing that their regular patronage would sustain not only the theater but Mexican cinema as a whole. As Fouce claimed, "There are two things that depend on your support: that the California remain open for artistic presentations and that national production receive assistance beyond its borders to yield new fruit. Mexico is paying attention to the attitude of the Mexican public of Los Angeles."[67]

Fouce's efforts, along with a more steady supply of Mexican films, stimulated a sudden resurgence of Spanish-language venues in downtown Los Angeles and a revival of nationalist consumption through film culture. Shortly after the California reopening, for instance, Carlos Emmanuel took over management of the Hidalgo and the México (both would subsequently be owned by Fouce before being demolished to make way for civic development in 1936). In November 1933 Fouce also began managing the second-run Teatro Eléctrico, promising that it "has a system of the highest quality, with impeccable photographic projection and sound. The theater is scrupulously maintained and all its employees speak Spanish. It's the ideal center for the Mexican working class that will now not have to travel far to see the films they like." Positioning the theater as an important community service, Fouce even altruistically asserted that "for us this is not a business, but rather a means of satisfying the desires of our working class."[68] His rhetoric here clearly coincides with that of his journalist counterparts who likewise situated consumption as key to the sustenance of a cohesive México de afuera, the construction of a transnational Mexican community that also functioned as a stable, identifiable audience to which he and others could market.

Despite the emphatically nationalist claims made by all such theaters during the early 1930s, the initial irregularity of Mexican production and a relatively unorganized distribution network (Fouce often traveled to Mexico personally to secure rights to new productions) resulted in a decidedly hybrid exhibition practice. Theaters alternated between Mexican films, the sporadic Spanish-language Hollywood productions, English-language films from Hollywood, and works from Spain and Argentina. Such mixed programming was also partially the result of double-feature programs (a fixture of the Depression era) that initially required more rentals than Mexico could produce. The mixed character of film exhibition, however, was consistently accompanied by presentations of a local nature, in a manner that capitalized on the emerging interdependence of different media and their assertion of Mexican identity. Premiers at the California during this period typically incorporated a prologue performed by local theatrical or musical talent such as Nelly Fernández, Rodolfo Hoyos, or Romualdo Tirado. The print advertisement for the premier of Fernando de Fuentes's *El prisionero 13* (1933), for instance, announced a prologue by the performers associated with the KMPC radio program *Hora de Hollywood* (The Hollywood hour), asking readers, "Have you heard it on the radio? See it in person today."[69]

Musical and theatrical performance, and the venues that supported them, indeed became increasingly and inextricably tied to cinema exhibition and cultural nationalism in Los Angeles as the 1930s progressed. The emergent popularity of Spanish-language radio and recording industries also shaped the programming of local theaters. With increasing frequency, venues hosted touring recording stars, pairing their appearances with a number of variety acts and local theatrical performances. A publicity poster for the Teatro California indicates the extent of interdependency between these venues and local radio programming.[70] On August 18–19, 1934, the theater presented *Revista de radio 1934* (1934 radio revue), written by Gabriel Navarro and featuring a number of performers that included Rodolfo Hoyos and Los Madrugadores (the band that regularly accompanied Spanish-language radio pioneer Pedro González).[71] The following Monday it hosted a benefit for El Eco de México radio station, complete with the performance of three radio dramas: "Pancho Villa," "La serenata de Los Angeles," and "Doña Chica en Jaligu."[72] Similar to the Hidalgo, the California also hosted live radio broadcasts in the early morning hours, allowing spectators to attend free of charge.[73] Not coincidentally, the 1930s also saw the emergence of an ongoing relationship between radio programming, vaudeville, and Hollywood production, particularly in the context of exhibition.[74] While the theatrical environment had transformed substantially since the 1920s, an increasingly steady supply of Mexican films, along with the successful intermedial business model embraced by local exhibitors like Frank Fouce, provided significant opportunities for a Mexican exhibition style to continue and flourish.

Due to the unparalleled success of *Rancho Grande*, Mexican producers quickly initiated a major cycle of ranchera films that encouraged this ongoing synergy of cultural nationalism between media and multiple texts in the context of exhibition and beyond. The more prominent of these productions over the next year included *Las cuatro milpas* (*The Four Corn Patches*, Ramón Pereda, 1937), *Amapola del camino* (Poppy of the trail, Juan Bustillo Oro, 1937), and *¡Jalisco nunca pierde!* (Jalisco never loses!, Chano Urueta, 1937) (not to mention the frequent rereleases of proven features like *Allá en el Rancho Grande* and *¡Ora Ponciano!* [Gabriel Soria, 1937]). Such was the impact of *Rancho Grande* that García Riera, in his encyclopedic, twelve-volume history of Mexican cinema, calls 1936 "The Year of *Rancho Grande*" and sarcastically labels 1937 "More Than Twenty Ranchos Grandes."[75] In fact, over half of the Mexican films produced in the next two years belong to this genre, in some form or fashion. The success of ranchera films exerted an immediate and transformative effect on the Spanish-language theaters downtown. By the summer of 1937, Fouce had capitalized on this craze by opening Teatro Roosevelt and premiering *¡Ora Ponciano!* simultaneously in three of his downtown venues, a practice that would be reserved almost exclusively for ranchera films over the next two years. Given the convergence of musical nationalism and cinema, the value of ranchera films relative to national sentiment was promoted in a predictably straightforward fashion. Print ads claimed that *¡Ora*

Ponciano! "enters into the depth of the national soul!" while *Allá en el Rancho Grande* was touted as "the film that makes you feel more Mexican."[76]

The intertextual dimension of the ranchera genre undoubtedly contributed to its popularity and the consequent success of the local theaters through constant repurposing and cross-promotion of successful properties. The titles of many such films were taken directly from popular songs, and print ads in *La Opinión* fully exploited these connections. The advertisement for *Las cuatro milpas*, for example, describes the film's title as "the name that evokes the most profoundly Mexican sentiments, woven around a song that has taken root in the soul of our people" and lists six additional songs featured in the film.[77] In the case of the other Mexican ranchera films based explicitly on popular songs, print advertisements prominently featured lyrics, capitalizing on the audience's familiarity with a known property through radio and records. As this musical emphasis suggests, the standardized, somewhat formulaic narratives of these films often functioned as a pretext for the inclusion of multiple songs and interludes of comic relief, a mode of presentation derived from popular theater (like carpas) and musical revues. Accordingly, these spectacular elements were readily extracted from the films and readapted to live performance in theaters where such conventions had already been established, constituting a mutually beneficial feedback loop. Los Angeles theaters thus began booking appearances by the stars of the comedia rancheras, from Tito Guízar (the star of *Allá en el Rancho Grande*) and Lorenzo Barcelata (who composed the music for many of these films) to Carlos López "Chaflán" and Leopoldo "Chato" Ortín, actors who most frequently provided the genre's comic relief (see fig. 23).

If exhibition practice and marketing capitalized on the familiarity of certain songs, the films then frequently became further promotional vehicles for subsequent uses of the musical material. This developed into a synergistic, mutually beneficial arrangement, particularly as many of these films (*Rancho Grande* included) were rereleased on multiple occasions. Although *Rancho Grande* was based on a well-known song, for instance, it also compelled many artists to record new versions of it or stage new interpretations. In addition to a version recorded by Los Angeles–based Azteca Records by the musical group La Panchita y Los Corporales (which included a rendition of "Cielito lindo" on the flipside), one recording by Los Tres Murciélagos even featured performances extracted from the film itself, a fact displayed prominently on the record's label.[78] Furthermore, several months after the premier of *Allá en el Rancho Grande* in Los Angeles, a touring musical review based on the film was booked at the Teatro California combining musical numbers with re-creations of key scenes (see fig. 24). This practice was pioneered by Campillo theater company in December 1934 when it staged a revista titled "La cucaracha" with the intent of capitalizing on the popularity of the song and the RKO film (which had premiered downtown the month before).[79] Other films received similar treatment subsequent to the success of

Fig. 23. Advertisement for a rerelease of *Allá en el Rancho Grande*. *La Opinión*, August 15, 1937. Reproduced courtesy of *La Opinión*.

Fig. 24. Advertisement for the musical revue based on *Allá en el Rancho Grande*. *La Opinión*, June 2, 1937. Reproduced courtesy of *La Opinión*.

Rancho Grande, including the ranchera film *¡Ora Ponciano!* and the 1934 melodrama *La mujer del puerto* (*The Woman of the Port*).

While scholars of Mexican cinema have characterized the narratives of these ranchera films as nostalgic and ideologically suspect (not to mention formulaic), contemporaneous critics and exhibitors instead would refer to the visual and musical elements of the films as possessing an entirely different appeal and function. To this extent, the approximate equation of ranchera content I cited earlier—"Seventy percent panoramas and music. The other thirty percent, dialogue and action"— aptly references the genre's reliance on spectacle over narrative cohesion.[80] The "non-narrative spectacle" that typifies Tom Gunning's concept of the "cinema of attractions" is indeed apparent in such films as "an undercurrent flowing beneath narrative logic and diegetic realism."[81] Pushing this logic further, one could easily argue that the spectacular dimensions of the genre at times overwhelm the narrative or render it irrelevant. More significant, the modularity of the films' spectacular elements, from comic sketches to musical interludes, were central to the genre's intermedial flexibility and its ability to appeal to multiple audiences. The objects of study that we refer to as *Allá en el Rancho Grande* and the comedia ranchera are consequently not equivalent to cinematic texts (as most scholarly analyses assume) but are instead spread across a range of artifacts and performances that converge in a particular context. In Mexican Los Angeles it was precisely these elements that became a point of contention over the genre's construction of Mexicanidad, with critics and audiences there uniquely positioned to appreciate (and debate) its canny negotiation of Mexican cultural nationalism and transnational appeal.

CONTESTED CONSTRUCTIONS OF MEXICANIDAD: THE COMEDIA RANCHERA DEBATE

If *Rancho Grande* consolidated an experience of Mexican cultural consumption across media that would sustain exhibition venues, journalists also understood it as a critical intervention in the representation of Mexico and Mexicans. Given the advocacy of Los Angeles critics for a Mexican cinema that integrated folkloric elements, the initial reception of *Rancho Grande* in *La Opinión* was predictably celebratory. A. Patiño Gómez celebrated the film as having proven "that it is not the 'social dramas' or works with 'internationalist' scripts that Mexican studios should be filming but works that are eminently 'folklorist,' local and even regionalist, with a provincial flavor and the particular customs and types of our environment," demonstrating that "Mexican films should stand out because of a certain 'something' that the cinematic works of other countries don't have," a strategy of differentiation that extended to exhibition and publicity.[82] According to like-minded critics, the film completely fulfilled the multiple functions of a properly national cinema. Rather than constituting a disruptive force associated with earlier forms of mass culture, Mexican cinema in Los Angeles suddenly (albeit momentarily) fostered a nationalist circuit of textual content, cultural criticism, and exhibition practice.

Despite the celebratory tone of these reviews, the ranchera genre would soon be at the center of a renewed debate about cinema and constructions of Mexicanidad. Crucially, the multimedia dimension of the comedia ranchera not only complicates our understanding of its historical significance and reception but also allows us to more appropriately understand the genre as a body of texts attributed with multiple meanings and imagined impacts. Obviously, theater publicity and initial critical reception often framed the film as an unabashed expression of nationalism. But this discourse obscures the way critics and audiences squared this with the operation of cultural nationalism and cinema as transnational enterprises. In the context of Los Angeles, this notion of positive or negative representations coincided again with the construction of urban space, and the contrast between discursive constructions of Main Street and Olvera Street in particular. Appropriately, it was the very transnational foundation of the film's production and circulation that shaped the terms of its contentious reception.

Comprehending the genre's varied impact also requires us to consider its various imagined audiences. In other words, if we understand cultural nationalism as part of an attempt to create or unite a community under a cohesive notion of national identity, we must also take into account its transnational motivations. In fact, the film critics of *La Opinión* consistently noted the potential popularity of this genre to non-Mexican audiences, an impetus consistent with the conception of a national cinema as an extension of public relations on an international level and of Mexican film culture as a potential intervention in local perceptions of Mexicans. Fidel Murillo, for instance, argued that *Rancho Grande* "constitutes the most beneficial propaganda for our country that has occurred outside its borders."[83] Likewise, Campos Ponce stated that through this genre, "finally, North American and European tourists happily encounter that which they had seen only in calendars or promotional brochures: charros, chinas poblanas, the women of Michoacán, etc., etc."[84] In fact, *La Opinión* made frequent reference to the unprecedented attendance of non-Mexicans at the downtown theaters, claiming that these films offered curious spectators a completely new and more authentic understanding of Mexico and its culture. Among the twelve thousand spectators who had attended a screening of *¡Ora Ponciano!* during its first week of release, Fouce noticed "a considerable percentage of North Americans who were attracted to the novelty as friends of our culture," many of them evidently Spanish students from universities and private schools.[85]

It was the attendance of this particular audience, along with the spectacular, multimedia dimension of the comedia ranchera, that some conceived of as a way to influence disparaging perceptions of Mexicans in Los Angeles and beyond. Main Street, the location of many of the downtown Mexican theaters, continued to be depicted in unsavory terms during this period. New waves of immigration, population growth, and the extension of the cheap entertainment district along this corridor inspired vehemently hostile reactions, reminiscent of the "ethnographic" journalism and sociological theses of the 1910s (see chapter 1).

In fact, a new round of scholarly studies examined downtown and reiterated the division of the entertainment landscape. In a sociological study of movie habits, for instance, Paul J. Crawford mapped the general spatial logic of the area: "the theaters may be classed according to the street on which they are situated; that is, Main Street, Broadway, and Hill Street. Each of these streets have [sic] theaters of certain characteristics, and there is remarkably little crossing over of the bound-aries. The Main Street shows are small, dirty and cheap."[86] The reputation of Los Angeles's Main (both North and South) as an epicenter of "cheap" entertainment evidently achieved national stature during this period, as Eric Schaefer justifiably speculates, since the trade press began referring to low-budget exploitation films as "Main Street movies."[87]

Perceptions of the entertainment offered there was, as in previous decades, inextricable from its notoriety as a destination for an ethnically heterogeneous working class. Another sociological survey of Main introduces its research proj-ect thusly: "The locality which is the object of study offers variety as to race, station in life, occupation, and character. Negroes, Filipinos, Chinese, Japanese, and Mexicans mingle with the Caucasian." The author further explains that "as the years passed and the small town grew into a city, the modern part of it moved westward, leaving Main Street to sink into a position of inferiority. Hotels which were once first-class became flop houses. Inferior second hand stores moved into many of its storerooms. Theaters where famous stars once played became the homes of burlesque . . . [and] taxi dance halls offered the society of white girls alike to the Filipino or white man."[88] Poet Blaise Cendrars, recounting his visit to Hollywood during the 1930s, penned an even more vehemently lurid account:

> As for *Main Street*, which is the hot street, the burning street of Los Angeles, it is lined with penny *cafeterias*, tiny three-cent *chileno* restaurants, nickel cin-emas, hourly hotels for a dime, clay-pipe shooting galleries, automated shops, billiard academies, bowling, miniature golf, burlesques and dance halls of the latest kind, pawnshops open through the night. *Main Street* is the customary promenade of prostitutes and female procurers, of Philipino [sic], Mexican, Asian, and Negro pimps, of sailors on leave from the fleet stationed at San Pedro who go there on binges, and of soldiers on a spree.[89]

The propaganda ostensibly offered by films like *Allá en el Rancho Grande* was thus not only regarded by critics as a key facet of the formation of a national audience–cum–community. It was also positioned as a potential corrective to racial discourses that sanctioned discrimination and inequality through concep-tions of the Mexican presence in Los Angeles as a perpetual problem. Ever the entrepreneur, Frank Fouce, for instance, rapidly announced plans to capitalize on new audiences for Mexican films and music, which he cleverly framed as a service to the nation and the Mexican community of Los Angeles. Noting the prolific production of ranchera films and their apparent popularity among non-Mexican audiences, Fouce planned to open a venue called the Mexican Music

Hall in the old Mason Opera House building as a means of attracting and even educating a broader audience. According to Fouce, the Music Hall would be "a center of attraction for all Californians and for tourists as well, because on its stage we will present what is typically ours, constituting a forum that will dignify us in the eyes of foreigners."⁹⁰ Significantly, Fouce planned for the theater to be a showcase for live musical performances and theatrical engagements, intending to employ Mexican artists whose careers had been adversely affected by the Depression and the popularity of cinema. In the pages of the *Los Angeles Times*, he also announced his ambitious plans to an English-speaking readership, promising to bring renowned theater actress Virginia Fábregas, the stock company of actor Fernando Soler, and operetta star Esperanza Iris to the Music Hall.⁹¹ This strategy of cultural elevation as a rhetorical rejection of local racial hierarchies would also emphasize the elements most popular with and familiar to audiences of Mexican descent and otherwise: typical Mexican music. Fouce believed that with this approach, the Music Hall "will lend prestige to Mexico, something that is sorely lacking in the United States."⁹² Significantly, this elevated bastion of national culture would be located not on Main, but on Broadway.

This harnessing of the visual and musical dimensions to present an elevated version of Mexicanidad for the benefit of non-Mexican audiences coincided with the aesthetic and discursive impetus of multiple, interrelated phenomena: the aforementioned development of Olvera Street (and the city's general embrace of the "Spanish fantasy heritage"), Hollywood's appropriation of Mexican music, and tourist promotions and imaginings. Mexico had also initiated a tourism campaign as part of its postrevolutionary nation-building initiatives, one that promoted a festive, picturesque, and exotic image of Mexico. The government's effort to create "a national identity that is sold, consumed, and negotiated" in this context paralleled analogous trends in cinema; the comedia ranchera and its traditional, festive atmosphere explicitly resonated with such efforts.⁹³ The genre indeed seemed to embody the aforementioned "tourist-attracting pictures" earlier proposed by government-funded film production.⁹⁴ While journalists apparently recognized that the appeal of the ranchera film hinged on a stereotypical version of Mexico and that "North Americans" may be attending "simply out of fondness for a spectacle that to them seems exotic," such representations were at least initially regarded as preferable to Hollywood's conception of a "trashy 'Mexico' unrecognizable to those of us born and raised in that country."⁹⁵ The convergence of ranchera iconography with "positive" imagery of tourism and fanciful reconstructions like Olvera Street, in the minds of some critics and theater owners, presented an opportunity to rehabilitate the Mexican image in Los Angeles . The promotional material and other visuals generated by all three clearly demonstrate their mutual affinity (see figs. 25 and 26). Once again, the mobilization of this regime of representation by Fouce and others hinged on distancing this imagery from the racial and class-based implications of "trashy 'Mexico'" and a "dirty and cheap" Main Street.

Fig. 25. Musician and dancer at Olvera Street, 1936. Los Angeles Public Library Photograph Collection.

Fig. 26. Lobby card for *Allá en el Rancho Grande*, 1936. Courtesy of the Agrasánchez
Film Archive, Harlingen, TX.

The connections between positive cinematic representation, tourism, and
urban space become apparent in other accounts of downtown penned during
the period. In his sweeping 1935 account of Los Angeles history (titled *Los Angeles: City of Dreams*), journalist Harry Carr frames his nearly four-hundred-page
narration as a story told to an elderly teacher visiting from Iowa. Meeting her
near Olvera Street, he explains, "For many years it was a dirty alley, abandoned
to slums and desolation. Then we picked up our traditions. . . . Now, to all intents
and purposes, it is the market-place of a Mexican town."[96] This clearly echoes
discourse that contrasted the supposed decline of ethnic heterogeneity with a
sanitized, tourist-oriented reconstruction of "Old Los Angeles." Over a dish of
enchiladas at La Golondrina Café, Carr's narrator explains to the "lady from
Dubuque" the meanings of the Mexican songs being sung at the café, including
"Cielito lindo," "Rancho Grande," and "Cuatro milpas." Not coincidentally, all of
these would soon serve as the basis of Mexican films, while also appearing in Hollywood films as musical representations of Mexico. In addition, Carr recognizes
several Mexican emissaries of Hollywood dining in the same restaurant: Ramón
Novarro, Dolores del Rio, and Leo Carrillo. Carr's impressionistic account of a
day on Olvera Street is thus indicative of the broader representational regime

with which the comedia ranchera potentially resonated and how its conception of Mexico was seen as rehabilitating its image in the eyes of non-Mexicans. Perhaps predictably, this rehabilitation paralleled the racial and class-based hierarchies apparent in Hollywood's projection of Mexico, the stardom of light-skinned Mexicans of "Spanish" descent, an exoticizing tourist gaze, the city's celebration of "Spanish heritage," and conceptual mappings of downtown Los Angeles.

Fouce's ambition for the Mexican Music Hall obviously sought to use Mexican film and live entertainment to capitalize on the potential touristic appeal of these media in keeping with this brand of imagery. While these plans never fully materialized, Fouce did reopen the Mason with a ten-day engagement of musician Lydia Mendoza (see fig. 27), and the venue became a center of live entertainment in Spanish until it was demolished to make way for civic construction in 1955.[97] Although Fouce apparently never rechristened the Mason as the Mexican Music Hall to attract a broader audience, he did regularly generate coverage of the venue through the *Los Angeles Times*, which occasionally reviewed the vaudeville-style programs he typically offered there, suggesting an ongoing attempt on his part to publicize these to a general audience. As early as 1940, for instance, Fouce placed an advertisement in the *Los Angeles Times* for Virginia Fábregas appearing at the Mason in the play *El monje blanco* (The white monk).[98] In a subsequent *Times* review of the play, Salvador Baguez suggested that Fouce's strategy was to some degree effective, noting that the Mason "has been the popular rendezvous of the local Latin-American colony as well as the numerous students of Spanish."[99]

This coincidence between the picturesque tourist version of Mexico (and Mexican Los Angeles), Hollywood film, the transnational consumption of Mexican music, and the ranchera genre was not lost on those who were decidedly more critical of its particular construction of Mexicanidad. While for some these dimensions of the genre would counter disparaging portrayals of Mexico by building on a transnational regime of representation, for others the replacement of greasers and bandidos with apparently more positive representations of Mexico hinged on exotic stereotypes nonetheless. For these individuals, this range of "positive" imagery presented the country and its people as cartoonish, colorful caricatures. Furthermore, this reaction derived at least partially from its transnational origins and circulation as an intermedial text in the form of music and folkloric imagery. In particular, while focusing on these aspects of cultural difference might prove a viable market strategy (for both cinema and tourism), it also resonated with Hollywood's tendency to portray Mexico as a land of perpetual song and dance. Indeed, some critics at least partially attributed the subsequent industrial crisis to producers' excessive reliance on folklore and music: the very foundation of the genre's transnational production and reception.

In a review of the 1937 film *Amapola del camino* (yet another film based on a popular song), for instance, Campos Ponce argued that although the film may have at one time been considered a superior effort, "being the tenth, the fifteenth,

Fig. 27. Advertisement for a performance by Lydia Mendoza at the Mason. *La Opinión*, December 1, 1937. Reproduced courtesy of *La Opinión*.

or twenty-fifth—we've already lost count—of these films about chinas and char-ros, peasants and oxen, songs and guitars, it is difficult to consider it justly from a technical standpoint, since it is, with very slight differences, a repetition of this 'Mexicanism' of which the public has decidedly grown weary." He added that scripts for such films "are not written for the cinema, but to be inserted into a song." With a total of eight songs, and no longer than a ten-minute inter-val between musical interludes, *Amapola del camino*, Campos Ponce quipped, would produce "musical indigestion" in the audience.[100] In another article, he criticized the limited, one-dimensional range of ranchera films and their ten-dency to reproduce a very narrow representation of Mexico's culture and heri-tage, forcefully arguing for the projection of a more varied and diverse image of Mexico to international audiences.[101]

Critics in the pages of *La Opinión* increasingly derided these productions as their numbers increased, despite the fact that they fueled the expansion of the Mexican industry and sustained local venues. Campos Ponce declared that "Mex-ican cinema's lack of initiative is absolute," complaining that a tendency toward imitation and repetition meant that "all the producers dedicated themselves to making films about charros and Indians, despite the fact that weeks earlier they had despised and rejected anything typically Mexican." He accordingly predicted that "in proceeding this way, some producers enrage the public and destroy any constructive effort they could have accomplished."[102] Gabriel Navarro likewise complained that the comedia ranchera genre represented the most deleterious trend afflicting Mexican cinema: "One would imagine that in Mexico there is nothing else but men on horses and women wrapped in shawls; that every per-son there is a traditional singer and every woman a revolutionary soldier. The plague of these films has reached such an extreme that it often seems that we are seeing the same film from last week, but with a different title."[103] An anonymous author likewise suggested that "our country is worth much, much more than the types that that parade across the screen as symbols of the Nation," contradicting those that praised the films for improving Mexico's image abroad.[104]

Rather than functioning as a straightforward expression of Mexican national-ism and traditional morality, *Allá en el Rancho Grande* and the comedia ranch-era instead presented a number of dilemmas and paradoxes central to those facing any national cinema: Exactly what does the "national" look and sound like? How can national expression so closely resemble Hollywood's version of Mexico? If a culturally specific national cinema must rely on international rec-ognition of national types and iconography, which of these are acceptable? What precisely constitutes positive or negative images? Is national cinema produced for a domestic, transnational, or international audience? If so, which of these should hold priority? The fact that an intermedial examination of the genre pro-vokes these questions rather than definitive answers (or at least generates *mul-tiple* possible answers) suggests the value of reevaluating national cinemas from a film culture methodology that incorporates exhibition, reception, and relevant intertexts (and the history of their circulation). In this way, we define our frame of analysis as the very debate over identity and representation. Films themselves are thus no guaranteed locus of the national, but a point of departure from which to gauge the contested terms of this category.

In the case of Los Angeles, *Rancho Grande*, by cannily navigating a number of key tensions (Hollywood vs. Mexico, technological polish vs. cultural specificity, domestic vs. international appeal), proposed a transnational conception of Mexicanidad that embraced modernization while evoking a folkloric past. This strategy, however, also generated representations that resonated with an exotic tourist imaginary and the revitalization of downtown. The central dilemmas occasioned by the comedia ranchera genre would persist and evolve over the next few years as critics confronted the challenges of constructing Mexicanidad in the face of substantial changes in the transnational film market, the impact of international sociopolitical developments, and shifts in the development of Los Angeles.

CODA: *ALLÁ EN EL RANCHO GRANDE* AND TEXTUAL ANALYSIS

By moving the analysis beyond the cinematic text in this chapter, my intention is not merely to suggest an alternative, yet monolithic reading of *Allá en el Rancho Grande* or the genre of comedia ranchera in general but to demonstrate that this genre relied so steadfastly on an ongoing exchange between multiple media (as did much of Mexican cinema of the period and beyond). Accordingly, its potential meanings reside both within the film text itself and in the way that intertextual and intermedial relations operated in specific, localized contexts, with exhibition serving as a key point of intersection in this regard. Thus, rather than positing a definitive reading, this case study suggests the inevitability of multiple readings; accounting for the film's success across the continent might produce a variety of results. Such an approach certainly does much to productively complicate the category of national cinema, while confirming Andrew Higson's foundational assertion that "the parameters of a national cinema should be drawn at the site of consumption as much as at the site of production of films."[105] It is precisely in the intermedial environment encompassed by the concept of Mexican film culture in Los Angeles, I argue, that *Rancho Grande* and the ranchera genre served as a site of contention over definitions of Mexicanidad and national culture, rather than some sort of definitive nationalist statement, conservative or otherwise.

When reading the existing scholarship on *Rancho Grande*, however, it occurred to me that although most of this material mounts a critique of the film based on narrative, setting, and iconography, almost none of it conducted a thorough textual analysis. My own viewings of the film, along with the critical discourse circulating in Mexican Los Angeles, for instance, convinced me that the spectacular elements of the film—cockfights, singing competitions, horse races, and comedy vignettes—were of equal or greater importance than the narrative itself, which in addition to being conventional would be recycled in other films of the genre. Aside from obvious historical considerations, it was because so many scholars and critics have leveled the recycled observation that the film is merely conservative or guilty of Porfirian nostalgia that I decided to revisit and reconsider the film and the genre as a whole.

It wasn't until I taught a course on Mexican cinema at the University of Michigan, however, that my faith in the *Rancho Grande* orthodoxy was thoroughly upended. I screen the movie every semester as part of a sweeping survey of Mexican film history. To my surprise, my students—most of whom begin the semester with absolutely no knowledge of Mexican film outside of more recent films like *Y tu mamá también* (Alfonso Cuarón, 2001)—consistently declare *Rancho Grande* to be one of their favorites of the semester. With the fresh perspective of the uninitiated (provoked by thoughtful scholarship), their assessments and analyses continue to astound and even challenge me. In the case of *Rancho Grande*, some of them quite understandably approach the film through the familiar lenses of genre (melodrama in particular) and auteur theory. In both cases, they are perplexed by the conclusion of the film: the attempted rape of Cruz presents no permanent obstacle to the lifelong friendship of Felipe and José Francisco; the comic subplot concludes when browbeaten husband, Florentino (Carlos López "Chaflán"), asserts his authority by beating his domineering wife, Angela (Emma Roldán), into submission; all principal characters across class and gender are suddenly reconciled in the final scene through a quadruple wedding that defies all credibility.

Having been introduced to scholarship on melodrama, students often declare this finale one of the most "excessive" of the semester. That is, its conclusion is such an abrupt reversal, the closing of it narrative threads so unconvincing, that it prompts us as viewers to question the film's supposedly unequivocal celebration of gender conventions and traditional morality. While the film is far from being progressive or radical, the supposition that it appealed to audiences based on its conservatism seems to be somewhat challenged by the text itself. Students, for instance, justifiably compare the film to Luis Buñuel's *Susana* (1951), in which a rural family on a hacienda (in a clear reference to the comedia ranchera) is disrupted by the destructive seductions of the titular character but is magically (and absurdly) restored in the very last minutes of the film. In her own textual analysis of the film, for instance, Joanne Hershfield argues that its conclusion "denies us the conventional pleasure of the classical melodrama by exposing the arbitrary nature not only of narratives but also of tradition and social mores."[106]

Our retrospective reading of *Susana* is no doubt colored by our perception of Buñuel as an auteur and the tendency to read his films through the lens of an iconoclastic career that includes his earliest surrealist productions and his later French art films. That is, although the director made Mexican films that adhered to generic formulas, scholars and critics typically (and justifiably) argue that "his approach to Mexican melodrama was somewhat mediated, cautious, self-conscious" so that *Susana* simultaneously adheres to the conventions of melodrama while functioning as a parody thereof.[107] Eager to apply the auteurist lens to Mexican cinema, my students often suggest that the career of Fernando de Fuentes might also be taken into consideration in our analysis of *Rancho Grande*, particularly as he directed *Vámonos con Pancho Villa* just a year earlier. While space precludes me from indulging in a production history or textual analysis of this particular film, it is notorious for undermining celebratory narratives of the Mexican Revolution (and Villa in particular) and is undeniably critical of masculine bravado. The contrast between *Vámonos con Pancho Villa* and *Rancho Grande* can be disconcerting from the perspective of an auteurist perspective and provokes a number of worthwhile questions: If revolutionary subject matter did not initially prove as popular as the comedia ranchera, was de Fuentes guided by purely economic considerations? If not, can his oeuvre inform our reading of *Rancho Grande* and, if so, in what ways? Can we even apply any model of auteurism to Mexican cinema of the 1930s? And given relevant critiques of auteurism, would this approach even be productive?

Between my own research and teaching, I've concluded that *Allá en el Rancho Grande* remains justifiably central to Mexican film studies for a number reasons. If a cursory textual analysis of the film provokes important questions, further approaching its circulation as a multimedia phenomenon holds additional implications. Rather than merely providing a model for cinematic nationalism, it was an agglomeration of multimedia texts that provoked debates about the terms of national identity and representation. Rather than being a fixed text with a determined set of meanings, its value and significance was subject to contextual factors of exhibition and reception. Rather than automatically dismissing it as conservative, furthermore, we might do better to understand it as site of struggle over the terms of the nation and representational politics on-screen and beyond. And rather than assigning it a stable or given place in the history of Mexican cinema, it is instead a case study that should prompt us to revisit the terms and methodologies with which this history—not to mention the history of other national cinemas—has typically been approached.

CHAPTER 5

NOW WE HAVE
MEXICAN CINEMA?

NAVIGATING TRANSNATIONAL MEXICANIDAD
IN A MOMENT OF CRISIS

If in the mid-1930s the comedia ranchera heralded a Mexican movie culture that involved the construction of postrevolutionary Mexicanidad across media, the late 1930s witnessed a significant disruption of this situation on multiple counts. In fact, transformations in multiple spheres would irrevocably alter the shape of Mexican film culture and hence the terms of its relation to conceptions of Mexicanness. Perhaps most notably, a number of the older theaters along Main Street began closing, either as a function of redevelopment construction or as a product of a gradual migration of downtown Mexican entertainment to Broadway (which would be completed in the postwar era). The Teatro Hidalgo and the Teatro México—mainstays of the Mexican entertainment landscape along Main—would both be demolished by the late 1930s, for instance. This shift was also accompanied by a decentering of the leisure landscape, as theaters in East Los Angeles also began targeting a multigenerational audience of Mexican immigrants and their children with a diverse range of film offerings. The multiple variants of Main Street discourse, at least relative to the Mexican population, consequently became less central to the representation of the leisure landscape downtown.

Conceptions of Mexicanidad circulating within this film culture underwent some important shifts at this moment. Perhaps most significantly, the brand of cultural criticism that framed consumption and identity in nationalistic terms fractured, while becoming open to more flexible notions of identity and community in the process. This situation could at least partially be attributed to the fact that many of the journalists responsible for sustaining the notion of México de afuera either returned to Mexico or ceased writing by the onset of World War II. Furthermore, the greater geographic dispersal of the Mexican-descent population was compounded by a generational divide: a maturing second generation increasingly did not identify as exclusively Mexican, but as American or Mexican American. All these circumstances presented a challenge to the construction of a cohesive, united Mexican community and would definitively undermine the notion of a transcendent national audience. In addition to these shifts of identification, the hybrid nature of film exhibition likewise obstructed the circuit of purely national production and consumption facilitated by the comedia ranchera phenomenon. Between an ascendant Argentine industry, a Mexican film industry in crisis, and emergent transnational trends in Hollywood, downtown theaters alternated between productions from a range of national origins while nonetheless striving to situate themselves as bastions of cultural nationalism.

As this tension suggests, the multiple transitions within and external pressures on Mexican film culture in Los Angeles generated competing constructions of Mexicanidad during this period of multiple transitions. On the one hand, exhibitors' publicity echoed certain critical positions that reiterated unabashed nationalism in the face of these factors. Publicity for downtown theaters, for instance, continued to claim an unconditional and unproblematic Mexican nationalist orientation and mission. Other individuals, however, began at least indirectly challenging the concept of México de afuera by considering negotiated notions of identity that more explicitly accounted for transnational subjectivity, Pan-Latino consciousness, and hyphenated identifications. As such, this period marks the initial decline of the cultural nationalism that had governed critical discourse and Mexican cinema culture in Los Angeles since the 1910s. Furthermore, it acknowledged a degree of fragmentation, fluidity, and heterogeneity obscured by earlier constructions of the Mexican population.

These shifting conceptions of Mexicanidad in the cultural realm become perhaps most apparent in the course of critical debates about the direction of Hollywood's renewed appeal to Latino and Latin American audiences. Most notably, Hollywood's collaboration with the Roosevelt's Good Neighbor Policy initiated in 1933 (a multifaceted effort to improve relations with Latin American nations and to alter perceptions of the United States in that region) and subsequent embrace of hemispheric Pan-Americanism during the lead-up to World War II generated new Pan-Latino cinematic representations intended to appeal (at least partially) to a broad, continental audience. Indeed, Alberto Sandoval-Sánchez, in his analysis of the careers of Carmen Miranda and Desi Arnaz, asserts that this cycle represents a watershed in the history of Latino representation in Hollywood, as the films "materialize the inaugural depictions and visualizations of *Latinidad* in the U.S. cultural collective imaginary."[1] Rather than reiterate Mexican specificity in the face of a generalized constructions of Latinidad, however, journalists protested this imagery while in turn proposing other forms of transnational identifications and affiliations that did not hinge on the exotic spectacles or the tourist gaze that permeated Pan-American films. These emerging constructions of transnational Mexicanidad were often (but not exclusively) manifest through the careers and reception of transnational stars, including Tito Guízar. As in previous decades, these varying notions of identity and community articulated through the sphere of Mexican film culture were guided by as much by economic considerations, marketing efforts, and personal investments therein as they were by sociohistorical and industrial shifts.

EXHIBITING THE TRANSNATIONAL:
THE FRAGMENTATION OF MEXICAN FILM CULTURE

As had been the case since the 1910s, the Mexican immigrant press continued a complex dialogue between constructions of identity, media representation, and the city's entertainment landscape. Important developments in multiple film industries, including Mexican production, greatly informed the direction of this discourse in the late 1930s. The emphasis on the relationship between cinema and national expression, always present in criticism and exhibition publicity in Los Angeles, became perhaps even more forcefully pronounced at this moment. Curiously, this shift occurred in spite of (or perhaps more counterintuitively, precisely as a result of) an increasingly hybrid programming practice, in which Mexican films were shown alongside Argentine and Hollywood production in Frank Fouce's downtown theaters. Indeed, it was precisely at this moment that both of these film industries constituted a potential threat to a struggling Mexican film industry. If exhibition programming proved necessarily diverse under these circumstances, the entertainment landscape also became increasingly dispersed as theaters more aggressively targeted the growing Mexican population of East Los Angeles, further challenging entrenched conceptions of the Mexican audience as a coherent community and the definition of Mexicanidad itself.

One of the more significant trends impacting this leisure landscape was the critical backlash against and momentary decline of Mexican cinema. Despite the apparent overproduction of costumbrista and comedia ranchera films, many in Los Angeles remained largely enthusiastic about the impact such productions had exerted on Los Angeles and the Mexican film industry. In early 1938 *La Opinión* published an article (a thinly disguised promotional piece for Azteca Films) boasting that the distributor "has in reality presented the biggest hits" of Mexican cinema, while offering a list of Azteca's forthcoming releases. The piece also praised Frank Fouce's Teatro California for supporting the national industry, claiming that audiences in the city "have been able to witness the relentless progress of the National Cinema Industry thanks to exhibitions in a theater that will undoubtedly pass into the history of the Colonia with a brilliant record of service." The concerted efforts of these businesses accordingly "have maintained in the soul of México de afuera a devotion to all of our culture, as immortal as it should be."[2] Another article unequivocally predicted that 1938 would constitute the "highest point of Mexican cinema in California," explaining that "our audiences, once resistant to the cinematic production of our country, considering it mediocre compared to Hollywood, have now developed a taste for our culture and pack theaters when a good film is presented. At the same time, distributors, impresarios, sign makers, an entire specialized class has flourished around the industry created by Mexican cinema."[3]

By the latter part of 1938, however, Mexican cinema had entered a period of crisis and reduced production, despite its recent resurgence and apparent movement toward consolidation. While critical voices in *La Opinión* reduced these difficulties to the formulaic production of comedias rancheras and union disputes, the matter was decidedly more complex. As Alfonso Pulido Islas argued in his 1939 assessment of the Mexican film industry, the production crisis resulted from a complex confluence of multiple factors and was just as much the result of a lack of infrastructure, the inability to establish an efficient division of labor observed by the U.S. studio system, rising production costs, the failure to sustain an effective star system, and the control of distribution by U.S. companies, among others. In this context, standardized production of ranchera films constituted an immediate (if shortsighted) and cost-effective solution for producers with limited resources, while any labor disputes exerted an exaggerated impact on a system already confronted by an array of difficulties and strain. Islas, diagnosing major obstacles and proposing a list of solutions, concluded his treatise with a warning: "The national film industry is in grave danger of entering a sharp decline, owing to causes internal to the film industry itself and to external causes that have their origin in the competition from the North American industry, from Argentina, and certainly in the future from Spain."[4]

In the pages of *La Opinión*, the ascendancy of Argentine cinema was in fact directly connected to the quality of Mexican films and regarded as a threat to the viability of a national cinema. As Tamara Falicov points out, Argentina went from producing twenty-two films in 1935 to releasing fifty in 1939, becoming "the most popular and prolific producer of films in Latin America, and was considerable competition to Hollywood in the Spanish-speaking world."[5] And, as Matthew B. Karush further notes, Argentina during this period boasted nine film studios and thirty independent production companies, allowing it to sustain this level of production through 1942.[6] In her review of the Mexican film *Rosa de Xochimilco* (Carlos Véjar, 1938), *La Opinión* columnist Hortensia Elizondo revealed local anxieties about these developments, sounding "a cry of alarm in order to stop these detrimental films that are, or soon will be, the definitive death of national cinema." According to Elizondo, such films were the reason "our own exhibitors accept Argentine productions and, in almost every case, reject national ones."[7] Other critics of the newspaper concurred, however reluctantly, that as Argentina indeed produced films of superior quality, it threatened the long-term viability of Mexican cinema. Tito Guízar's starring role in the Argentine film *De México llegó el amor* (Love arrived from Mexico, Richard Harlan, 1940) was, not coincidentally, regarded as a clear indication of Mexico's inability to produce films worthy of major stars and Argentina's successful exploitation of their bankability. With the release of this film, Elizondo again warned producers that "Argentina is leaving Mexico behind as far as cinematic production," arguing that despite their use of a "disagreeable" Argentine accent and a heavy reliance on regional culture, "the majority of Argentine films are praiseworthy and well-made and, furthermore, as much as it hurts to admit, outdo our own."[8]

If journalists increasingly expressed anxiety about the crisis afflicting Mexican cinema and repeatedly predicted an impending competition between national industries, the resurgence of Hollywood Spanish-language production in the late 1930s generated perhaps the most sustained and heated contention during this period. An article in *Motion Picture Herald* succinctly summarized the concerns occasioned by these developments:

> Stiff competition from Hollywood in the form of top flight pictures in Spanish is making itself felt in Mexico's film industry, particularly in production. Also, Hollywood is attracting many of the best Mexican players and the Hollywood product is finding good acceptance throughout Latin America, causing Mexican producers to worry about their exports. Finally there is the drag of mediocre films produced by Mexican companies.[9]

This trend was partially motivated by the onset of World War II and its effect on Hollywood, not to mention the industry-wide anxiety about an impending crisis in the late 1930s.[10] On both counts, the U.S. industry made concerted attempts to capitalize more fully on the Latin American market, as European and Asian countries either restricted the importation of Hollywood products or entered into a period of extreme instability and turmoil. The *Hollywood Reporter*, for instance, noted that multiple studios were currently producing films targeting Latin America, with some even planning to establish production facilities in a number of nations, in hopes that employing "native actors will forestall possible boycotts induced by native producers." The trade paper subsequently summarized the logic of the studios: "with the decrease in European grosses imminent as a result of quotas, boycotts, and squeeze-outs, cultivating Latin markets is necessary in order to keep the average of foreign gross returns."[11] As Lisa Jarvinen has also noted, Hollywood's efforts in this arena were also motivated by potential competition in this market from the emergent Mexican, Argentine, and Spanish film industries.[12]

Significantly, these production trends coincided with the initiation of Roosevelt's Good Neighbor Policy toward Latin America in 1933 and a renewed emphasis on fostering cooperative hemispheric relations. If the Argentine film industry threatened to overtake Mexico in the Spanish-language markets, Hollywood's full entry into the production of Pan-American features represented a threat of a different order. In cooperation with the U.S. government, Hollywood by the late 1930s began producing films that would ostensibly build continental goodwill, encourage Latin America's allegiance to the Allied effort, promote U.S.

products throughout the region, and safeguard U.S. investments. As a cultural phenomenon, this trend became a wartime fixture of mass culture that included cinema, concert tours, radio programming, and print culture. Many of these efforts would, by 1940, be coordinated by the Office of the Coordinator of Inter-American Affairs (OCIAA), a government agency headed by Nelson Rockefeller, whose mission was "to improve hemispheric solidarity so as to stem the tide of Nazi economic and ideological (and, later, military) incursions into Latin America while increasing the flow of trade—economic and cultural—along a north-south axis."[13]

While Hollywood's participation in this initiative served to demonstrate its dedication to the Allied cause, it also coincided fortuitously with the industry's struggle to garner increased revenue from Latin America, given the closing of the European markets. While studios produced several historical epics toward these ends, including Warner Bros.'s *Juarez* (William Dieterle, 1939) and a significant amount of documentaries, the bulk of Pan-American feature production consisted of musicals and low-budget features with Latin American settings and singers.[14] Starring imported talent like Carmen Miranda and featuring multiple musical interludes, such films were designed to attract Latin American audiences and appeal to U.S. audiences by capitalizing on the Latin music craze in the United States, while promoting Latin America as a colorful tourist destination.

Despite the best intentions of Hollywood and the OCIAA, these films provoked a continental response that unleashed much of the same critical vitriol directed at Hollywood's previous efforts to produce films for the Latin American market and their construction of and appeal to a continental audience. Abandoning the aforementioned "mythical kingdoms" to once again represent specific locales and peoples, Hollywood's Pan-American version of "Latinness" often involved a bewildering mixture of national and cultural signifiers. As Allen L. Woll has noted, Latin American critics "were annoyed by the misrepresentations of their culture which occurred frequently despite the plethora of technical advisors available to screenwriters," and they "resented the inter-American unity message which was clearly evident in each film."[15] Ana M. López further argues that the "ethnographic" impulse evident in such films crafted "cultural interpretation and representation" of "Latins" that in addition to conflating or confusing national cultures, continued to frame Latin Americans as definitive others (although through more apparently positive characterizations).[16] As in previous decades, Hollywood's construction of Latin America and its peoples generated a considerable degree of backlash in Los Angeles. *La Opinión* columnist A. A. Loyo, after watching *Argentine Nights* (Albert S. Rogell, 1940) at the Paramount downtown, predicted that Latin American audiences "will reject this film as they have rejected many others (even those made in Spanish on this side of the border) because U.S. producers insist on presenting our customs in a distorted manner or in a decidedly theatrical way."[17]

During this cycle of production, studios self-consciously worked to avoid demeaning and offensive images in the name of hemispheric goodwill, but their projection of Latin America relied on conceptions of the region as an exotic spectacle inspired by the imagery of tourism. Nonetheless, these apparently more positive representations tended to flatten out differences within the region and consistently associated the continent with a limited range of characteristics that framed the region as "a postcard, a photograph, a tourist attraction, [or] a night club."[18] In other words, studios and their regulatory mechanisms consistently failed to understand that ongoing, misguided attempts to construct a pancontinental "Latin" were perhaps just as offensive to audiences and critics as so-called negative stereotypes.

Eventually, Will Hays of the MPPDA hired Addison Durland (a banker with extensive ties to Mexico) to monitor the Good Neighbor representations of Latin America by Hollywood films through the Production Code Administration. While local journalists predicted that, given Durland's extensive experience across the continent, "there will be no more errors, nor anachronisms, nor humiliations" in Hollywood films about Latin America, the results of his interventions were decidedly more ambiguous.[19] As Brian O'Neil notes, his censorship efforts tended to coincide with the interests of Latin American elites, and his policies promoted Latin America as "modern, clean, and especially in the cases of Brazil and Argentina, European in complexion," an approach that left intact decades of cinematic convention in which "the 'Hollywood Latin' retains one-dimensional entertainment value."[20] As it had during the heyday of Spanish-language production in the early 1930s, Hollywood aspired primarily to eliminate the more offensive dimensions of on-screen representations, refusing to abandon the generalized representations of the "Latin" that theoretically would allow them to appeal to a broad Latin American audience while not violating long-standing perceptions of the region held by the domestic audience. Despite the fact that the implications of this representational impulse shaped by the MPPDA's intervention coincided with notions of racial and cultural elevation promoted by many Mexican journalists in Los Angeles, for instance, these critics nonetheless vocally rejected these befuddling, amalgamated constructions of the Latin American.

All these production trends influenced and paralleled developments in the realm of exhibition in Mexican Los Angeles. Despite claims that the downtown venues and their audiences were authentically Mexican, the very basis of this notion became contested terrain. Up until the end of 1937, all of Fouce's downtown venues featured combined programs consisting largely of Mexican films and live performances. In fact, during this year alone, Fouce opened the Teatro Roosevelt and the Teatro Mason (the intended Mexican Music Hall), a decision undoubtedly influenced by the steady supply of Mexican films and by the popular musicians and musical variety troupes that toured in support of such productions. By 1938, as the supply of new Mexican releases dwindled, Fouce increasingly booked a more diverse range of productions and also relied heavily on double features. In

June 1938, for instance, the first-run California and Eléctrico Theaters announced the premier of the Cantinflas film *¡Así es mi tierra!* (That's how my country is!, Arcady Boytler, 1938), which was paired with the Edward G. Robinson film *The Last Gangster* (Edward Ludwig, 1937).[21] Meanwhile, the second-run Roosevelt often screened reliable hits, particularly those of the comedia ranchera genre. On the same week of June 9, for instance, the Roosevelt advertised yet another revival of the ranchera film *¡Ora Ponciano!*, supported by a programmer starring Ronald Reagan titled *Love Is on the Air* (Nick Grinde, 1937).[22]

As early as 1938, Argentine films were also increasingly being shown in Fouce's theaters downtown, often as part of a double bill framed in the press as a "showdown" between national industries. When the Argentine comedy *Melgarejo* (Luis Moglia Barth, 1937) was paired with the rerelease of *Allá en el Rancho Grande* at the California Theater, *La Opinión* established the program as a competition, declaring that "Mexico and Argentina, in a manner of speaking, are going '*mano a mano*' today on the screen of the California," a turn of phrase used frequently in the years to come.[23] Indeed, as reports in *La Opinión* and the Mexican trade journal *Cinema Reporter* warned of an impending crisis, Fouce relied increasingly on English-language and Argentine features.[24] This was particularly the case by 1940, as the backlog of Mexican features was gradually exhausted. Not surprisingly, the exhibition of Argentine cinema in the United States was in fact directly and consistently linked to the declining quality of Mexican cinema. *Cinema Reporter* published multiple articles about the decreasing revenues from the U.S. market, claiming that exhibitors in the border region were forced to reduce ticket prices and to regularly offer double features and raffles.[25] In a subsequent article, Rafael Calderón and Juan and Alberto Salas Porras (the owners of the Azteca distribution company) complained that only seven of the fifty-seven films they acquired from Mexico were actually worthy of distribution. As a result, the distributor began carrying more Argentine films, as a way to ensure steady revenues and uphold their own reputation.[26] Fouce even declared the situation in 1940 to be worse than the earliest years of Mexican film exhibition in California. According to him, his theaters had experienced a 40 percent drop in revenue, forcing him to reduce admissions, increase the quality of live performances, and to raffle $125 dollars. In his estimation, 80 percent of Mexican films were of poor quality and were directly responsible for these circumstances.[27]

The hybrid exhibition programming that increasingly held sway during these years was also accompanied by a geographic dispersal of Mexican entertainment. This shift was to a great extent the product of the increasing movement of the Mexican population across the river into East Los Angeles. Crowded out of downtown by higher rents, industrial development, and civic construction over the course of the 1930s, immigrants gravitated toward this neighborhood to take advantage of more affordable housing options while racially restrictive covenants prevented them from residing in other areas of town. The establishment of reliable and inexpensive interurban rail lines also facilitated this transition. By the late 1920s, the Belvedere neighborhood housed approximately thirty thousand individuals of Mexican descent, more than any other in the city. As had been the case with downtown, however, East Los Angeles neighborhoods like Boyle Heights housed a remarkably diverse population. For instance, an estimated ten thousand Jewish households lived in this neighborhood by 1930, and Brooklyn Avenue functioned as the epicenter of Jewish life in Los Angeles.[28]

Not only were Fouce's new Mason and Roosevelt located away from the original epicenter of Mexican cultural life along Main, but these years also witnessed extension of Mexican cinema culture to East Los Angeles, albeit on terms distinct from its manifestation downtown. The Unique was among the earliest of such theaters, located on First Street near Rowan. Although it hosted films and local theater performances since at least 1932, the venue typically exhibited double features of subsequent-run Hollywood films.[29] In this regard, it was hardly an exception. During the 1930s the Eastside boasted a number of neighborhood theaters, including the Teatro Bonito, the Strand, the Crystal Theater, and the Jewel Theater. Most of these were dedicated to double features of U.S. films, with the Strand initially offering vaudeville programs with each screening.[30] In 1933 *La Opinión* explained the attraction of such theaters, despite the existence of multiple venues operating concurrently downtown:

> As they are removed from the center of the city, the Mexican families of Belvedere have resolved the problem of entertainment in an intelligent and encouraging way. To attend a downtown theater, a family of three without an automobile, for example, would have to spend a minimum of forty cents to ride the streetcars or the bus that offer service here. This amount, added to the admission charged in the downtown theaters, created the necessity of establishing theaters in the heart of the neighborhood itself, at least on an improvised basis, to satisfy the spiritual necessity of artistic diversion.[31]

Indeed, working-class families were a significant portion of the population in this area, as many Mexicans had moved from the crowded (and increasingly expensive) housing options downtown to buy single-family homes in neighborhoods like Belvedere, Boyle Heights, and Maravilla (see fig. 28).

Despite the overwhelming presence of Mexican-descent families in this area, however, the cinemas located there relied heavily on production from Hollywood through the mid-1930s. To some extent, such programming decisions were likely a function of the products available to such venues. In 1933, for instance, as Fouce and Carlos Emmanuel were finally capable of operating downtown theaters that screened primarily Mexican film, the Unique Theater began offering "Mexican Thursdays" dedicated exclusively to films in Spanish. While this practice was eventually suspended, the Teatro Bonito in East Los Angeles began showing Spanish-language films on Tuesdays, Wednesdays, and Thursdays in 1935, bookings undeniably facilitated by the theater's relationship with the newly established distribution office of Azteca Films. From this point on, the theater

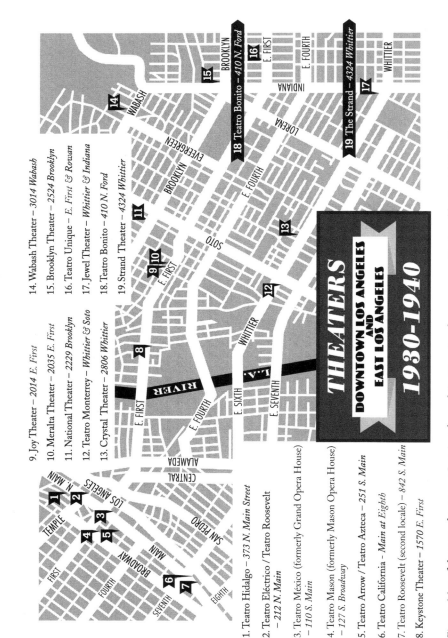

9. Joy Theater – *2014 E. First*

10. Meralta Theater – *2035 E. First*

11. National Theater – *2229 Brooklyn*

12. Teatro Monterrey – *Whittier & Soto*

13. Crystal Theater – *2806 Whittier*

14. Wabash Theater – *3014 Wabash*

15. Brooklyn Theater – *2524 Brooklyn*

16. Teatro Unique – *E. First & Rowan*

17. Jewel Theater – *Whittier & Indiana*

18. Teatro Bonito – *410 N. Ford*

19. Strand Theater – *4324 Whittier*

1. Teatro Hidalgo – *373 N. Main Street*

2. Teatro Eléctrico / Teatro Roosevelt – *212 N. Main*

3. Teatro México (formerly Grand Opera House) – *110 S. Main*

4. Teatro Mason (formerly Mason Opera House) – *127 S. Broadway*

5. Teatro Arrow / Teatro Azteca – *251 S. Main*

6. Teatro California - *Main at Eighth*

7. Teatro Roosevelt (second locale) – *842 S. Main*

8. Keystone Theater – *1570 E. First*

Fig. 28. Map of theaters, downtown Los Angeles and East Los Angeles, 1930–1940. Designed by Daniel González.

became a third- or fourth-run theater for such features. As an example, *Allá en el Rancho Grande* was finally shown there in July 1938, after it had already been released on three separate occasions in Fouce's theaters downtown.[32] As Mexican films became more regularly available, the Teatro Monterrey opened on Whittier Boulevard in East Los Angeles in late 1939, promising one night of Mexican films each week.[33] In the same year the Unique also reinstated its policy of screening Spanish-language films once a week, beginning with the ranchera film *Ojos tapatíos* (Jaliscan eyes, Boris Maicon, 1938). An advertisement for the theater billed the new Spanish-language features as "a treat for those who understand Spanish—an opportunity for those who wish to study it" (see fig. 29).[34]

The diverse programming practices of such theaters might be partially explained by the continued diversity of East Los Angeles before World War II. While the Monterrey and Unique at least occasionally screened Mexican films by the late 1930s, others in the area continued to show primarily Hollywood fare. The theaters owned by Jack Y. Berman, including the Meralta, the Joy, the Wabash, the Brooklyn, and the National, when not exhibiting double features of this sort, apparently served the Jewish clientele of the area. In 1938, when more than ten thousand "Jews and Jewish sympathizers" paraded down Brooklyn Avenue (now César E. Chavez) in Boyle Heights to protest Nazi Germany's treatment of Jews, Berman closed the National Theater, placing a notice on the marquee: "CLOSED TONITE: PROTEST NAZI HORROR" (see fig. 30).[35] Several weeks later Berman's Brooklyn Theater screened twenty minutes of documentary footage of the protests that took place in Boyle Heights and Hollywood.[36] The National Theater (likewise located on Brooklyn Avenue) also regularly screened films in Yiddish.[37] Not surprisingly, when Berman did begin exhibiting films in Spanish, he did so at the Joy Theater located in Belvedere, a neighborhood more decidedly Mexican in composition. Imitating the policies of the Unique and Monterrey, the Joy offered Spanish-language films on Tuesday, Wednesday, and Thursday, inaugurating this practice in June 1939 with a revival of *Allá en el Rancho Grande* and continuing with other popular films of the ranchera genre.[38]

These exhibition practices, along with other elements of East Los Angeles movie culture, may have also emerged as a function of generational difference. In addition to the ethnic diversity of the neighborhood, theaters likely attempted to attract a younger generation of spectators with Hollywood films while appealing to an older generation of Mexican immigrants (and new arrivals) with Spanish-language programming and emphasizing its value relative to cultural and linguistic retention. Furthermore, the newspapers established in East Los Angeles, including the *Belvedere Citizen* and the *Eastside Journal*, although technically bilingual, published overwhelmingly in English—a function again of the ethnic and generational heterogeneity of the area. A notice placed by the Teatro Bonito in the *Belvedere Citizen* makes this dynamic even more apparent. Titled "A Message to the Spanish-Speaking Colony," the piece

Fig. 29. An example of the weekly program at the Unique Theater during the late 1930s.
Belvedere Citizen, August 4, 1939.

asserts that "the ownership of the Teatro Bonito of this city, wishing to cooper-
ate with the distinguished Mexican colony, has joined the great effort made by
Mexico and the rest of Latin America to promote the florid language of our
ancestors, and one of the more efficient ways to achieve this noble end is to
promote all cinema in Spanish." The article continues, encouraging parents "to
let your children see and hear more films of our countries so that they become
familiar with our customs, our stories, our music, our landscapes and in a word
become familiar with the true homeland of their parents."[39] Despite these occasional notices, the cinema culture of East Los Angeles—including press culture,
programming practices, and theater publicity—was a far cry from the cultural
nationalism typically associated with downtown theaters.

By contrast, Fouce's incessant assertions that the exhibition of Mexican cinema
constituted a service to the nation and to Mexicans within and beyond national
borders often belied the actual exhibition practices of his chain, particularly as

Fig. 30. Marquee of the National Theater on the evening of the anti-Nazi protest. *Eastside Journal*, November 28, 1938.

the Mexican industry slowed production. Nonetheless, evocations of the nation and an emphasis on the retention of Mexican culture arose forcefully at a moment of crisis for the Mexican film industry and of prolific transnational production and exhibition programming. Given the prevalence of the concept of México de afuera and its centrality to the middle-class and elite economic and cultural networks, Fouce and other exhibitors downtown had a clear incentive to adopt this rhetoric in their own promotion. In particular, the entrepreneur consistently positioned his "empire" as the epicenter of Spanish-language entertainment in the city, while also constantly reiterating his business endeavors as crucial to the maintenance of Mexican identity in Los Angeles. Fouce articulated these connections in theater publicity, press interviews, and even in the decor of his theaters, which featured paintings of Mexican historical figures (see figs. 31 and 32).

One particular episode proves indicative of Fouce's powerful influence over the Mexican cultural sphere, showing how he mobilized the rhetoric of

Fig. 31. Painting of Father Hidalgo in the interior of the Teatro California. Photograph by John Miller. Tom B'hend and Preston Kaufmann Collection, Margaret Herrick Library, Academy of Motion Picture Arts and Sciences.

Fig. 32. Painting of Benito Juárez in the interior of the Teatro California. Photograph by John Miller. Tom B'hend and Preston Kaufmann Collection, Margaret Herrick Library, Academy of Motion Picture Arts and Sciences.

unflagging nationalism as a central component of his commercial endeavors. In 1939, with a variety of Spanish-language products available, a group of unnamed investors opened the Teatro México (not to be confused with the venue that occupied the former Grand Opera House) in the former location of the Burbank Theater. Opening on Cinco de Mayo with a premier of the "great and truly Mexican" film *Perjura* (*Perjurer*, Rafael J. Sevilla, 1938), the theater owners made a concerted effort to establish the México as a venue "dedicat[ed] with all its heart to the Mexican colony."[40] Preparations for the premier included "decorating the theater with Mexican motifs, installing the best sound reproduction and projection equipment," and hiring "a truly Mexican staff."[41] In addition to promising to book only Mexican films, the operators of the México intended to adopt the intermedial approach so crucial to the success of Mexican cinema, promising that the venue "will also present weekly theatrical functions since it has one of the best stages in Los Angeles. These works will include drama, musicals, [and] comedies and will feature the most prominent talent of the colony."[42]

The emergence of this theater, particularly as it publicized a list of forthcoming releases to premier there, provoked a prompt response from distributor Azteca Films that itself cloaked commercial investments in lofty nationalist pronouncements. In a full-page advertisement in *La Opinión*, the distributor described its relationship to Frank Fouce in these terms:

> It was eight years ago, when nobody believed in the future of films in Spanish, that "Azteca Films Distributing" from El Paso, Texas, and Mr. Francisco Fouce, impresario from California, began a struggle that now seems titanic, to create affection for Mexican productions in the spirit of our public. The work was rough. First, there was a lack of theaters in which to show the few films that Mexico produced; then there was not enough production to maintain the constant enthusiasm of fans. The obstacles were imposing and dangerous. It was necessary to open a path, to work as pioneers, to establish in California something that had never existed, with the aggravation of a very serious competition from Hollywood producers.

After years of incessant struggle, Fouce and Azteca were thus able to finally declare, "Now we have Mexican cinema; now we have theaters in which to exhibit it and a public that is interested, finally, in films made in our countries." Mexicans in Los Angeles finally had "their own theaters: venues that exclusively exhibited films that portrayed their life, that were faithful reflections of their customs." Echoing concurrent critical discourse about Mexican cinema and its relation to national identity, the advertisement also assured readers that "our desire, we repeat, is to promote Mexican Cinema, because we hold the firm conviction that its future is intimately tied to the future of Mexico itself and with the Hispano-American nations in general." This rhetoric, however, was here mobilized to reiterate Frank Fouce's control over the exhibition of Mexican cinema in downtown Los Angeles. Affirming that Azteca and Fouce "are tied by the same moral obligation, which is the improvement of Mexican cinema abroad," the piece forcefully declares (in all capital letters): ALL OF THE MEXICAN FILM PRODUCTIONS CONTROLLED BY [AZTECA], WILL IN THE FUTURE BE PREMIERED EXCLUSIVELY IN THE THEATERS OF THE FRANCISCO FOUCE COMPANY."[43]

Obviously, this circuit of national consumption echoed rhetoric generated by the immigrant press since the 1910s. Just as then, the representation of the business and its audience as authentically Mexican and Spanish speaking was economically expedient. In a subsequent interview with *La Opinión*, Rubén A. Calderón, the Los Angeles manager of Azteca, further encouraged the public "to patronize the movie theaters where these pictures are shown, so that Mexico can continue producing and fully develop its efforts in favor of a definitive improvement of the film industry."[44] While again emphasizing the connections between Mexican cinema and the maintenance of national identity in the United States, this atypically large advertisement was also obviously published to publicly consolidate the connections between Azteca, Fouce, and the Mexican film industry, while also implicitly questioning the legitimacy and motivation of rival exhibitors. Not coincidentally, the Nuevo Teatro México soon disappeared from the entertainment landscape, whether as a result of this public relations campaign or through the termination of its relationship with Azteca. In fact, Fouce advertised the Los Angeles premier of the film *Perjura* at the California Theater in 1940, as if the Teatro México had somehow never existed.[45]

This unabashed embrace of nationalist Mexicanidad at least partially accounts for the regular exclusion of East Los Angeles theaters from entertainment coverage in *La Opinión*. Given the ideological orientation of *La Opinión*, coverage of activities in East Los Angeles theaters was by contrast typically scant and usually consisted of a simple listing. Despite their frequent theatrical events, charity benefits, and the often Mexican-oriented nature of their publicity, the programming of the Unique and Monterrey apparently did not easily coincide with the agenda of the newspaper or with the more steadfastly nationalist claims of Fouce (actual programming practices aside). It's also quite likely that these theaters did not generate the level of advertising revenue as Fouce's downtown theaters. An editorial by A. A. Loyo makes explicit the logic of the near exclusion of these theaters from the broader critical discourse:

> the theaters of Main Street (North and South) presented their typical film programs, sometimes mixed, that is, with one art film in Spanish and another in English, and sometimes "one hundred percent" in the language of our birth. The shows in "the other Mexican district," for their part, preferred to offer their clientele only double features in English, but just as in other theaters and cinemas, both Mexican and American, they also offered their clientele, at least in one instance, "metallic" prizes that attract so many people. In summary, this week held nothing extraordinary, passing into history like so many others.[46]

While this assessment somewhat misrepresents the differences between East Los Angeles and downtown (as my own summary has shown), it does aptly demonstrate that the theaters and its owners operated outside the economic and cultural networks united and defined by Mexican nationalism.

The issue of (contested) Mexican identity also arose frequently in other sections of the paper during this period, with editorialists continuing to promote the salience of a cohesive México de afuera in the face of generational difference and with the increasingly undeniable prospect of a permanent and sizable population of Mexican descent remaining within the United States. One such editorial, titled "The Great Mexican Problem," exemplifies the efforts to retain conventional notions of Mexican national identity against the influence of U.S. culture in a decidedly transnational context. Evoking a mythical, invented past, the author of this piece recalls that Mexicans, upon first arriving in the United States, "were a solid root of identical beings, with one language, one faith, and one flag." With immediate return to Mexico delayed, these immigrants strove to "resuscitate the life they left, fulfill their spiritual necessities, and so were born in the United States the Spanish-language press, theater in this language, bookstores that disseminated through immigrant camps the spirit and the sustenance of the race." Characterizing the birth of a new generation as a "painful divorce," the author then describes the influences that placed a "wall of incomprehension" between these children and the culture of their parents: education, the English language, sports, and cinema. Predictably, the editorial proposes language retention as the key to resolving this dilemma: "The Castilian language, passed from parents to children, has been forced to become an amalgamation of beings and a point of conversion for all common interests. The Mexican homes where Spanish is spoken on a daily basis have seen that the spiritual divorce between parents and children has been only an unfulfilled threat."[47]

While such an editorial might be regarded as somewhat unremarkable, particularly as it reproduced discourse prevalent in La Opinión over the course of two decades, it also revealed anxiety about demographic and generational transformations occurring in Los Angeles and elsewhere. If cinema was situated as a potentially corrupting influence in this regard, attempts by La Opinión and theater owners to promote and defend the Spanish language and Mexican cinema culture can be regarded simultaneously as marketing strategies and as part of a larger effort to sustain Mexican national identity in the United States. The relevance of mass culture to this arrangement by the late 1930s had become increasingly central, both in Mexico and the United States. Not only had cinema, radio, and recording industries assumed the aesthetic and vocabulary of cultural nationalism, but in the context of Los Angeles, the retreat of the Mexican Consulate from cultural life in the city also placed a greater burden on the press and film exhibitors to act as repositories of Mexican culture. Not surprisingly, these discursive efforts become particularly urgent in the face of transition, often with insistent and uncompromising conceptions of nationalism serving as a disavowal of intercultural and transnational exchange and the culturally hybrid consumption practiced by immigrant audiences in both downtown and East Los Angeles.

Toward a Transnational Mexicanidad: Critical Discourse and Negotiated Identity

This period of uncertainty and transition also generated a range of responses from journalists that departed from the stricter terms of nationalism espoused by Fouce, Azteca, and like-minded journalists. While there persisted a marked tendency to reiterate a conventionally national version of Mexicanidad as a market strategy and defense of the Mexican film industry, there also emerged more attenuated positions that acknowledged the fact and necessity of transnational exchange, particularly between Hollywood and Mexico. Appropriately, I trace these competing constructs through a transnational critical debate that accompanied the brief resurgence of Spanish-language production by Hollywood studios as part of a broader strategy to garner Latin American audiences, and its perceived impact on Mexican national cinema and film culture in general. The terms of this debate echoed many of the same concerns voiced during Hollywood's initial foray into foreign-language production and involved many of the same individuals. Just as significantly, this series of exchanges between critics readily demonstrates the transnational circulation of cultural criticism and the multiple investments that particular individuals possessed in both the U.S. and Mexican film industries. Beyond the ever-present concerns about the site of production and textual content, the issue of labor resurfaced in these debates, particularly as several critics (Gabriel Navarro included) were contracted by Hollywood or the Mexican industry. The transnational dimensions of both cinemas and the peculiar position of talent (including journalists) within and between them, reveal the multiple and changing conceptions of what it meant to be Mexican in light of these developments.

As production on the new cycle of Spanish-language films got under way in 1938, critic Gabriel Navarro initially reacted with the same brand of cultural nationalism typical of his criticism since the 1920s. Restating many of the same critiques he had launched during the transition to sound, for instance, Navarro (despite his often pessimistic assessments of the Mexican industry) mounted a vigorous defense of Mexican cinema relative to Hollywood Spanish-language production, opening his article with this epigraph from Frank Fouce: "None of the Hispano pictures made in Hollywood—except those of [Carlos] Gardel and [José] Mojica, which were supreme attractions—have ever given as much at the box office as Mexican productions. The best of those films has not yielded even half of that of the best of those filmed in our country. This is a painful truth." Navarro goes on to explain that although Mexican films suffer from "bad sound, bad photography, [and] a poverty of technical execution," audiences in Los Angeles prefer them, as they possess "an indisputable sincerity, a full identification with Hispano sentiment, [and] a simple and charming reality." Hollywood Spanish-language films, although "they are very close to excellence," suffer from "a cold and cruel beauty that says nothing to the heart, nor the mind." Reiterating this dichotomy, the critic also recounted a list of familiar complaints about these films, including linguistic inconsistencies, the employment of non-Latino directors, and the direct translation of scripts.[48]

What proved remarkable about Navarro's new, somewhat predictable, offensive directed at Spanish-language Hollywood films on the basis of nationalism is that it no longer represented a critical consensus. This dynamic would become more apparent as the debates about these films continued, revealing a number of positions on the relationship between site of production, cultural authenticity, and national (or transnational) identity. Responding directly to Navarro, for instance, studio consultant and dialogue director Miguel de Zárraga defended the efforts of Hollywood, while also using the controversy to promote his latest production. Emphasizing that Latin American film industries have made commendable progress in recent years, he argued nonetheless that these national cinemas produce quality films only as an exception, as they "still lack technical elements, and their artists still need a great deal of practice before they can succeed and continue improving." But, in Hollywood, there is never a need "to resort to risky improvisations," since an unending supply of resources and capital are available "to instantly bring here any desired actor, writer, or musician."[49]

As an example, de Zárraga cites Cantabria Film's forthcoming release *Verbena trágica* (Tragic festival, Charles Lamont, 1939), listing its prestigious international cast and declaring it "THE BEST HISPANO FILM EVER PRODUCED IN HOLLYWOOD." Released by Columbia, the film features Mexican actor Fernando Soler and takes place in a Latino neighborhood in New York. Not coincidentally, de Zárraga was responsible for adapting the script into Spanish. In a sly rhetorical move, he accused critics like Navarro of excessive nationalism, reminding them that "the spirit is not only in the cities and fields of the homeland and not only reflected in national monuments." Because the film in question takes place in an immigrant enclave, it thus demonstrates that "outside our countries, in lands officially foreign, there are enormous groups of our fellow countrymen that continue to speak our language and to feel the same emotions as us." Sidestepping the objections of Navarro, de Zárraga characterized his complaints as an insult to the immigrant population of the United States and thus to the readership of *La Opinión*.[50]

Navarro was allowed to respond in the same issue and reminded readers of de Zárraga's role in the production of *Verbena trágica* and further questioned his impartiality by pointing out the larger role he had played in Hollywood Spanish-language productions since the early 1930s: "he has always lived off the industry, and has written almost all of the adaptations, and is part of the publicity staff of one of the studios."[51] In addition, Navarro challenged the foundation of de Zárraga's argument on several counts. First, although de Zárraga referred to a lack of artistic development among Mexican actors, Navarro pointed out that these are precisely the individuals imported by Hollywood for the production of Spanish-language features, with Fernando Soler and Tito Guízar among the most prominent. Navarro also denied that he had somehow impugned Latino immigrants, instead arguing that it is precisely because of this population that "we demand that they be offered something that agrees with their sentiment, instead of ideological translations that say nothing to their Latino perspective." While reiterating the box office success of Mexican films in Los Angeles, the critic nonetheless praised *Verbena trágica* as a worthy accomplishment (and would later pen a positive review of the film). At the same time, he also emphasized that "the success of one production does not in any sense destroy our argument that Hispano pictures should be written, acted, and felt in Spanish, under the direction of Hispano talent."[52] On this last point, de Zárraga wholeheartedly agreed, while admitting in a subsequent column that Hollywood had committed multiple errors in their Spanish-language productions. Nonetheless, he maintained that Los Angeles could indeed serve as a new center of Hispanic production, arguing that emerging cinemas in Mexico and Argentina are "not incompatible with what we could do in Hollywood if they let us, in an analogous form and an identical spirit."[53]

If such critical debates emerge from an ongoing history of interpersonal animosity and individual investment in particular projects and industries, they also revived the discussion of what might constitute a proper Spanish-language cinema and how such a cinema might successfully transcend national boundaries by appealing to the common cultural sensibilities of an entire continent. The debate once again centered on issues of cinematic content, industry labor, and the construction and representation of Latinos both on-screen and as an audience. It also coincided with a renewed attempt on the part of multiple entities to define a Pan-Latino spirit, to target a Latin American market, and to consequently abandon a purely national frame of reference that guided earlier film criticism. In contrast to a strictly nationalist orientation, for instance, director Jaime Salvador (who had recently completed the independently produced *Castillos en aire* [Castles in the air, 1938], with de Zárraga as screenwriter) proposed a more Pan–Latin American approach to Spanish-language production:

> In speaking of cinema in Spanish, we must make it with all the Spanish-speaking populations in mind, as their racial affinity constitutes an immense nation that has only political borders, but corresponds to a single sentiment, a single basic culture, a single literature—values that through their antiquity and beauty occupy a prominent place among the ancient cultures and literatures of the Universe.[54]

If such a declaration apparently coincided with Roosevelt's brand of Pan-Americanism and Hollywood's construction of the generalized Latin American as an image and an audience, some important distinctions remained, guiding critical forays into articulating a Pan–Latin American or transnational Mexicanidad. Perhaps most notably, unlike the earlier period of U.S. foreign-language production, the recent and prolific output of the Mexican industry provided an ostensibly authentic body of work, an intermedial articulation of cultural nationalism against which to compare the efforts of Hollywood. Even more important, as I outlined in the last chapter, this national industry was able to absorb international talent and influences while cultivating a continental appeal. In terms of textual content and its reliance on Latin American labor, the Mexican film industry itself represented an example of transnational Mexicanidad against which to evaluate the parallel efforts of Hollywood film. So, while critics like Navarro often attempted to mark clear distinctions between the national industries, these debates also demonstrate the extent to which such boundaries were consistently challenged, particularly by the transnational activities of talent and studios. More than working to devise criteria by which to evaluate an industry and its output, these formulations of transnationalism also functioned as a way by which these critics understood their own careers, an indication of their movement between nations and industries, and an attempt to account for the uniquely transnational positions of their constituency: immigrant movie audiences.

Beyond this initial round of critical sparring, the production and reception of a series of films starring Tito Guízar proved emblematic of emerging trends in Hollywood and the way critical discourse engaged with decidedly transnational modes of production and labor. As part of Hollywood's renewed production of Spanish-language and Latin American–themed films, Paramount Pictures released a number of features starring Guízar (which are apparently no longer extant). As a celebrity who had already gained significant fame in both the United States and Mexico, he was uniquely positioned to act in such films, particularly given their emphasis on musical performance. He had already established his career as a singer for a New York radio station in 1931, and his leading role in *Allá en el Rancho Grande* solidified his popularity on both sides of the border and throughout Latin America. Not surprisingly, Paramount contracted him to appear in English-language films that highlighted his musical abilities, including *Tropic Holiday* (Theodore Reed, 1938) and *St. Louis Blues* (Raoul Walsh, 1939), and in Spanish-language films in which he occupied more of a central role: *Mis dos amores* (My two loves, Nick Grinde, 1938), *El trovador de la radio* (The radio troubadour, Richard Harlan, 1938), *El otro soy yo* (The other man is me, Richard Harlan, 1939), *Papá soltero* (Single father, Richard Harlan, 1939), and *El rancho del pinar* (The pine ranch, Richard Harlan and Gabriel Navarro, 1939). From the perspective of star studies, figures like Guízar appealed to audiences by embodying or reconciling key tensions and contradictions. In this instance, the discourse surrounding Guizar (and other transnational stars) was particularly fixated on the way such individuals navigated the movement between two countries with their Mexican identity intact and how they reconciled national loyalty with the representational conventions of Hollywood. To this extent, his star persona and its reception coincided with broader concerns about transnational cinemas and coincident identity constructions.

The contracting of Guízar, along with other Latin American talent, was evidently calculated to avoid the interrelated controversies about representation and labor discrimination that accompanied the earlier period of Spanish-language production. Studio publicity often boasted about the hiring of Latin American talent, individuals like Guízar whose participation would guarantee a renewed authenticity of representation. Referring to *Tropic Holiday*, producer Arthur Hornblow Jr., in an interview with the *New York Times*, listed the Mexican talent hired for the production, assuring readers that they "were permitted to perform as they saw fit without any concessions to Hollywood's conception. They were not treated patronizingly, which is a common fault in the Southwest. . . . In other words, satisfactory results were obtained." The strategy, Hornblow explained, was to ensure that such films "will not only retrieve the market below the Rio Grande, but will provide America with a new type of entertainment."[55] As the *Hollywood Reporter* noted, this early stage of production oriented toward Latin America left producers "admitting they don't know which way it will go, but that it will be 'different.'"[56] Part of this difference consisted of drawing talent that sustained careers in two or more national industries, allowing U.S. productions to claim representational authenticity by association. Guízar's own career, while certainly exceptional, was also indicative of the tendency of many actors to move with relative freedom between the U.S. and Mexican industries (he also worked in Argentina). After his work with Paramount, for instance, he returned to Mexico to star in *Allá en el trópico* (Over in the tropics, Fernando de Fuentes, 1941), a rehashing of the ranchera genre that reunited the original cast of *Rancho Grande*.

Despite his popularity, however, Guízar's negotiation of an openly transnational stardom often drew criticism, particularly as his career defied a strictly national frame of reference and involved a regular movement between industries. To a large extent, this backlash was at least partially an extension of the way the Pan-American cycle constructed its audiences and represented the continent. On the one hand, his films often drew directly and unabashedly from an aesthetic of cultural nationalism as embodied by the comedia ranchera. In addition to his lighter skin, the charro costuming apparent in a publicity still for *Mis dos amores* (with costar Blanca de Castejón) is drawn directly from such films and would seem consistent with the visual construction of authentic Mexicanidad typical of the genre (see fig. 33). While undoubtedly intended to appeal to Latin American audiences, the same sort of iconography, when directed toward a U.S. audience, simultaneously evoked festive, exotic stereotypes typical of the imagery produced by tourism industries; they would soon become a mainstay of Pan-American musicals. This dilemma of bifurcated reception (whereby the

En Pleno Idilio

En una de las escenas de la cinta Cobián-Paramount, "Mis dos Amores", aparecen aquí foto-grafiados Tito Guízar y Blanca de Castejón, estrella e intérprete femenina principal, respectiva-mente. Nótese el traje típicamente mexicano de los artistas, cuya labor es juzgada en el artículo que aparece en esta misma página.   —Foto Ramos Cobián

Fig. 33. Publicity still from the Cobián-Paramount film *Mis dos amores*, starring Tito Guízar. *La Opinión*, August 21, 1938. Reproduced courtesy of *La Opinión*.

national in one context was perceived as exotic in another) was evident in the backlash against the comedia ranchera. While the visual and aural iconography of his U.S. films might resonate with the genre, they also clearly reproduced one-dimensional stereotypes.

The way that he and his films were promoted by Paramount, for instance, predictably reinforced conceptions of the musical Mexican and of Mexico as a colorful, exotic tourist destination. The press book for *The Llano Kid* (1939), for instance, suggested intermedial tie-ins along these lines, advising theater owners to partner with radio stations and local music stores that might promote guitars and Guízar's records. As the movie capitalized on "'the South American way' in music" the press book also suggested hiring a Mexican singer to perform live prologues, dressing him in a "colorful Mexican cowpuncher costume," and mak-ing "him part of a Mexican carnival in front of the theater." The press book also counseled exhibitors to transform their theater with plenty of Mexican tone to get across the atmosphere and locale of the picture. . . . A good plan would be to cover your front with compo board surfaced with tan plaster to resemble an adobe building. Cactus and tropical leaf outlines can be cut from green cardboard and applied to this front. Green, white, and red streamers of crepe paper, in Mexican national colors, can be suspended under the marquee and draped about the front and box office. . . . If you can get an attractive sombrero for your cashier, dress her up in a Mexican outfit with a colorful blouse, silver jewelry, etc.[57]

While this imagery indeed corresponds closely to the iconography of the ranchera's version of an authentic Mexico, it also reveals the motivations behind critics' discomfort with this visual and aural vocabulary and the way it was harnessed by the U.S. film industry to generate supposedly positive, authentic Mexican stereotypes.

As he participated in this regime of representation, Guízar often provoked resentment and suspicion among Mexican critics who questioned his loyalty to Mexico because of his constant movement between contexts and his popularity among multiple audiences. Perhaps as a proof of his loyalty, Guízar maintained a consistent presence among the Mexican population of Los Angeles. Within a single month in 1938, for instance, *Allá en el Rancho Grande* and *Amapola del camino* (Poppy of the trail, Juan Bustillo Oro, 1937) were rereleased at the Teatro California, and his films were apparently among the highest grossing in such venues. Guízar also made frequent live appearances, often performing at local premiers or benefit concerts. On June 20, 1938, he served as the guest of honor at a fundraiser organized by Mexican consul Adolfo de la Huerta, which was intended to contribute to the debt incurred by Mexico when it nationalized the petroleum industry in the same year.[58] While such appearances are undoubtedly evidence of the actor's generosity, they also served to emphasize his unflagging dedication to Mexican audiences. At a subsequent benefit for the health care fund of the Hispano American Alliance, Guízar affirmed that "I owe all that I am primarily to the Mexican public. And so I want to give them something of value. I have the true desire to be among my people, to extend my hand to my compatriots, and to contribute in some form to the work [the Alliance] is doing."[59]

Despite such efforts, Guízar and his work in Hollywood were met by continued ambivalence by the Spanish-language press. Even the title of Fidel Murillo's review of *Tropic Holiday* expresses a typical range of mixed feelings in this regard: "An Absurd Delight That Dignifies Our People." In this piece, Murillo admits that the film "correct[s] the concept held by North Americans of our romantic, Indo-Latino countries, emphasized by the films of years past." And although the production presents a wildly inaccurate "tropical salad" that mixes costumes from different regions, Murillo blames Mexican costumbrista productions for inspiring these absurdities, arguing that "at least Hollywood has the excuse of distance to account for its inexact ignorance of our popular characteristics."[60] Navarro offered a similarly ambivalent review of Guízar's next production, *Mis dos amores*. Most of the film's defects, he argued, resided in the script and its adaptation, and he speculated that "the dialogist sees life through a chronic indigestion, without finding the grotesque, without understanding the sense of humor that marks each of our actions." At the same time, Navarro, citing the musical performances and the unparalleled continental appeal of Guízar, predicted that "Spanish America is on the verge of seeing a film that it will like extraordinarily, despite its defects."[61]

The next of Guízar's Paramount productions, *El trovador de la radio*, proved significant on a number of levels. First, the film's director, Richard Harlan, was of Peruvian descent, a fact celebrated by critics as an important advance, an indication that by finally heeding the advice of Navarro and others, "producers have begun to see the light of reason."[62] Second, Navarro himself was employed to do Spanish script adaptation and dialogue direction on the production, and he served in this capacity on three additional films starring Guízar. Significantly, this marked his first involvement in Hollywood Spanish-language production, after years of launching criticism at the industry for its misguided practices in this area. Furthermore, for at least one critic, the film had achieved the ideal level of transnational exchange, adhering to a formula frequently proposed for both Mexican film and Spanish-language Hollywood productions. A. A. Loyo's glowing review of the film declared that the film "has at its base a union of international factors that have produced the combination of American technology with 'Hispano' ambience," a division of labor coinciding precisely to the perceived sensibilities of each nation.[63]

Perhaps most notably, however, the production of this film reignited a fierce transnational debate between advocates of Spanish-language Hollywood films and journalists defending the Mexican industry. Part of this conflict apparently erupted on the set of *El trovador de la radio*, when de Zárraga complained to Paramount about "incorrect phrases" being spoken by actors. He subsequently authored an article in a Mexican magazine (reprinted in *La Opinión*), denouncing writers hired by the studio (presumably Navarro) as "clumsy literary apprentices" and arguing that Hollywood should "close the door to intrusive and presumptuous illiterates."[64] Naturally, this initiated another round of hostile exchanges between the two, with Navarro accusing de Zárraga of systematic discrimination, reminding readers that he was "the first Mexican hired to write the dialogue for a film in Spanish" because "Spanish writers had taken it upon themselves to inform producers that Mexicans are ignorant of the language."[65]

While renewed Spanish-language production rekindled prolific debates about language usage, issues of representation, and labor discrimination, it also spurred a conflict between Latin American journalists and those working in Los Angeles. In particular, Mexican director Ramón Peón declared in *Hollywood Reporter* that because of its technological superiority, "Hollywood is the place to make Spanish pictures, and [that] the majors have the proper facilities for distribution."[66] Of course, Peón stressed the importance of tailoring such films to Latin American sensibilities and offered producers a set of eight guidelines to ensure the success of productions in both first-run venues and neighborhood theaters. The ensuing critical exchange between authors in *La Opinión* and the Mexican trade journal *Cinema Reporter* has been compellingly analyzed by Brian O'Neil and centered on two main issues: "(1) the perceived detrimental effects in terms of competition for markets and talent that Hollywood's Spanish film production would have on Mexico's own film industry and (2) the ability, or lack thereof, of Hollywood to produce high quality, 'authentic' Cine Hispano."[67]

The initial points of the debate were thus outlined in terms that stressed the inauthenticity of Hollywood production and the industry's tendency to co-opt international talent like Guízar. Roberto Cantú Robert of *Cinema Reporter* accordingly labeled Peón "Enemy number one of Hispano cinema" and declared that Hollywood Spanish-language films had traditionally exhibited "a lack of ambience and of characters truly identified with the idiosyncrasies of our peoples."[68] Nationalist rhetoric was also deployed to denounce the apparent exodus of other Mexican talent to Hollywood to participate in such productions, with Arturo de Cordova, Andrea Palma, and Jorge Negrete apparently among such notable personalities. *Cinema Reporter* conveyed the anxiety this migration occasioned among the Mexican industry and unions, predicting that such trends would further accelerate a crisis for national cinema and urging Mexican producers to pay high-profile talent promptly.[69] Another anonymous contributor, conceding that Hollywood Spanish-language films might become an inevitable fixture, nonetheless advocated for the maintenance of strict national distinctions, proposing that all such films be prominently labeled: "SPANISH CALIFORNIA MADE."[70] Not coincidentally, Mexican films during this period typically displayed a title that proudly declared their nation of origin.

If Navarro had once been accused of excessive, narrow-minded nationalism, this episode marks a shift in his own conception of Mexicanidad, one whose flexibility allowed for transnational conceptions of identity. As O'Neil has astutely pointed out, Navarro's intervention appropriately attempted to stake out a territory between a nationalist discourse emanating from Mexico and a celebratory embrace of Hollywood productions.[71] In a lengthy editorial, Navarro sarcastically criticizes a brand of Mexican nationalism that eschewed pragmatism and effectively denied the fact of transnational exchange: "Our patriotism touches the limits of intransigency. Mexico should be for Mexicans and no one else. By the same token, all things accomplished beneath the sky of our homeland belong to us completely." He further challenges the righteousness of Mexican journalists, declaring that he would "bet two to one that the cinema journalists of Mexico would not think twice before accepting a proposal to write scripts, dialogue, or publicity in the shadows of the studios of Hollywood. . . . Accepting money in exchange for artistic services does not necessarily mean renouncing nationality."

Defending the actors who had already traveled to Hollywood, he notes that they will earn more money in the United States but will also gain significant knowledge and experience, returning to Mexico with "a more solid capacity to act in front of the cameras."[72]

For a later article, Navarro interviewed director Gabriel Soria and actors Fernando Soler and Arturo de Cordova, allowing them the opportunity to defend themselves from the accusations of the Mexican press and further validate the journalist's own assertions. Soler affirmed that "we have come, because in all honesty, we have much to learn from the North Americans on a technical level if we want to improve the artistic level of our production." De Cordova further assured Navarro that "our trip, far from damaging Mexican cinema, benefits it, because whatever we manage to learn will be put into practice there, which is where our true place remains."[73] Navarro also predicted that the "publicity machine" of the studios would convert them into celebrities, further enhancing the prestige of Mexican cinema in the process. Again emphasizing the transnational dynamic apparently denied by Mexican critics, Navarro points out that "it is crucial to remember the fact—painful but true—that our prestigious figures always need to be consecrated abroad, so that the Hispano public recognize in them any value whatsoever," an arrangement apparently already confirmed by the fame of stars like Tito Guízar, Lupe Velez, and Dolores del Rio.[74]

Spanish-language Hollywood films in the late 1930s, particularly as they offered employment to Mexican journalists like Navarro and Los Angeles–based playwright and journalist Adalberto Elías González, thus prompted a somewhat conditional revision of conventional nationalism within film criticism. In subsequent articles Navarro continues to defend himself and others against accusations that they are somehow less Mexican or betraying their homeland by working in Hollywood. Thus he affirms that "twenty years of residence in the United States has not been able to extinguish my affection for that which is ours" and reminds readers that he has steadfastly argued that "cinema over there [Mexico] is superior to cinema here in its sincerity, color, and spirit."[75] In a letter to *Cinema Reporter*, González likewise defends the Spanish-language Hollywood production of *La inmaculada* (The immaculate woman, Louis J. Gasnier, 1939), reminding the publication's readers that many Mexicans, himself included, had worked on the film. Again, challenging notions of authenticity apparently espoused by nationalist critics, he forcefully asserts, "I believe that Mexicans that live here have just as much right to work and eat as our compatriots living over there. Consequently, attacking a film just because it was produced in Hollywood is a flagrant injustice."[76]

By espousing a position that allowed for qualified support of both the Mexican and U.S. industries, and the talent that moved between them, Navarro and others proposed an attenuated compromise between the more extreme discourses on either end of the continuum. Citing Navarro's own personal investment in Hollywood production, O'Neil points out that this sort of compromise produced a level of inconsistency and even apparent contradiction in his defense, as "the production of Spanish-language films in Hollywood allowed him to have his cake and eat it too. By defending the policy, he could argue that he was supporting Mexican artists and filmmakers while remaining true to his nationalist mantra of how Hispanic cinema must be made in Spanish."[77] As I have suggested, however, Navarro's position within and between film industries, rather than invalidating his argument, increasingly indicates an attempt to come to terms with the ambiguities of working on a transnational level, to articulate a coherent working philosophy for artists moving between contexts and confronted by multiple expectations.

Just as important, this marks an important shift in the conception of Mexicanness within Mexican immigrant press culture, creating a space for transnational and hyphenated identifications. Rather than wanting to merely "have his cake and eat it too," Navarro increasingly worked to articulate what it meant to be Mexican outside of Mexico and how one might sustain multiple loyalties and affiliations, a more complex, fluid notion of identity. Perhaps most tellingly, the articles written by Navarro in the course of this debate mark a significant adjustment of his and his cohort's initial positions, which had remained relatively consistent since the early 1930s: a condemnation of Spanish-language Hollywood films and a nearly unequivocal support for those produced in Mexico. His willingness to develop a new standpoint on both counts, however apparently inconsistent, thus marks a key transition. While still refusing to relinquish the centrality of the Spanish language and inveighing against the "hybridity" of assimilation, he nonetheless created an important discursive space from which to comprehend transnational production and even identity. While it would certainly be reductive to regard such a shift as the emergence of the Mexican American sensibility noted by George J. Sánchez or the articulation of a "third space" or "borderlands" discourse, it does suggest the necessity and willingness of such authorities to develop new conceptual frameworks and the waning centrality of the notion of México de afuera and its explanatory force.[78]

This moment does indeed mark the definitive decline of the concept of México de afuera in press culture and otherwise. Part of this was inevitably occasioned by a younger generation less likely to identify as Mexican nationals and the realization on the part of others (especially those with children) that a return to Mexico was increasingly unlikely or undesirable. Just as significantly, a number of the critics that espoused this philosophy either returned to Mexico or simply stopped producing criticism. In 1942, for instance, Frank Fouce organized a "grandiose farewell" for La Opinión journalist Gabriel Navarro upon his return to Mexico.[79] Quite appropriately, the function included the performance of one of his plays, a film screening, and a range of musical performances paying tribute to his substantial cultural impact on Mexican Los Angeles. The return of many of the exiled elite to Mexico during this period also heralded an equally crucial shift whereby San Antonio's La Prensa and Los Angeles's La Opinión began publishing in two languages, reflecting the fact that "bilingualism and biculturalism—Mexican Americanism—had begun."[80] The control exerted by elite cultural authorities and the middle-class economic network in Los Angeles further eroded with demographic shifts. As Sánchez notes, "the steady movement of Chicanos into East Los Angeles reduced the influence of Plaza-area merchants and professionals who had grouped around the consul to define the local agenda for Mexicans."[81]

World War II also witnessed the emergence of Mexican cinema's golden age, a prolific period of national production paradoxically supported by the U.S. State Department and Hollywood studios. While the OCIAA encouraged Hollywood to intensify its efforts in Latin America after the United States declared war on Axis nations, the financial and critical failures of Hollywood's Pan-American and Spanish-language films of the late 1930s convinced government officials and the film industry to adopt a different strategy. Namely, the OCIAA believed that by providing technical and financial support to the Mexican industry, it would indirectly serve as a pro-Ally (or at least non-Axis) ambassador to the rest of Latin America. A number of Hollywood studios constructed production facilities in Mexico (RKO invested heavily in the construction of what would become the nation's largest studio, Churubusco), while the entire industry allowed Mexican cinema, in the spirit of hemispheric cooperation, to garner a larger share of the Latin American market. These circumstances ushered in a prolific period of film production that earned critical and popular success on an international scale. Indeed, for many, the Golden Age has become synonymous with Mexican national cinema itself. This steady supply of quality films, along with a steady stream of immigration, would ensure the stability of Spanish-language exhibition in the city for a number of decades to come. Significantly, the intermedial synergy established during the mid-1930s only intensified during the Golden Age, as the Mexican industry finally produced a stable star system that was sustained in part through regular public appearances in downtown theaters. On all counts, the Golden Age marked the end of Mexican film culture as an inherently precarious, contested, and volatile phenomenon.

Curiously enough, Frank Fouce participated in the transnational production of nationalism represented by the Golden Age, taking advantage of his unique position as an exhibitor operating between the Mexican film industry and Hollywood. Just as he had regularly traveled to Mexico to secure productions for his theaters, he also began to act as an ambassador between the film communities of each nation. In 1941 Fouce organized the Motion Picture Producers Goodwill Fiesta in Mexico City, traveling with a significant numbers of Hollywood celebrities, including Wallace Beery, Frank Capra, Kay Francis, Laurel and Hardy, Mickey Rooney, and Norma Shearer. The itinerary included public appearances, a dinner with the Mexican Motion Picture Producer's Association and a meeting with President Ávila Camacho.[82] Alejandro Buena, head of the Mexican Department of Tourism, subsequently presented Fouce an award for spearheading this event, bestowing on him the title of "Ambassador of Goodwill."[83] Given his efforts in this arena, Fouce was subsequently employed by the OCIAA as a liaison to the Mexican film industry, heading a commission that assessed the capacity and needs of this sector and making recommendations to U.S. government and Hollywood.[84] Not only did this prolific output in turn secure the viability of Spanish-language theaters in downtown Los Angeles (and elsewhere), but this context of exhibition itself had provided a key interface through which this exchange would be facilitated in decades to come.

CODA: THE CALIFORNIA DEMOLISHED

The study ends at the point when Main Street ceased to be synonymous with Mexican entertainment, a shift already perceptible in my account of the late 1930s and the emergence of competing conceptions of transnational Mexican identity. Indeed, this historical moment marks a number of key transitions almost as drastic as those with which I began the book: the entrance of the United States into World War II; the flourishing of Mexican cinema's Golden Age; a renewed influx of immigration spurred by the guest worker, or Bracero Program (initiated in 1942); the embrace of a Mexican American identity by a younger second generation; the almost complete obsolescence of the México de afuera discourse; the closure of theaters along Main to make way for new construction; and the acceleration of white flight from downtown. The intermedial approach I have adopted in my analysis of the pre–World War II era would perhaps prove as useful to mapping these contextual and discursive factors relative to the ongoing representation and construction of Mexicanidad through film culture.

Perhaps the most notable of these developments initiated in the 1940s, particularly in terms of the history of Mexicans in Los Angeles, was the emergence of the Broadway district as the city's epicenter of Mexican cinema culture. In 1949, for instance, Fouce began operating the Million Dollar Theater, a movie palace constructed in 1918 and originally operated by Sid Grauman. Fouce converted the venue into the epicenter of Mexican cinema culture in Los Angeles, a showplace in which he would present the most recent releases from Mexico and feature performances by some of Mexico's most popular celebrities. By the 1960s the Corwin family would begin operating a number of theaters along this corridor, as the area became overwhelmingly dedicated to businesses serving the Latino immigrant population. By 1978 Spanish-language films continued to be shown in an impressive number of theaters along Broadway, including the Million Dollar, the Broadway, the Rialto, the Globe, the Roxie, and the United Artists, while the Los Angeles and the Orpheum exhibited Hollywood films with Spanish subtitles.[85]

Although this corridor and its relation to the Mexican immigrant population has yet to receive extensive scholarly attention, it nonetheless remains central to the historical memory of Mexican cinema and entertainment. The Los Angeles

Conservancy, for instance, has worked assiduously to preserve the buildings and character of the Broadway corridor, including its history as a Latino entertainment district. The organization collaborates each year with the nonprofit Latin American Cinemateca of Los Angeles (LACLA) for one evening of the Last Remaining Seats program, screening a classic Latin American film in a Broadway theater each year. While acknowledging and commemorating an important element of the city's past (and present), this act of historical memory almost entirely obscures the origins of Mexican film culture along North Main. Civic construction, the 101 Freeway, revitalization, and selective preservation (like Olvera Street) have largely erased its traces from the urban fabric. If Main may have once functioned as Broadway's ethnically heterogeneous other, its historical significance has been largely forgotten. And although reconstructions of this district, like the *Calle Principal* exhibition at the LA Plaza de Cultura y Artes, work to revive its memory, they do so at the expense of the complexity and contention at the heart of the city's cultural history. Main Street has been almost entirely exiled from civic memory.

The reasons for this erasure (physical and otherwise) are multifaceted and very much linked to the expediency and economic viability of urban history and civic preservation. This dynamic becomes evident in the story of the last Mexican theater along Main to be destroyed. In 1990 the California Theater, on Main Street and Eighth in Los Angeles, was demolished to make way for a parking structure. Built in 1918 as one of the city's first and most ornate picture palaces, the theater spent the 1980s as an adult theater before finally falling into disuse. The owners of the building—brothers Steve, Mark, and Dennis Needleman—had initiated these plans several years earlier but endured multiple delays as the city's Community Redevelopment Agency conducted a survey of the potential impact of new development on downtown historical buildings. Despite the best efforts of the Los Angeles Historic Theatre Foundation and others to have the theater designated as a landmark, the agency, in consultation with the Los Angeles Conservancy, concluded that preservation of the building would not be viable. Steve Needleman (echoing nearly a century's worth of Main Street discourse) cited conditions in the surrounding area as a key factor guiding this decision: "the theater is a health hazard, an absolute detriment to the area, a drug hangout." He predicted that "even if the theater were rehabilitated . . . the transients, prostitutes, and junkies who live in the area around the California would frighten off potential theatergoers." Bruce Corwin, whose Metropolitan Theater Corporation had once operated the venue, concurred, "There is no way for that theater to do business in that location. . . . The only thing to do is move on."[86]

As such comments suggest, the potential preservation of the theater hinged particularly on its potential for future use and, consequently, its compatibility with existing plans for downtown development. The late 1980s witnessed an acceleration of development proposals and investment in the area, a process shaped by ongoing negotiation between developers, city agencies, and multiple nonprofit organizations. Discussing the preservation of historical sites in Los Angeles, Jean Bruce Poole and Tevvy Ball have summarized the kind of factors that guide such decisions: "the site's historical value, the aesthetic and architectural values of its buildings and art, its importance to society as a place of living culture, its symbolic meanings to various segments of the community, its economic value as a place that generates revenue through tourism and commercial ventures, and so on."[87] Despite competing visions for the direction of preservation and development, a general consensus had emerged that efforts in both areas would be concentrated two blocks west along the Broadway Theater and the commercial district, which had already been placed on the National Register of Historic Places. With an unrelenting focus on Broadway and its potential for revitalization and profit, the fate of the California seemed peripheral and inevitable. Jay Rounds, executive director of the conservancy, explained it accordingly, "Had it been located on Broadway as a part of that district, it would have been possible to look at the chance of revitalizing it as a part of that group . . . but we haven't been able to come up with a viable solution. It should come down" (see fig. 34).[88]

Fig. 34. The California Theater in 1988. Photograph by John Miller. Tom B'hend and Preston Kaufmann Collection, Margaret Herrick Library, Academy of Motion Picture Arts and Sciences.

Obviously, the ongoing persistence of such discourse readily resonates with the rhetoric of "blight" and "slum" that city officials and developers have historically mobilized in the name of revitalizing and historicizing downtown Los Angeles. What remains absent from such constructions of Main Street, however, is an account of the businesses that flourished there and the potential significance they held for the city's immigrant populations. Indeed, prevalent narratives of decline and development frequently overshadow alternative conceptions and uses of urban space. Furthermore, the district's stigmatized status—namely, the ongoing equation of marginalized populations with criminality and vulgar entertainment—accounts for the relative neglect of such venues by the contemporaneous press, conservationists, and historians alike. Not coincidentally, limited archival traces remain of these theaters, their programming practices, and their patrons. Compounding this, by the 1980s the physical traces of this history had been almost completely replaced by civic buildings, highway construction, and assorted development, an erasure compounded by the distance of time and the vagaries of civic memory.[89] But the California Theater (and others in the area) is part of a crucial dimension of Los Angeles history during this period that scholars have only recently begun to investigate. By reconstructing this frequently overlooked history, this book has thus aspired to provide a new understanding of the urban development of Los Angeles during this period, the complexity of the city's entertainment landscape, the convergence of multiple film industries, and the way its Mexican-descent population was both affected by and contributed to all these phenomena.

❧

CONCLUSION

In the decades since the dispersal of Main Street as a Mexican entertainment destination, Los Angeles has experienced a range of far-reaching transformations and a spectacular growth. Aside from the aforementioned preservations of Broadway and Olvera Street, the physical landscape of downtown would likely prove unrecognizable to a Mexican immigrant of the 1920s and 1930s. North Main itself has been cut through by the 101 Freeway and occupied by civic construction. Even South Main, which preserved its seedy reputation well into the 1990s, has emerged as one of downtown's premier corridors of residence and nightlife for a population of young urban professionals; it is currently packed with fashionable wine bars, lofts, coffee shops, pet boutiques, and art galleries. In the past decade or so, Main has transformed from a de facto symbol of downtown's unseemly decline to a prime example of the incredible amount of investment dedicated to the area's rapid gentrification and redevelopment.

As the city has grown and changed, so has its Latino population. In addition to successive generations of immigrants from Mexico, Los Angeles has become home to a substantial Central American presence since the 1970s. Despite the end of restrictive housing covenants, many of the region's Latinos remain relegated by economic disparity to low-income neighborhoods. While still subject to discrimination and segregation at multiple levels, Latinos are nonetheless dispersed throughout Southern California, securing the area's reputation as the country's premiere Latino metropolis. While it is beyond the scope of this short conclusion to trace the changing relationship between this population, competing conceptions of urban space, the history of Los Angeles, and trends in media cultures since the 1930s, I would nonetheless like to demonstrate the ways in which such connections are still mobilized. This suggests the relevance and applicability of the method and framework I have pursued in this book to the analysis of contemporary media cultures and questions of transnational identity.

Although radio, television, print, and new media are inescapable elements of a Spanish-language or Latino media culture in the contemporary period (and thus worthy of analysis on their own terms), I will briefly examine the ways that the Hola México Film Festival mobilizes intermedial synergies in a manner continuous with yet distinct from arrangements in the early twentieth century, particularly relative to notions of transnational cinema. Despite hosting a significant number of Latino-oriented film festivals, this is currently Los Angeles's most prominent showcase dedicated exclusively to Mexican cinema. Held each May (and expanding each year), the festival was established by Samuel Douek in 2009, after he had inaugurated a similar venture in Australia. Although clearly possessing its own unique origins and history, the festival is to some degree an extension (or replacement) of a similar festival organized by the Mexican Consulate in the early twenty-first century in an effort to capitalize on Mexican cinema's apparent "New Wave" following the global success of *Amores perros* (Alejandro González Iñárritu, 2000) and *Y tu mamá también* (Alfonso Cuarón, 2001).

Similar to its predecessor, Hola México celebrates Mexican national cinema while situating it as a transnational phenomenon. As in the past, this dynamic relative to the site specificity of Los Angeles is linked not only to the distribution of films but to perceived audience composition and the binational circulation of talent. Speaking specifically of Hola México's attraction to local audiences, Douek explains that "part of the unique experience that this film festival [is] all about is that [it] allows the Mexican community, that by choice or circumstance cannot return to their native country . . . to enjoy the same cultural and film experiences that their friends and relatives have had in their native land." While evoking cinema as an element of transnational community formation and affirmation, the festival also integrates a more "exceptional" type of migrant into its articulation of the relationship between Mexico and Hollywood. As one online article explains, "the Opening Night red carpet of HMFF [Hola México Film Festival] has become legendary with an A-list of celebrities, including Mexican actors working in Hollywood, Hollywood actors, and Latin music stars coming together to celebrate the best works in Mexican cinema."[1] The *Los Angeles Times* aptly summarized the logic of the festival in its inaugural year: "L.A. audiences would seem to need no introduction to Mexican cinema. The city has the nation's largest Mexican American population, it's the adopted home of many of Mexico's leading actors, directors, cinematographers, and designers, and there are numerous venues and festivals here that regularly screen Mexican films."[2] The relations among Los Angeles, Mexican cinema, and the construction of "Mexican" as a transnational category, although perhaps typical of a globalized film economy, clearly resonates with iterations of Mexican cinema culture and the cross-border circulation of talent from Dolores del Rio and Lupita Tovar in the 1920s to more contemporary examples like Gael García Bernal and Guillermo del Toro.

To this extent, the festival also positions Mexican cinema as transnational public relations for the nation and its citizens (whether at home or abroad), a rhetoric that emerged with the earliest Mexican silent films of the 1920s. As in the past, this function is situated as a response to images of Mexico circulated by the U.S. mainstream media. As Douek has explained, "Mexico is not what is seen on current television networks or select news reports."[3] Elaborating on this logic, the Mexican consul for Cultural Affairs, Alejandro Pelayo, predicted in 2009 that "there is going to be a great opportunity for Mexico to show the world that we don't just generate problems and conflicts . . . but that we also generate riches of culture—past, present, and future."[4] The terms of difference between positive and negative images in this context echoes similar distinctions made in the past. Just as Pelayo attributes to Mexican cinema the capacity to correct the image of Mexico as a source of "drug-related violence [and] swine-flu outbreaks" (referencing the evocations of disease and violence common since at least the 1910s), Douek also claims that the variety of films selected present "a Mexico that's more modern, more cosmopolitan."[5]

While working against the positioning of Mexico on the wrong side of the divides between civilized and savage, cultivated and culturally backward, cleanliness and filth, political stability and lawlessness, and so on (with all the racial implications embedded in such terminology), Hola México also wages this representational battle on the familiar grounds of stereotypes. In the festival's 2012 promotional video titled "Adios Clichés," a Mexican gunslinger reminiscent of a bandido walks into a saloon and begins shooting the various embodiments of cinematic stereotypical icons of Mexico (actually, each side of his oversized mustache wields a pistol): a Mexican wrestler (or *luchador*), a mariachi musician, an Aztec dancer, a Chihuahua, a bottle of tequila, and a plate of nachos (even Frida Kahlo finds herself in the crosshairs). "Why am I mad?" asks the narrator. "Because I'm Mexican and Mexico is so much more than clichés."[6] As a parody and quotation of these clichés, the video's message is clear: that by screening films demonstrating the country's complexity and authenticity (which is paradoxically absent from the promotional piece itself), the festival works to counteract the problematic constructions of Mexico circulating in the mainstream media.

While this rhetorical framing corresponds to the multiple cultural functions typically ascribed to national cinemas, the festival also serves as a promotional vehicle for Mexican films in a foreign market. Its proximity to Hollywood is strategic in this sense, as it generates visibility for these films (and by proxy Mexican cinema) in an industry town, while nonetheless marking their distinction from Hollywood productions and addressing a specialized market. In this respect, the festival embodies the transnational dimensions of national cinema and their somewhat paradoxical relationship with Hollywood. Just as in the case with the comedia ranchera films, advocates of Mexican cinema work to create a necessary distance (in terms of content and cultural representation) from Hollywood while simultaneously aspiring to international distribution and sharing affinities (from generic conventions to talent) with the dominant film industry. While the exact terms of this alternation between competition and collusion with Hollywood has

changed over the decades, the continuity of this central dilemma within the production and distribution of Mexican cinema is nonetheless remarkable.

As is the case with other festivals, Hola México is not a mere reflection of
some preexisting conception of "Mexican cinema"; rather such events and their
programmers are among the agents that give shape to the very category itself. As
Liz Czach has noted, in the case of Canadian film festivals and the formation of
national cinema, "the festival circuit and festival screenings function to gather
potential critical, public, and scholarly attention for individual films and directors. While sales, foreign distribution deals, and the interest of talent agents are
some of the hoped-for outcomes of festival exposure, those films and directors
regularly represented in festivals are also likely to garner something else—critical
capital."[7] This is the kind of cultural distinction that facilitates a film's inclusion
within the category of national cinema and its history, particularly when national
cinema is framed almost exclusively as a body of prestigious, critically acclaimed
features. Consequently, I am less interested here in drawing conclusions about
the films screened at the festival based on thematic or generic concerns than I
am with highlighting the assumed equation between national cinema and the
narrative feature format. I do so not for the purposes of lamenting the exclusion
or marginalization of experimental, short, multimedia, and documentary works
(although this is, of course, worth noting). Rather, in the context of Hola México,
the feature format and its relation to national cinema serve a particular economic
function tied to its location in Los Angeles and its Latino population.

As with past iterations of Mexican film culture, Hola México operates within
and hence mobilizes a range of intermedial connections and cultural-economic
networks. Not surprisingly, these forces are instrumental to the construction
of and marketing to a Latino population. Of course, the festival is publicized
across media directly targeting the city's Latino population, including the web-
sites LatinoLA and Remezcla and the newspaper *La Opinión*, among others. As
with organs of press and publicity in the past, such venues share a mutually beneficial address to a Latino audience ostensibly united by cultural consumption.
The sponsorships of the film festival in 2013 alone reflect a similar orientation,
representing a cross-section of the enterprises most invested in the conception
of a Latino market: radio (97.9 La Raza), television (the local Telemundo station
and Dish Latino), and Alaska Airlines (which offers regular service to Mexico).

While this range of economic connections and investments are hardly surprising given the contemporary nature of niche and ethnic marketing in Los Angeles
and elsewhere, they have specific implications for the promotion and conception of Mexican national cinema. That is, while the almost exclusive focus on
features adheres to a conventional festival format and may indeed hold implications for the range of expression possible within such a context, it also indicates
the ongoing expediency of the format. That is, despite changes in technology
and an apparently ever-shifting landscape of distribution windows (and the
diminished significance of theatrical exhibition), the feature film still remains

the predominant form of international cinematic exchange. To this extent, sponsors like Dish Latino and Telemundo continue to be invested in the construction of Mexican cinema (and its appeal to Latino audiences) as it lends them visibility at a major event and indirectly promotes potential Mexican and Latino content for media platforms that identify themselves as such. In other words, if these platforms construct a Latino audience to attract advertisers, programming such content affirms and assists in this construction, in a manner reminiscent of the marketing discourse that promoted downtown theaters before World War II as truly Mexican. All parties involved in such an endeavor are hence invested in the conception and maintenance of this category through the production, distribution, and consumption of cinema.

As a town whose economy is fueled to a large degree by entertainment and culture, events like Hola México also serve as public relations marketing for the city itself. That is, if Los Angeles has branded itself as a cultural destination through a particular construction of the Mexican since the early twentieth century, its status as a global and culturally vital city also depends on sustaining this appeal. In a contemporary environment in which cities compete for investment and tourism, such unique, high-profile cultural events have become important factors that mark distinctions between places. As Julian Stringer has argued, film festivals have become a prominent component of the ways in which "cities have sought to establish a distinct sense of identity and community—an aura of specialness and uniqueness."[8] Not coincidentally, the locations of the 2013 festival situate this celebration of Mexican cinema within expedient evocations of the city's history tied to development and renewal. This bears out Cindy Hing-Yuk Wong's assertion that "film festivals provide a unique network through which all those involved in cinema may view the past, explore the present, and create the future," a dynamic that extends from the construction of national cinema to a festival's relation to its host city.[9] In the case of Hola México, not only did events take place at the aforementioned LA Plaza de Cultura y Artes across from the original Plaza and in one of Broadway's historical movie palaces, but the majority of screenings occurred at the LA Live complex. Featuring the Staples Center, the Nokia concert venue, a high-rise hotel, a multiplex, and an assortment of restaurants, the complex is a key facet of the rebranding of downtown Los Angeles as a major destination and economic engine.

Although this particular festival evokes history to situate the contemporary category of Mexican as marketable commodity—through film, related cultural events, and conceptions of the city—its particular construction of this category may defy or work against the familiar dichotomy of negative (violent, diseased, and nonwhite) and positive (pastoral, musical, and Spanish) images circulated during the early twentieth century. That is, if denigrating images facilitated earlier development schemes in downtown Los Angeles and positive constructions framed the Mexican as a potential tourist attraction, the concept of Mexicanness circulating through events like Hola México do not necessarily reproduce this stark binary, particularly as its brand of Latinidad is primarily pitched toward a Latino audience. Nonetheless, as in the past, constructing and representing the category of Mexican through cinema still proves expedient for a network of mutually dependent entities, including the marketing of Los Angeles as a global, cosmopolitan, and culturally diverse city.

More than simply asserting the fundamental role assumed by Mexican immigrants and their descendants in the shaping and very conception of Los Angeles, I hope to have demonstrated the utter centrality of visual and discursive representations thereof (through cinema culture in particular) to this equation. Examining the intermedial connections of film culture in both the historical and contemporary moment (and perhaps even the connections between them) still allows us to understand the discursive and physical sites of Mexican cinema as contested and ever-evolving terms. Conversely, while the construction of this population across media and borders for the purposes of marketing is a familiar fixture of contemporary culture industries, examining the origins of these dynamics in the early twentieth century fundamentally alters our understanding of the functioning of and intersection between Hollywood, Mexican cinema, immigrant cultural production and consumption, exhibition practices, and conceptions of urban space.

NOTES

INTRODUCTION

1. For accounts of the importance of Main Street to Mexican Los Angeles, see Douglas Monroy, *Rebirth: Mexican Los Angeles from the Great Migration to the Great Depression* (Berkeley: University of California Press, 1999), 44–45; and George J. Sánchez, *Becoming Mexican American: Ethnicity, Culture, and Identity in Chicano Los Angeles, 1900–1945* (New York: Oxford University Press, 1993), 171–187. For an overview of Mexican film exhibition in Los Angeles (primarily after World War II), see Rogelio Agrasánchez Jr., *Mexican Movies in the United States: A History of the Films, Theaters, and Audiences, 1920–1960* (Jefferson, NC: McFarland, 2006), 47–69.

2. Charles Ramírez Berg, "Colonialism and Movies in Southern California, 1910–1934," *Aztlán: A Journal of Chicano Studies* 28, no. 1 (2003): 84.

3. These population figures are drawn from U.S. Bureau of the Census numbers, as cited in Robert M. Fogelson, *The Fragmented Metropolis: Los Angeles, 1850–1930* (Berkeley: University of California Press, 1993), 77–78.

4. Josh Sides, *L.A. City Limits: African American Los Angeles from the Great Depression to the Present* (Berkeley: University of California Press, 2003), 15.

5. Robert Howard Ross, "Social Distance as It Exists between the First and Second Generation of Japanese in the City of Los Angeles and Vicinity" (master's thesis, University of Southern California, 1939).

6. Junko Ogihara, "The Exhibition of Films for Japanese Americans in Los Angeles during the Silent Film Era," *Film History* 4, no. 2 (1990): 81–82. See also Denise Khor, "Asian Americans at the Movies: Race, Labor, and Migration in the Transpacific West, 1900–1945" (PhD diss., University of California, San Diego, 2008), 1–2.

7. Linda España-Maram, *Creating Masculinity in Los Angeles's Little Manila: Working Class Filipinos and Popular Culture, 1920s–1950s* (New York: Columbia University Press, 2006), 5–6.

8. Mark Wild, *Street Meeting: Multiethnic Neighborhoods in Early Twentieth-Century Los Angeles* (Berkeley: University of California Press, 2005), 38. See also Carey McWilliams, *Southern California: An Island on the Land* (Salt Lake City: Gibbs-Smith, 1973), 289–294.

9. William Deverell, *Whitewashed Adobe: The Rise of Los Angeles and the Remaking of Its Mexican Past* (Berkeley: University of California Press, 2004), 6.

10. See William David Estrada, *The Los Angeles Plaza: Sacred and Contested Space* (Austin: University of Texas Press, 2008), 216–217.

11. Ricardo Romo, *East Los Angeles: History of a Barrio* (Austin: University of Texas Press, 1983), 11.

12. Matt Garcia, *A World of Its Own: Race, Labor, and Citrus in the Making of Greater Los Angeles, 1900–1970* (Chapel Hill: University of North Carolina Press, 2001), 139.

13. For an account of the factors motivating this shift, see Steven J. Ross, "How Hollywood Became Hollywood: Money, Politics, and Movies," in *Metropolis in the Making: Los Angeles in the 1920s*, ed. Tom Sitton and William Deverell (Berkeley: University of California Press, 2001), 255–276.

14. Richard Koszarski, *An Evening's Entertainment: The Age of the Silent Picture* (Berkeley: University of California Press, 1990), 104.

15. Mark Shiel, *Hollywood Cinema and the Real Los Angeles* (London: Reaktion Books, 2012), 7.

16. For a history and analysis of these stereotypes in U.S. cinema, see Juan J. Alonzo, *Bad Men, Bandits, and Folk Heroes: The Ambivalence of Mexican American Identity in Literature and Film* (Tucson: University of Arizona Press, 2009).

17. Jacqueline Najuma Stewart, *Migrating to the Movies: Cinema and Black Urban Modernity* (Berkeley: University of California Press, 2005), 17.

18. Key monographs in this area include Lizabeth Cohen, *Making a New Deal: Industrial Workers in Chicago, 1919–1939* (New York: Cambridge University Press, 1990); Peter Conolly-Smith, *Translating America: An Immigrant Press Visualizes American Popular Culture, 1895–1918* (Washington, DC: Smithsonian Books, 2004); Sabine Haenni, *The Immigrant Scene: Ethnic Amusements in New York, 1880–1920* (Minneapolis: University of Minnesota Press, 2008); Andrew R. Heinze, *Adapting to Abundance: Jewish Immigrants, Mass Consumption, and the Search for American Identity* (New York: Columbia University Press, 1990); and Kathy Peiss, *Cheap Amusements: Working Women and Leisure in Turn-of-the-Century New York* (Philadelphia: Temple University Press, 1986).

19. See Monroy, *Rebirth*; Vicki L. Ruiz, "'Star Struck': Acculturation, Adolescence, and the Mexican American Woman, 1920–1950," in *Building with Our Hands: New Directions in Chicana Studies*, ed. Adela de la Torre and Beatríz M. Pesquera (Berkeley: University of California Press, 1993), 109–129; and Sánchez, *Becoming Mexican American*.

20. Laura Isabel Serna, *Making Cinelandia: American Films and Mexican Film Culture before the Golden Age* (Durham, NC: Duke University Press, 2014), 11.

21. Denise Khor, "'Filipinos Are the Dandies of the Foreign Colonies': Race, Labor Struggles, and the Transpacific Routes of Hollywood and Philippine Films, 1924–1948," *Pacific Historical Review* 81, no. 3 (2012): 386–387; Khor, "Asian Americans," 30.

22. See Andrew Higson, "The Concept of National Cinema," *Screen* 30, no. 4 (1989): 36–47.

23. Laura Isabel Serna, "Exhibition in Mexico during the Early 1920s: Nationalist Discourse and Transnational Capital," in *Convergence Media History*, ed. Janet Staiger and Sabine Hake (New York: Routledge, 2009), 69.

24. Desirée J. Garcia, "'The Soul of a People': Mexican Spectatorship and the Transnational *Comedia Ranchera*," *Journal of American Ethnic History* 30, no. 1 (2010): 73, 74.

25. Aaron Gerow, *Visions of Japanese Modernity: Articulations of Cinema, Nation, and Spectatorship, 1895–1925* (Berkeley: University of California Press, 2010), 21.

CHAPTER 1 — CONSTRUCTING MEXICAN LOS ANGELES

1. For an overview of these slum discourses and the transformations of urban space they facilitated in the post–World War era, see Eric Avila, *Popular Culture in the Age of White Flight: Fear and Fantasy in Suburban Los Angeles* (Berkeley: University of California Press, 2004).

2. These population figures are drawn from U.S. Bureau of the Census numbers, as cited in Fogelson, *Fragmented Metropolis*, 77–78.

3. Edward J. Escobar, *Race, Police, and the Making of a Political Identity* (Berkeley: University of California Press, 1999), 22.

4. For a more comprehensive account of the factors contributing to this unprecedented movement of population, see Monroy, *Rebirth*; Sánchez, *Becoming Mexican American*; and David Gutiérrez, *Walls and Mirrors: Mexican Americans, Mexican Immigrants, and the Politics of Ethnicity* (Berkeley: University of California Press, 1995).

5. Romo, *East Los Angeles*, 31.

6. Ibid., 29.

7. Wild, *Street Meeting*, 38–61.

8. Sides, *L.A. City Limits*, 18.

9. See Elena Boland, "Old Show Magnates Irked by Bonds of Retirement," *Los Angeles Times*, October 27, 1929, B13. Other early nickelodeons along South Main included the Rounder Theater and the Picture Theater. See "Motion Picture Theaters of Los Angeles," *Rounder*, October 29, 1910, 86.

10. Throughout the manuscript I alternate between the designations "theater" and "teatro" to indicate the transition between entertainment options and audience composition of a particular venue, although both terms (with a few exceptions, as noted) refer to the same physical building.

11. "Los Angeles, Studio Center, Has Pioneer Exhibitors," *Moving Picture World*, July 15, 1916, 416.

12. Bruce W. LaLanne, "From Main Street to Broadway: Los Angeles Theaters, the Early Years, 1781–1932," folder 387, Tom B'hend and Preston Kaufmann Collection, Margaret Herrick Library, Academy of Motion Picture Arts and Sciences, Los Angeles, 18.

13. Henry O. Melveny, quoted in Paul Herbold, "Sociological Survey of Main Street, Los Angeles, California" (master's thesis, University of Southern California, 1936), 35.

14. See Jan Olsson, "Hollywood's First Spectators: Notes on Ethnic Nickelodeon Audiences in Los Angeles," *Aztlán: A Journal of Chicano Studies* 26, no. 1 (2001): 189.

15. Historic Resources Group, "Merced Theater Historic Structure Report," December 1997, El Pueblo de Los Angeles Historical Collection, 14.

16. Monroy, *Rebirth*, 19.

17. Stephanie Lewthwaite, *Race, Place, and Reform in Mexican Los Angeles: A Transnational Perspective, 1890–1940* (Tucson: University of Arizona Press, 2009), 41.

18. See Larry May, *Screening Out the Past: The Birth of Mass Culture and the Motion Picture Industry* (Chicago: University of Chicago Press, 1980), 43–59.

19. For an account of the initiatives reformers targeted toward immigrant women in New York, see Peiss, *Cheap Amusements*.

20. See Ruth Vasey, *The World according to Hollywood, 1918–1939* (Madison: University of Wisconsin Press, 1997), 22–23. See also Lee Grieveson, *Policing Cinema: Movies and Censorship in Early Twentieth Century America* (Berkeley: University of California Press, 2004).

21. Jan Olsson, *Los Angeles before Hollywood: Journalism and American Film Culture, 1905 to 1915* (Stockholm: National Library of Sweden, 2008), 189–222, 208.

22. Richard Butsch, "Changing Images of Movie Audiences," in *Going to the Movies: Hollywood and the Social Experience of Cinema*, ed. Richard Maltby, Melvyn Stokes, and Robert Allen (Exeter: University of Exeter Press, 2007), 300.

23. Olsson, *Los Angeles before Hollywood*, 253.

24. Lewthwaite, *Race, Place, and Reform*, 36, 53.

25. Phoebe S. Kropp, "Citizens of the Past? Olvera Street and the Construction of Race and Memory in 1930s Los Angeles," *Radical History Review*, no. 81 (2001): 37.

26. Olsson, *Los Angeles before Hollywood*, 168.

27. Henry Christeen Warnack, "Atmosphere to Main Street," *Los Angeles Times*, August 1, 1915, sec. 3, p. 1.

28. See Harry C. Carr, "The Film Show Boom in Los Angeles and Some of Its More Vivid Results," *Los Angeles Times*, October 13, 1907, sec. 3, p. 1. For Olsson's analysis of this image, see "Hollywood's First Spectators," 187–188.

29. See the Estelle Lawton Lindsey, *Los Angeles Record*, February 25, 1913, 4.

30. See Sánchez, *Becoming Mexican American*, 97.

31. William Wilson McEuen, "A Survey of the Mexicans in Los Angeles" (master's thesis, University of Southern California, 1914), 76–77, 70–71.

32. Ramírez Berg, "Colonialism and Movies," 81.

33. Giorgio Bertellini, *Italy in Early American Cinema: Race, Landscape, and the Picturesque* (Bloomington: Indiana University Press, 2010), 214. For other accounts of the "Americanization" and respectability of U.S. cinema during the period, see Richard Abel, *The Red Rooster Scare: Making Cinema American, 1900–1910* (Berkeley: University of California Press, 1999); Peter Decherney, *Hollywood and the Culture Elite: How Movies Became American* (New York: Columbia University Press, 2006); and William Uricchio and Roberta E. Pearson, *Reframing Culture: The Case of Vitagraph Quality Films* (Princeton, NJ: Princeton University Press, 1993).

34. Daniel Bernardi, "The Voice of Whiteness: D. W. Griffith's Biograph Films (1908–1913)," in *The Birth of Whiteness: Race and the Emergence of U.S. Cinema*, ed. Daniel Bernardi (New Brunswick, NJ: Rutgers University Press, 1996), 108.

35. Ramírez Berg, *Latino Images in Film: Stereotypes, Subversion, Resistance* (Austin: University of Texas Press, 2002), 68.

36. For more about this cycle of silent "greaser" films, see Gary D. Keller, *Hispanics and United States Film: An Overview and Handbook* (Tempe, AZ: Bilingual Press/Editorial Bilingüe, 1994): 13–16; and Frank Javier Garcia Berumen, *The Chicano/Hispanic Image in American Film* (New York, Vantage, 1995), 1–4.

37. See Richard Abel, "G. M. Anderson: 'Broncho Billy' among the Early 'Picture Personalities,'" in *Flickers of Desire: Movie Stars of the 1910s*, ed. Jennifer M. Bean (New Brunswick, NJ: Rutgers University Press, 2011), 22–42.

38. Arthur G. Petit, *Images of the Mexican American in Fiction and Film* (College Station: Texas A&M University Press, 1980), 40.

39. Ramón A. Gutiérrez, "Hispanic Identities in the Southwestern United States," in *Race and Classification: The Case of Mexican America*, ed. Ilona Katzew and Susan Deans-Smith (Stanford, CA: Stanford University Press, 2009), 186.

40. See Lewthwaite, *Race, Place, and Reform*, 32.

41. See David Montejano, *Anglos and Mexicans in the Making of Texas, 1836–1986* (Austin: University of Texas Press, 1987), 117–125.

42. See Claire Fox, *The Fence and the River: Culture and Politics at the U.S.-Mexico Border* (Minneapolis: University of Minnesota Press, 1999), 41–68.

43. Margarita de Orellana, *Filming Pancho: How Hollywood Shaped the Mexican Revolution* (New York: Verso, 2009), 8–9. See also Zuzana Pick, *Constructing the Image of the Mexican Revolution: Cinema and the Archive* (Austin: University of Texas Press, 2010), 39–68; and Aurelio de los Reyes, *Con Villa en Mexico: Testimonios sobre camarógrafos norteamericanos en la revolución, 1911–1916* (Mexico City: Universidad Nacional Autónoma de México/Instituto de Investigaciones Estéticas, 1985). See also Margarita de Orellana, *La mirada circular: El cine norteamericano de la revolución mexicana, 1911–1917* (Mexico City: Artes de México, 2010), 153.

44. For a comprehensive account of the "Brown Scare," see Romo, *East Los Angeles*, 89–111. See also Ramírez Berg, "Colonialism and Movies," 85–88.

45. Estrada, *Los Angeles Plaza*, 134.

46. Romo, *East Los Angeles*, 98.

47. Escobar, *Political Identity*, 55.

48. See Estrada, *Los Angeles Plaza*, 139–142, 150. For more on the Christmas Day Riot of 1913, see Escobar, *Political Identity*, 42–49.

49. Olsson, *Los Angeles before Hollywood*, 253.

50. Natalia Molina, *Fit to Be Citizens? Public Health and Race in Los Angeles, 1879–1939* (Berkeley: University of California Press, 2006), 54. For another account of the racializing impact of discourses on disease in Los Angeles, see the "Ethnic Quarantine" chapter in Deverell's *Whitewashed Adobe*, 172–206.

51. Norman M. Klein, *The History of Forgetting: Los Angeles and the Erasure of Memory* (New York: Verso, 1997), 55.

52. Nicolás Kanellos, "A Brief History of Hispanic Periodicals in the United States," in *Hispanic Periodicals in the United States, Origins to 1960: A Brief History and Comprehensive Bibliography*, ed. Nicolás Kanellos, with Helvetia Martell (Houston: Arte Público, 2000), 37.

53. See Sánchez, *Becoming Mexican American*, 108–125.

54. Doris Meyer, *Speaking for Themselves: Neomexicano Cultural Identity and the Spanish-Language Press, 1880–1920* (Albuquerque: University of New Mexico Press, 1996), 109.

55. For a more complete overview of Lozano's life and career (and *La Prensa* in particular), see Onofre di Stefano, "*La Prensa* of San Antonio and Its Literary Page, 1913–1915" (PhD diss., University of California, Los Angeles, 1983), 100–126. See also Richard A. Garcia, *Rise of the Mexican American Middle Class: San Antonio, 1929–1941* (College Station: Texas A&M University Press, 1991), 223–233; Francine Medeiros, "*La Opinión*, a Mexican Exile Newspaper: A Content Analysis of Its First Years, 1926–1929," *Aztlán: A Journal of Chicano Studies* 11, no. 1 (1980): 67–68; and Nora Ríos-McMillan, "A Biography of a Man and His Newspaper," *Americas Review* 17, nos. 3–4 (1989): 136–149.

56. See Dennis J. Parle, "The Novels of the Mexican Revolution Published by the Casa Editorial Lozano," *Americas Review* 17, nos. 3–4 (1989): 163–168.

57. Medeiros, "*La Opinión*," 75.

58. Di Stefano, "*La Prensa*," 86.

59. R. Garcia, *Mexican American Middle Class*, 233.

60. Juan Bruce-Novoa, "*La Prensa* and the Chicano Community," *Americas Review* 17, nos. 3–4 (1989): 150.

61. See Aurelio de los Reyes, "El gobierno mexicano y las películas denigrantes, 1920–1931," in *México Estados Unidos: Encuentros y desencuentros en el cine*, ed. Ignacio Durán, Iván Trujillo, and Mónica Verea (Mexico City: Universidad Nacional Autónoma de México, 1996), 26–27.

62. "Lo que nunca deberian hacer los mexicanos: Las películas denigrantes para México," *El Heraldo de México*, January 31, 1918, 2.

63. "Censura de películas," *El Heraldo de México*, February 17, 1918, 1.

64. Vasey, *World according to Hollywood*, 19.

65. Laura Isabel Serna, "'As a Mexican I Feel It's My Duty': Citizenship, Censorship, and the Campaign against Derogatory Films in Mexico, 1922–1930," *Americas* 63, no. 2 (2006): 225–244. See also Helen Delpar, "'Goodbye to the Greaser': Mexico, the MPPDA, and Derogatory Films, 1922–1926," *Journal of Popular Film and Television* 12, no. 1 (1984): 34–40.

66. John Mraz, *Looking for Mexico: Modern Visual Culture and National Identity* (Durham, NC: Duke University Press, 2009), 26.

67. Luis G. Pinal, "'El pasado' de Manuel Acuña adaptado a la pantalla," *El Heraldo de México*, July 19, 1925, 5.

68. "El actor Ben Wilson hará películas mexicanas," *El Heraldo de México*, July 19, 1925, 5.

69. Emory Bogardus, *The Mexican in the United States* (Los Angeles: University of Southern California, 1934), 60.

70. Gabriela F. Arredondo, *Mexican Chicago: Race, Identity, and Nation, 1916–1939* (Urbana: University of Illinois Press, 2008), 143.

71. Alexandra Minna Stern, "Eugenics and Racial Classification in Modern Mexican America," in Katzew and Deans-Smith, *Race and Classification*, 152, 160.

72. Sides, *L.A. City Limits*, 23.

73. Octavia B. Vivian, "The Story of the Negro in Los Angeles" (San Francisco: R and E Research Associates, 1970), 32.

74. For an account of how the presence of Mexican labor often disadvantaged African American workers in the decades before World War II, see J. McFarline Ervin, *The Participation of the Negro in the Community Life of Los Angeles* (San Francisco: R and E Research Associates, 1973), 26–37.

75. Khor, "Filipinos Are the Dandies," 386–387.

76. See España-Maram, *Creating Masculinity*, 128.

77. Khor, "Asian Americans," 18–64.

78. Arlene Dávila, *Latinos, Inc.: The Marketing and Making of a People* (Berkeley: University of California Press, 2001), 9.

79. Advertisements for Repertorio Musical Mexicano, *El Heraldo de México*, May 19, 1918, 2; January 2, 1918, 2.

80. "Por el Teatro Hidalgo," *El Heraldo de México*, May 30, 1918, 1.

81. Agustín Gurza, "A Cultural Treasure for the Ages," in *The Arhoolie Foundation's Strachwitz Frontera Collection of Mexican and Mexican American Recordings*, ed. Agustín Gurza, with Jonathan Clark and Chris Strachwitz (Los Angeles: UCLA Chicano Studies Research Center, 2012), 6.

82. Subscription advertisement for *El Heraldo de México*, in *El Heraldo de México*, May 20, 1919, 4. Similar language is used in a subsequent article that chronicles the paper's history. See 'El Heraldo de México' cuenta algo de su propia vida," *El Heraldo de México*, July 1, 1919, 5.

83. Advertisement for Mayo y Compañía, *El Heraldo de México*, May 10, 1919, 2.

84. "Lo que es y lo que puede hacer la Liga Protectora Mexicana de California," *El Heraldo de México*, March 13, 1918, 2.

85. See Richard Griswold del Castillo, *The Los Angeles Barrio, 1850–1890: A Social History* (Berkeley: University of California Press, 1979), 131–138.

86. Sánchez, *Becoming Mexican American*, 113.

87. See "El Heraldo de México," 5.

88. "Sesión solemne y pública en el Teatro Hidalgo el 15 de septiembre a las 9:30 A.M.," *El Heraldo de México*, September 5, 1918, 1.

89. See "Llamamiento a los músicos mexicanos," *El Heraldo de México*, September 12, 1918, 8.

90. Advertisement for Islas Brothers Music Company, *El Heraldo de México*, November 23, 1918, 8.

91. "La educación del pueblo mexicano," *El Heraldo de México*, June 23, 1918, 4.

92. "Arte Latino," *El Heraldo de México*, February 17, 1918, 8.

93. Advertisement for Teatro Hidalgo, *El Heraldo de México*, February 10, 1918, 6.

94. "Los Cancioneros Mexicanos," *El Heraldo de México*, February 21, 1918, 6.

95. *Calle Principal*, LA Plaza de Cultura y Artes, accessed July 22, 2014, lapca.org/la-calle-principal.

96. *Calle Principal* wall text, LA Plaza de Cultura y Artes, Los Angeles.

97. *Calle Principal*, http://lapca.org.

98. Hector Tobar, "A Valuable New L.A. Asset: Museum Tells Stories We Need to Know, but There Are Missteps," *Los Angeles Times*, April 22, 2011, A2.

99. Louis Adamic, quoted in Estrada, *Los Angeles Plaza*, 174.

100. See Nicolás Kanellos, *A History of Hispanic Theater in the United States: Origins to 1940* (Austin: University of Texas Press, 1990), 35–36.

101. Meyer, *Speaking for Themselves*, 7.

CHAPTER 2 — SPECTACLES OF HIGH MORALITY AND CULTURE

1. Charles Musser, "Towards a History of Theatrical Culture: Imagining an Integrated History of Stage and Screen," in *Screen Culture: History and Textuality*, ed. John Fullerton (Eastleigh, UK: Libbey, 2004), 3, 5.

2. Robert Knopf, introduction to *Theater and Film: A Comparative Anthology*, ed. Robert Knopf (New Haven: Yale University Press, 2005), 9.

3. Maxine Schwartz Seller, introduction to *Ethnic Theater in the United States*, ed. Maxine Schwartz Seller (Westport, CT: Greenwood, 1983), 6.

4. I of course draw this term from Benedict Anderson's foundational work *Imagined Communities: Reflections on the Origin and Spread of Nationalism* (London: Verso, 1983).

5. See Colin Gunckel, "Ambivalent Si(gh)tings: Stardom and Silent Film in Mexican America," *Film History* (forthcoming).

6. El Mago de Hollywood [Gabriel Navarro], "El cristal encantado, *La Prensa*, March 28, 1926, 12.

7. See Richard Maltby, "Introduction: 'The Americanisation of the World,'" in *Hollywood Abroad: Audiences and Cultural Exchange*, ed. Melvyn Stokes and Richard Maltby (London: British Film Institute, 2004), 2–20.

8. See Monroy, *Rebirth*, 165–207.

9. The actual dates of the revolution continue to be a matter of dispute. See Alan Knight, "Weapons and Arches in the Mexican Revolutionary Landscape," in *Everyday Forms of State Formation: Revolution and the Negotiation of Rule in Modern Mexico*, ed. Gilbert M. Joseph and Daniel Nugent (Durham, NC: Duke University Press, 1994), 24–66.

10. See in particular the anthology *The Eagle and the Virgin: Nation and Cultural Revolution in Mexico, 1920–1940*, ed. Mary Kay Vaughan, and Stephen E. Lewis (Durham, NC: Duke University Press, 2006).

11. "La 'Anahuac Film Corporation' es ya un hecho," *El Heraldo de México*, October 20, 1920, 2.

12. "El arte cinematográfico en Los Angeles, como medio de diffusion de la cultural mexicana," *El Heraldo de México*, October 4, 1921, 5.

13. "El Orfeón Popular Mexicano y Escuela de Artes de la Palabra ha tenido completo éxito," *La Prensa*, October 20, 1921, 1.

14. See Rogelio Agrasánchez Jr., *Guillermo Calles: A Biography of the Actor and Mexican Cinema Pioneer* (Jefferson, NC: McFarland, 2010), 44–45.

15. Agrasánchez, for instance, claims that Cuautla indeed dissolved after the release of its first film. *Guillermo Calles*, 46.

16. Advertisement for Teatro Hidalgo, *El Heraldo de México*, February 10, 1918, 6.

17. "Notas teatrales de 'El heraldo,'" *El Heraldo de Mexico*, February 25, 1920, 3.

18. See, for instance, the advertisement for the Fifth Annual Paramount Week, *Los Angeles Times*, September 3, 1922, sec. 3, p. 24.

19. Advertisement for Teatro Eléctrico, *El Heraldo de México*, April 10, 1919, 2.

20. "Revista Teatral," *El Heraldo de México*, August 8, 1920, 8.

21. Advertisement for Teatro Columbia, *El Heraldo de México*, May 29, 1921, 3.

22. Advertisement for Teatro Eléctrico, *La Prensa*, October 19, 1921, 5.

23. Advertisement for Teatro Plaza, *El Heraldo de México*, September 12, 1925, 6.

24. Kanellos, *History of Hispanic Theater*, 21.

25. Romo, *East Los Angeles*, 80.

26. Estrada, *Los Angeles Plaza*, 118.

27. Ibid., 109. See also Becky M. Nicolaides, *My Blue Heaven: Life and Politics in the Working-Class Suburbs of Los Angeles, 1920–1965* (Chicago: University of Chicago Press, 2002), 18–19.

28. Fogelson, *Fragmented Metropolis*, 154.

29. Richard Longstreth, *City Center to Regional Mall: Architecture, the Automobile, and Retailing in Los Angeles, 1920–1950* (Cambridge, MA: MIT Press, 1997), 5.

30. Camille Naomi Rezutko Bokar, "A Historical Study of the Legitimate Theater in Los Angeles, 1920–1929, and Its Relation to the National Theatrical Scene" (PhD diss., University of Southern California, 1973), 242.

31. In 1925 alone, as an example, West Coast Theaters planned to construct eighteen new theaters, and seven within the Los Angeles city limits. None of these were to be constructed downtown. See Arthur L. Brewer, *West Coast Theaters, Inc.: A Sketch of the Company and the Motion Picture Exhibiting Business from the Stand Point of the Bond House and the Conservative Investor* (Los Angeles: Banks, Huntley, 1925), 18.

32. See "What Shall It Be? Waldeck's Casino," *Los Angeles Times*, November 25, 1903, A4.

33. "Sheriff Ousts Casino Crowd," *Los Angeles Times*, February 20, 1905, sec. 1, p. 13. See also "Hoodoo's Prey Loses His Leg," *Los Angeles Times*, July 23, 1906, sec. 1, p. 13.

34. See Empress Theatre Program, July 22, 1911, Empress Theatre folder, box 4, Theater Program Collection (1146), Seaver Center for Western History Research, Los Angeles.

35. See "Baseball Fans Have Wild Time at Empress," *Los Angeles Times*, October 9, 1915, 16.

36. See "Italian Hercules to Wrestle Jim Londos," *Los Angeles Times*, September 25, 1919, sec. 3, p. 2; and advertisement for Teatro Zendejas, *El Heraldo de México*, September 26, 1919, 3.

37. "El teatro 'Latino' de Los Angeles," *La Opinión*, July 31, 1927, 10.

38. Lawrence W. Levine, *Highbrow/Lowbrow: The Emergence of Cultural Hierarchy in America* (Cambridge, MA: Harvard University Press, 1988), 184.

39. See Schwartz Seller, introd. to *Ethnic Theater*, 5-11.

40. Haenni, *Immigrant Scene*, 59.

41. Nina Warnke, "Immigrant Popular Culture as Contested Sphere: Yiddish Music Halls, the Yiddish Press, and the Process of Americanization, 1900-1910," *Theatre Journal* 38, no. 3 (1996): 323.

42. Bertellini, *Italy*, 273.

43. Elizabeth C. Ramírez, *Footlights across the Border: A History of Spanish-Language Professional Theater on the Texas Stage* (New York: Lang, 1990), 129.

44. Peter C. Haney, "*Carpa y teatro, sol y sombra*: Show Business and Public Culture in San Antonio's Mexican Colony, 1900-1940" (PhD diss., University of Texas at Austin, 2004), x.

45. Schwartz Seller, introd. to *Ethnic Theater*, 9.

46. For a history of Cantinflas's embodiment of the pelado from the *carpa* (tent theaters that attracted a primarily working-class audience) to the cinema, see Jeffrey Pilcher, *Cantinflas and the Chaos of Mexican Modernity* (Wilmington, DE: Scholarly Resources, 2001), 1-64.

47. Kanellos, *History of Hispanic Theater*, 20.

48. This estimated number is based on the research of Elizabeth C. Ramírez. For a list of the different positions occupied by individuals within each *cuadro*, see *Footlights across the Border*, 54.

49. Advertisement for Teatro Hidalgo, *El Heraldo de México*, July 11, 1918, 6.

50. M. Alison Kibler, *Rank Ladies: Gender and Cultural Hierarchy in American Vaudeville* (Chapel Hill: University of North Carolina Press, 1999), 11. For other scholarship on the ways in which the vaudeville industry strove to create entertainment that attracted audiences across multiple divisions of class, gender, and ethnicity, see Kathryn J. Oberdeck, *The Evangelist and the Impresario: Religion, Entertainment, and Cultural Politics in America, 1884-1914* (Baltimore: Johns Hopkins University Press, 1999); and Robert W. Snyder, *The Voice of the City: Vaudeville and Popular Culture in New York* (New York: Oxford University Press, 1989).

51. "Teatros," *El Heraldo de México*, March 9, 1924, 6.

52. "Teatrales," *El Heraldo de México*, August 29, 1924, 6.

53. Salvador Gonzalo Becerra, "Teatrales," *El Heraldo de México*, January 2, 1925, 5.

54. "Teatrales: Nuestros autores," *El Heraldo de México*, September 16, 1924, 5.

55. Medeiros, "*La Opinión*," 71.

56. "La crisis teatral en Los Angeles va de mal en peor," *El Heraldo de México*, July 28, 1925, 5.

57. Tomás Ybarra-Frausto, "Rasquachismo: A Chicano Sensibility," in *CARA: Chicano Art; Resistance and Affirmation*, ed. Richard Griswold del Castillo, Teresa McKenna, and Yvonne Yarbro-Bejarano (Los Angeles: UCLA Wight Art Gallery, 1991), 158.

58. See Rita E. Urquijo-Ruiz, "Las figuras de la peladita/el peladito y la pachuca/el pachuco en la producción cultural chicana y Mexicana de 1920 a 1990" (PhD diss., University of California, San Diego, 2004), 11–70.

59. Nicolás Kanellos, "Recovering and Re-constructing Early Twentieth-Century Hispanic Immigrant Print Culture in the US," *American Literary History* 19, no. 2 (2007): 448.

60. Daniel Venegas, *The Adventures of Don Chipote; or, When Parrots Breast-Feed* (Houston: Arte Público, 2000), 116–117.

61. Ibid., 117.

62. Tomás Ybarra-Frausto, "'I Can Still Hear the Applause': La farándula chicana; Carpas y tandas de variedad," in *Hispanic Theater in the United States*, ed. Nicolás Kanellos (Houston: Arte Público, 1984), 53.

63. For discussions of intergroup stereotypes and their function within other immigrant theater cultures, see Conolly-Smith, *Translating America*; and Schwartz Seller, introd. to *Ethnic Theater*, 8.

64. Urquijo-Ruiz, "Figuras de la peladita," 12, 16.

65. "Los precios de entrada en el Capitol," *El Heraldo de México*, April 18, 1925, 6.

66. Luis Alvear V., "Balance del año teatral en español de la ciudad," *La Opinión*, January 1, 1927, 4.

67. "El 'alma' del 'folklore' mexicano," *El Heraldo de México*, August 4, 1926, 3.

68. "Sonado triunfo de Guz Aguila en 'Exploración presedencial,'" *El Heraldo de México*, June 28, 1924, 5.

69. "El triunfo colossal del aplaudido autor Guz Aguila, en el Teatro 'Hidalgo,'" *El Heraldo de México*, June 13, 1924, 5.

70. Alvear V., "Balance del año teatral," 4.

71. See Monroy, *Rebirth*, 165–207.

72. Brief summaries of both works are included in Kanellos, *History of Hispanic Theater*, 51–52.

73. See Gunckel, "Ambivalent Si(gh)tings."

74. "El teatro 'Latino,'" 10.

75. Amber J. Arruza, "El triunfo de las revistas," *El Heraldo de México*, January 24, 1926, 3.

76. Carlos J. Vargas, "Teatrales," *El Heraldo de México*, January 8, 1926, 7.

77. Nicolás Kanellos, "Two Centuries of Hispanic Theater in the Southwest," in *Revista Chicano Riqueña: Mexican Theater Then and Now*, ed. Nicolás Kanellos (Houston: Arte Público, 1983), 29.

78. See Ramírez, *Footlights across the Border*, 74.

79. John Koegel, "Crossing Borders: Mexicana, Tejana, and Chicana Musicians in the United States and Mexico," in *From Tejano to Tango: Latin American Popular Music*, ed. Walter Aaron Clark (New York: Routledge, 2002), 99.

80. See 'El asesino del martillo,' nuevo drama de Adalberto González, en el 'Hidalgo,'" *El Heraldo de México*, October 11, 1923, 6.

81. Willis Knapp Jones, *Behind Spanish American Footlights* (Austin: University of Texas Press, 1966), 491.

82. See Elizabeth C. Ramírez, *Chicanas/Latinas in American Theatre: A History of Performance* (Bloomington: Indiana University Press, 2000), 18.

83. Gabriel Navarro, "¿Qué pasa con el teatro español en Los Angeles?" *La Opinión*, July 31, 1927, 4.

84. "Espectáculos de la semana," *La Opinión*, September 26, 1926, 5.

85. "Los teatros locales," *La Opinión*, December 8, 1928, 4.

86. Arturo J. Aldama, *Disrupting Savagism: Intersecting Chicana/o, Mexican Immigrant, and Native American Struggles for Self-Representation* (Durham, NC: Duke University Press, 2001), 35–68.

87. Manuel Gamio, *The Life Story of the Mexican Immigrant* (New York: Dover, 1971), 183.

88. Aldama, *Disrupting Savagism*, 49.

89. Manuel Gamio, *El inmigrante mexicano: La historia de su vida; Entrevistas completas, 1926–1927*, ed. Devra Weber, Roberto Melville, and Juan Vicente Palerm (Mexico City: Porrúa, 2002), 293, 340, 293.

90. Ibid., 329.

91. Ibid., 374.

92. Gamio, *Life Story*, 4.

93. Gamio, *Inmigrante mexicano*, 122, 231.

CHAPTER 3 — THE AUDIBLE AND THE INVISIBLE

1. Among these works are James Lastra, *Sound Technology and the American Cinema: Perception, Representation, Modernity* (New York: Columbia University Press, 2000); Douglas Gomery, *The Coming of Sound* (New York: Routledge, 2005); and, perhaps most notably, David Bordwell, Janet Staiger, and Kristin Thompson, *The Classical Hollywood Cinema: Film Style and Mode of Production to 1960* (New York: Columbia University Press, 1985).

2. Malte Hagener, "*Prix de beauté* as a Multiple Intersection: National Cinema, Auteurism, and the Coming of Sound," *Cinema et Cie*, no. 4 (2004): 109.

3. See Mary C. Beltrán, *Latina/o Stars in U.S. Eyes: The Making and Meanings of Film and T.V. Stardom* (Urbana: University of Illinois Press, 2009), 26; and Hershfield, *The Invention of Dolores del Rio* (Minneapolis: University of Minnesota Press, 2000), 20–25.

4. Vasey, *World according to Hollywood*, 115–122.

5. Richard Maltby, introduction to *Identifying Hollywood's Audiences: Cultural Identity and the Movies*, ed. Melvyn Stokes and Richard Maltby (London: British Film Institute, 1999), 5.

6. Beltrán, *Latina/o Stars in U.S. Eyes*, 39.

7. Romo, *East Los Angeles*, 142.

8. Richard Maltby and Ruth Vasey, "'Temporary American Citizens': Cultural Anxieties and Industrial Strategies in the Americanisation of European Cinema," in *"Film Europe" and "Film America": Cinema, Commerce, and Cultural Exchange, 1920–1939*, ed. Andrew Higson and Richard Maltby (Exeter: University of Exeter Press, 1999), 51.

9. For U.S. distribution and marketing efforts, see Jens Ulff-Moller, "Hollywood's 'Foreign War': The Effect of National Commercial Policy on the Emergence of the American Film Hegemony in France, 1920–1929," in Higson and Maltby, *Film Europe*, 181. Quote from Vasey, *World according to Hollywood*, 67.

10. Andrew Higson, "Polyglot Films for an International Market: E. A. Dupont, the British Film Industry, and the Idea of a European Cinema, 1926–1930," in Higson and Maltby, *Film Europe*, 284.

11. Maltby and Vasey, "Temporary American Citizens," 32.

12. Ginette Vincendeau, "Hollywood Babel," *Screen* 20, no. 2 (1988): 28.

13. Luis Reyes de la Maza, introduction to *El cine sonoro en México*, ed. Luis Reyes de la Maza (Mexico City: Universidad Nacional Autónoma de México, 1973), 13. For more on the perceived consequences of sound film in Mexico, see Angel Miquel, *Disolvencias:*

Literatura, cine y radio en México (1900–1950) (Mexico City: Fondo de Cultura Económica, 2005), 66.

14. Alejandro Aragón, "Vanidad de vanidades," *El Ilustrado*, January 3, 1929; see also "El cine de porvenir es el cine de voz viva," *Excelsior*, April 21, 1929, both repr. in Reyes de la Maza, *Cine sonoro en México*, 36, 73–76.

15. For "American propaganda," see, for instance, "El cine mexicano," *El Universal*, May 26, 1929; for "one of the pillars," see "El cine hablado y el idioma," *Continental*, June 1929, both repr. in Reyes de la Maza, *Cine sonoro en México*, 89, 108.

16. See Gilbert G. González, *Culture of Empire: American Writers, Mexico, and Mexican Immigrants, 1880–1930* (Austin: University of Texas Press, 2004).

17. See Monroy, *Rebirth*, 165–207. This intergenerational tension, particularly as it related to young women, has also been described by Ruiz in "Star Struck."

18. Gunckel, "Ambivalent Si(gh)tings."

19. Martine Danan, "Hollywood's Hegemonic Strategies: Overcoming French Nationalism with the Advent of Sound," in Higson and Maltby, *Film Europe*, 225.

20. Gabriel Navarro, "La pantalla: La película parlante en español y sus primeros pasos; 'Sombras de Gloria,' 'Charros, gauchos y manolas' y otras producciones hispano americanas," *La Opinión*, March 22, 1930, 4.

21. "Spanish Shorts Made at Fort Lee," *Variety*, October 2, 1929, 5.

22. For *Sombras de gloria*, see "Del cinema sonoro: La producción en español ha entrado en un período de franca actividad," *La Opinión*, November 14, 1929, 6; for *Charros, gauchos y manolas*, see "Intérprete de *Rosas rojas*," *La Opinión*, November 21, 1929, 6.

23. "Hoy es el estreno mundial en el Teatro México de la cinta 'Sombras Habaneras,'" *La Opinión*, December 4, 1929, 6.

24. See Robert G. Dickson, "Los orígenes y desarrollo del cine hispano," in Durán, Trujillo, and Verea, *México Estados Unidos*, 137.

25. "Par Made 82 Versions: 1930," *Variety*, January 21, 1931, 6.

26. See Abé Mark Nornes, *Cinema Babel: Translating Global Cinema* (Minneapolis: University of Minnesota Press, 2007); and Gaizka S. de Usabel, *The High Noon of Films in Latin America* (Ann Arbor: UMI Research Press, 1982).

27. De Usabel, *High Noon*, 80, 79.

28. "U.S. Execs Think Foreign Lands Will Feel Film Shortage This Winter: Situation Still Chaotic," *Variety*, September 8, 1931, 7.

29. Clarence J. North and Nathan D. Golden, "The Latin-American Audience Viewpoint on American Films," *Journal of the Society of Motion Picture Engineers* 17, no. 1 (1931): 21.

30. Mary C. Lanigan, "Second Generation of Mexicans in Belvedere" (master's thesis, University of Southern California, 1932), 51.

31. Henry Blanke to H. A. Bandy, October 23, 1930, Warner Bros. Archive, University of Southern California, Los Angeles.

32. These films were *La llama sagrada*, *El hombre malo*, *Los que danzan*, and *La dama atrevida*.

33. Vasey, *World according to Hollywood*, 96.

34. Rafael M. Saavedra, "La producción de películas habladas en nuestra idioma no está todavía orientada," *La Opinión*, December 10, 1929, 4.

35. "El cinema sonoro: Los cartabones de Hollywood—ofensiva contra las fotofónicas en México—el problema de los filarmónicos," *La Opinión*, January 1, 1930, 6.

36. Marvin D'Lugo, "Aural Identity, Genealogies of Sound Technologies, and Hispanic Transnationality on Screen," in *World Cinemas, Transnational Perspectives*, ed. Nataša Ďurovičová and Kathleen Newman (New York: Routledge, 2010), 166.

37. Hagener, "*Prix de beauté*," 102.

38. "El idioma español causa desorientación en Hollywood: Hay disparidad de criterio sobre si debe o no el acento neto de Castilla," *La Opinión*, December 22, 1929, 14.

39. Juan B. Heinink and Robert G. Dickson, *Cita en Hollywood: Antología de las películas habladas en castellano* (Bilbao, Spain: Mensajero, 1990), 50.

40. "Coast Worrying over Spanish Accent Talkers," *Variety*, December 4, 1929, 4.

41. "El problema de las cintas hispano-parlantes está a punto de desaparecer aquí," *La Opinión*, March 11, 1930, 4.

42. See Committee on Foreign Production memorandum, February 6, 1930, Foreign Language Committee: Foreign Language Problems, box 2, Academy Archives, Margaret Herrick Library, Academy of Motion Picture Arts and Sciences. See also T. Navarro Tomás, *El idioma español en el cine parlante* (Madrid: Tipografía de Archivos, 1930), 95.

43. Rafael M. Saavedra, "Punto final: La desorientación que sobre el lenguaje español existia en Hollywood, ha terminado; Los productores nos dan la razón," *La Opinión*, February 16, 1930, 6.

44. Committee on Foreign Production, quoted in Navarro Tomás, *Idioma español*, 95.

45. Lisa Jarvinen, *The Rise of Spanish-Language Filmmaking: Out from Hollywood's Shadow, 1929–1939* (New Brunswick, NJ: Rutgers University Press, 2012), 35.

46. Gabriel Navarro, "La pantalla," *La Opinión*, April 1, 1930, 4.

47. See Hagener, "*Prix de beauté*," 111.

48. Dickson, "Orígenes y desarrollo," 135.

49. Gabriel Navarro, "Un fotodrama intensamente humano, 'La Llama Sagrada,'" *La Opinión*, February 3, 1931, 4.

50. Gabriel Navarro, "La revolución del cine hispano," *La Opinión*, September 27, 1931, 5.

51. See Blanke to Felipe Mier, June 30, 1930, Warner Bros. Archive.

52. See Blanke to Bandy, June 30, 1930, Warner Bros. Archive.

53. See Heinink and Dickson, *Cita en Hollywood*, 50.

54. *El hombre malo* trailer script, folder 6, box 24, Warner Bros. Archive.

55. Letter to Jack Warner, May 26, 1930, Warner Bros. Archive.

56. Quote from Baltasar Fernández Cué, ibid.

57. Bandy to Blanke, June 3, 1930, Warner Bros. Archive.

58. "Problema de las cintas," 4.

59. See "To the Motion Picture Producers," *Hollywood Filmograph* 10, no. 5 (1930): 19.

60. Navarro Tomás, *Idioma español*, 54, 67.

61. See Archibald Reeve, "Como invadir los estudios del cinema," *La Opinión*, August 5, 1928, 14.

62. Navarro, "Fotodrama intensamente humano," 4, 5.

63. "Un proyectado boicot a las películas en castellano," *La Opinión*, May 25, 1930, 4.

64. Guillermo Prieto Yeme, "The American Made Spanish Talkies," *International Photographer*, August 30, 1930, 14.

65. John V. Wilson to Lester Cowan, Academy Archives. See also Guillermo Prieto Yeme, "Plan for Academia de Español Teatral," Academy Archives.

66. "La intriga de Hollywood," *La Opinión*, May 11, 1931, 4.

67. Gabriel Navarro, "La pantalla," *La Opinión*, June 5, 1930, 7.

68. Margot Valdez Peza, "Con Lupita Tovar en Hollywood," *El Ilustrado*, November 13, 1930, repr. in Reyes de la Maza, *Cine sonoro en México*, 226.

69. For perhaps the most methodical attempt to assess the composition of labor in Spanish-language Hollywood, see Carlos F. Borcosque, "La producción hispano parlante de 1931," *Cinelandia*, March 1932, 50.

70. "Teatrales," *La Opinión*, October 15, 1929, 5.

71. See, for instance, "Our Mexican Residents," *Los Angeles Times*, May 25, 1927, A4; and "Hands Off!," *Los Angeles Times*, February 18, 1928, A4.

72. For a full discussion of this rhetoric, see Camille Guerin-Gonzales, *Mexican Workers and American Dreams: Immigration, Repatriation, and California Farm Labor, 1900–1939* (New Brunswick, NJ: Rutgers University Press, 1996), 25–47. See also D. Gutiérrez, *Walls and Mirrors*, 46–56.

73. Monroy, *Rebirth*, 149.

74. Francisco E. Balderrama and Raymond Rodríguez, *Decade of Betrayal: Mexican Repatriation in the 1930s* (Albuquerque: University of New Mexico Press, 2006), 136.

75. Nicolás Kanellos, "An Overview of Hispanic Theater in the United States," in Kanellos, *Hispanic Theater*, 10–11.

76. Gabriel Navarro, "Teatrales," *La Opinión*, July 21, 1931, 4.

77. "End of Downtown's De Luxers Seen in Neighborhooder's Draw," *Variety*, May 13, 1931, 12.

78. Robert G. Dickson, "California Theater in the 1930s," *Marquee* 26, no. 4 (1994): 6.

79. Bruce W. LaLanne, "Fred Miller's New California Theater," folder 449, Tom B'hend and Preston Kaufmann Collection, Margaret Herrick Library, Los Angeles, 5.

80. "White Opens California as Spanish Theater: This Will Be Tryout Here for Spanish Made Pictures," *Hollywood Filmograph* 10, no. 10 (1930): 14.

81. "Spanish Film to Open California Theater Friday," *Los Angeles Examiner*, August 27, 1930, n.p. See also "Spanish Talker Roadshow for U.S. 'Foreign' Spots," *Variety*, April 9, 1930, 12.

82. See "Miller Installs Art Gallery in New California," *Los Angeles Examiner*, September 1, 1930, n.p.

83. "President's Aide Wires Praise of Miller Theater," *Los Angeles Examiner*, September 6, 1930, n.p.

84. See Gregory Goss, "Miller to Offer Notable List of New Features," *Los Angeles Examiner*, November 22, 1930, n.p.; and "L.A. Theater for Only Foreign Version Films," *Variety*, August 6, 1930, 13.

85. Dickson, "California Theater," 6.

86. Gabriel Navarro, "Una película que va a gustar al público latino: 'La Mujer X,'" *La Opinión*, April 12, 1931, 7.

87. "Una verdadera estrella de la cinematografía española ha surgido con 'Noche de Bodas,'" *La Opinión*, May 24, 1931, 7.

88. Gabriel Navarro, "Un peligroso 'boomerang,'" *La Opinión*, October 4, 1931, 5.

89. Curtis Marez, "Subaltern Soundtracks: Mexican Immigrants and the Making of Hollywood Cinema," *Aztlán: A Journal of Chicano Studies* 29, no. 1 (2004): 57–82. See also Curtis Marez, *Drug Wars: The Political Economy of Narcotics* (Minneapolis: University of Minnesota Press, 2004), 146–222.

90. Fidel Murillo, "De como la carencia de films hispanos ha resultado en una favorable reacción teatral," *La Opinión*, November 21, 1931, 4.

91. Gabriel Navarro, "La reapertura del Teatro 'México,'" *La Opinión*, July 17, 1932, 7.

92. Fidel Murillo, "Ha muerto el teatro hispano en Los Angeles: Hay que llorarlo," *La Opinión*, August 8, 1934, 4.

93. Fidel Murillo, "Crónica teatral," *La Opinión* December 21, 1934, 4.

94. "Teatrales," *La Opinión*, December 12, 1934, 4.

95. Rielle Navitski, "The Tango on Broadway: Carlos Gardel's International Stardom and the Transition to Sound in Argentina," *Cinema Journal* 51, no. 1 (2011): 30.

96. D'Lugo, "Aural Identity," 164.

97. Charles O'Brien, *Cinema's Conversion to Sound: Technology and Film Style in France and the U.S.* (Bloomington: Indiana University Press, 2005), 27.

98. Estrada, *Los Angeles Plaza*, 184.

99. Philip K. Scheuer, "Tourist-Critic Discovers el Teatro Leo Carrillo," *Los Angeles Times*, May 15, 1932, B13.

100. See Lee Shippey, "The Lee Side o' L-A," *Los Angeles Times*, June 15, 1932, A4.

101. "To Save Reminders of the Past," *Los Angeles Times*, May 18, 1924, 25.

102. Leo Carrillo, *The California I Love* (Englewood Cliffs, NJ: Prentice Hall, 1961), 8, 240.

103. Brochure for the Leo Carrillo Theater, 1932, Leo Carrillo Theater folder, box 4, Theater Program Collection (1146), Seaver Center for Western History Research, Los Angeles.

104. For a discussion of this fantasy heritage and its relation to Olvera Street, see Carey McWilliams, *North from Mexico: The Spanish-Speaking People of the United States* (New York: Greenwood, 1968), 35–47.

105. For "new playwrights," see brochure for the Leo Carrillo Theater, 1932, Seaver Center for Western History Research; for "plays and dancing," see Shippey, "Lee Side o' L-A," A4; for "dominion," see "Teatro Leo Carrillo Dedicated with Pomp," *Los Angeles Times*, June 13, 1932, A1, and "Teatro Leo Carrillo to Be Formally Dedicated," *Los Angeles Times*, June 12, 1932, B8; for "early Spanish ritual," see "Christening of Theater Will Be Gay," *Los Angeles Times*, June 11, 1932, A3.

106. See "New Theater Selects Play," *Los Angeles Times*, March 19, 1932, A7.

107. See "Leo Carrillo Theater Scene of Dance Revue," *Los Angeles Times*, November 13, 1932, B14.

108. Edwin Schallert, "'Passion Flower with Nance O'Neil Starred, Blooms Attractively in Olvera-Street Setting," *Los Angeles Times*, May 19, 1932, A16.

109. "Noted Stage and Screen Sponsors Theater on Historic Olvera Street: Leo Carrillo Backs Project," *Los Angeles Times*, March 1, 1932, A7.

110. Monroy, *Rebirth*, 10.

CHAPTER 4 — FASHIONABLE CHARROS AND CHINAS POBLANAS

1. Aurelio de los Reyes, *Medio siglo de cine mexicano (1896–1947)* (Mexico City: Trillas, 1987), 126.

2. Baltazar Fernández Cué, "Hollywood y las películas en español," *El Universal Ilustrado*, August 6, 1931, 44; De los Reyes, *Medio siglo*, 117.

3. See Higson, "Concept of National Cinema," 37.

4. Nataša Ďurovičová, "Vector, Flow, Zone: Toward a History of Cinematic *Translatio*," in Ďurovičová and Newman, *World Cinemas*, 94.

5. José María Sánchez García, quoted in Emilio García Riera, *Historia documental del cine mexicano*, vol. 1, *1929–1937* (Guadalajara, Mexico: University of Guadalajara, 1992), 211.

6. "Concesionario de la cinta *Santa*," *La Opinión*, May 14, 1932, 5.

7. Gabriel Navarro, "Ha surgido ya un competidor de Hollywood," *La Opinión*, April 3, 1932, 5.

8. "El Teatro México sera abierto por una empresa netamente mexicana," *La Opinión*, September 8, 1932, 4.

9. "Como se juzga en la prensa Americana la producción de cine en nuestro país," *La Opinión*, January 7, 1933, 1.

10. Helen Delpar, *The Enormous Vogue of Things Mexican: Cultural Relations between the United States and Mexico, 1920–1935* (Tuscaloosa: University of Alabama Press, 1992), 5.

11. "Una compañia nueva en la B. California," *La Opinión*, August 28, 1934, sec. 2, p. 6.

12. Gabriel Navarro, "Por que el cine de México es superior al hispano de aquí," *La Opinión*, May 21, 1934, 4.

13. Gabriel Navarro, "Los tres defectos de la película hispana," *La Opinión*, July 16, 1933, sec. 2, p. 3.

14. "La industria del cine en México," *La Opinión*, November 21, 1933, 4.

15. Gabriel Navarro, "Hagamos cine 'en español' y no cine 'traducido al español,'" *La Opinión*, December 25, 1932, suplemento ilustrado, 3.

16. Roberto Cantú Robert, "Instantáneas de la producción nacional," *La Opinión*, December 24, 1933, sec 2, p. 3.

17. Luis F. Bustamante, "Se han hecho cargos concretos a dos productores del cine nacional, en un escándalo que amenaza crecer todavía," *La Opinión*, March 13, 1935, 4.

18. X. Campos Ponce, "El cinema," *La Opinión*, June 9, 1936, 4.

19. A. Patiño Gómez, "El cine nacional en el mercado exterior," *La Opinión*, July 19, 1936, sec. 2, p. 6.

20. Fidel Murillo, "Otra película nacional, está ya rodándose," *La Opinión*, October 29, 1933, sec. 2. p. 3.

21. Fidel Murillo, "*Pro-patria*," *La Opinión*, July 10, 1932, sec. 2, p. 5.

22. Advertisement for the Gran Teatro México, *La Opinión*, December 17, 1935, 4.

23. Advertisement for *Juárez y Maximiliano*, *La Opinión*, February 3, 1935, sec. 2, p. 3.

24. Hortensia Elizondo, "El cinema en México," *La Opinión*, November 11, 1934, sec. 2, p. 6.

25. Ibid.

26. Ibid., December 29, 1935, sec. 2, p. 6.

27. "Un peligro para el cine," *La Opinión*, March 28, 1936, 3.

28. Ibid.

29. Kathleen Mullen Sands, *Charrería Mexicana: An Equestrian Folk Tradition* (Tucson: University of Arizona Press, 1993), 75; see also 237–263.

30. Olga Nájera Ramírez, "Engendering Nationalism: Identity, Discourse, and the Mexican Charro," *Anthropological Quarterly* 67, no. 1 (1994): 7.

31. Mraz, *Looking for Mexico*, 28–29.

32. Erica Segre, *Intersected Identities: Strategies of Visualization in Nineteenth- and Twentieth-Century Mexican Culture* (New York: Berghahn Books, 2007), 5.

33. Thomas Turino, "Nationalism and Latin American Music: Selected Case Studies and Theoretical Considerations," *Latin American Music Review* 24, no. 2 (2003): 175.

34. Mary Kay Vaughan and Stephen E. Lewis, introduction to Vaughan and Lewis, *Eagle and the Virgin*, 15.

35. See Mraz, *Looking for Mexico*, 31. See also Mauricio Tenorio-Trillo, *Mexico at the World's Fairs: Crafting a Modern Tradition* (Berkeley: University of California Press, 1996).

36. Joy Elizabeth Hayes, "National Imaginings on the Air: Radio in Mexico, 1920–1950," in Vaughan and Lewis, *Eagle and the Virgin*, 247.

37. Daniel Sheehy, "Popular Mexican Musical Traditions: The Mariachi of West Mexico and the Conjunto Jarocho of Veracruz," in *Music in Latin American Culture: Regional Traditions*, ed. John M. Schechter (New York: Schirmer Books, 1997), 46.

38. See Gurza, with Clark and Strachwitz, "El Mariachi: From Rustic Roots to Golden Era," in *Strachwitz Frontera Collection*, 116.

39. Eduardo de la Vega Alfaro, "Origins, Development, and Crisis of the Sound Cinema (1929–1964)," in *Mexican Cinema*, ed. Paulo Antonio Paranaguá (London: British Film Institute, 1995), 81. For more on Lara's impact on the recording and film industries, see Miquel, *Disolvencias*, 46.

40. See Sánchez, *Becoming Mexican American*, 124. For a history of the relationship of the consulate with the Mexican immigrant population, see Francisco E. Balderrama, *In Defense of la Raza: The Los Angeles Mexican Consulate and the Mexican Community, 1929–1936* (Tucson: University of Arizona Press, 1982).

41. Socorro Merlín, *Vida y milagros de las carpas: La carpa en México, 1930–1950* (Mexico City: Instituto Nacional de Bellas Artes/Centro Nacional de Investigación y Documentación Teatral Rodolfo Usigli, 1995), 19, 22.

42. A. Padilla Mellado, "De la hoja de plata," *La Opinión*, July 7, 1936, 4.

43. "Nueva oficina distribuidora de películas," *La Opinión*, October 13, 1935, 7.

44. James Lockhart, "Cinema Attendance Up in Mexico City," *Motion Picture Herald*, July 18, 1936, 34.

45. X. Campos Ponce, "México empieza a refaccionar a los productores del cinema," *La Opinión*, March 26, 1936, 4. For more on the cinema initiatives of the Cárdenas administration, see Seth Fein, "Hollywood and United States–Mexico Relations in the Golden Age of Mexican Cinema" (PhD diss., University of Texas, 1996).

46. A. Patiño Gómez, "Cinegramas," *La Opinión*, August 27, 1936, 4.

47. A. Patiño Gómez, "El cinema en México," *La Opinión*, August 26, 1936, 4.

48. "La formula de éxito para el cine mexicano," *La Opinión*, October 25, 1936, sec. 2, p. 6.

49. "Historia de nuestra producción parlante," *El Cine Gráfico Anuario, 1945–1946*, 1946, 173.

50. Ana M. López, "A Cinema for the Continent," in *The Mexican Cinema Project*, ed. Chon A. Noriega and Steve Ricci (Los Angeles: UCLA Film and Television Archive, 1994), 9.

51. De la Vega Alfaro, "Origins, Development, and Crisis," 83.

52. López, "Cinema for the Continent," 8.

53. Ibid.

54. Emilio García Riera, "The Impact of *Rancho Grande*," in Paranaguá, *Mexican Cinema*, 130.

55. Nájera Ramírez, "Engendering Nationalism," 9–10.

56. For a history of the Hollywood singing cowboy film, see Peter Stanfield, *Horse Opera: The Strange History of the 1930s Singing Cowboy* (Urbana: University of Illinois Press, 2002).

57. For an analysis of Autry's "Mexican" films, see DeeDee Halleck, "Las imágenes contradictorias del México de Gene Autry: Un análisis de dos películas; *South of the Border y Down Mexico Way*," in Durán, Trujillo, and Verea, *México Estados Unidos*, 37–40.

58. See Donald Andrew Henriques, "Performing Nationalism: Mariachi, Media, and the Transformation of a Tradition (1920–1942)" (PhD diss., University of Texas, 2006), 87–120.

59. "Mexico Will Institute Ten-to-One Film Quota," *Hollywood Reporter*, August 21, 1935, 1.

60. "Industry Now Considering Color in Films Seriously," *Hollywood Reporter*, October 28, 1935, 4.

61. X. Campos Ponce, "Cinegramas," *La Opinión*, January 28, 1936, 4.

62. X. Campos Ponce, "'Cielito lindo' sera llevado a la pantalla," *La Opinión*, April 12, 1936, sec. 2, p. 6.

63. In a series of articles reprinted in *La Opinión*, de Fuentes relates the production history of the film, including its debt to *Nobleza baturra*. See "Fernando de Fuentes relata la historia de '*Allá en el Rancho Grande*,'" *La Opinión*, February 5, 1939, sec. 2, p. 6.

64. "La llorona se estrenará en el California," *La Opinión*, September 3, 1933, sec. 2, p. 3.

65. Advertisement for the California Theater, *La Opinión*, September 3, 1933, sec. 2, p. 3.

66. "El 'California' abre hoy de nuevo sus puertas a las colonias," *La Opinión*, September 14, 1933, 4.

67. "Hoy se estrenerá *Sobre las olas*," *La Opinión*, October 11, 1933, 4.

68. La empresa de 'California' ha tomado a su cargo el 'Eléctrico,'" *La Opinión*, November 28, 1933, 4.

69. Advertisement for the California Theater, *La Opinión*, November 25, 1933, 4.

70. Publicity poster for the California Theater, Teatro de la Raza folder, box 17, Theater Program Collection (1146), Seaver Center for Western History Research, Los Angeles.

71. See also "Teatrales," *La Opinión*, August 14, 1934, sec. 2, p. 6.

72. Publicity poster for the California Theater, Seaver Center for Western History Research.

73. This practice was described in Chris Strachwitz, with James Nicolopulos, eds., *Lydia Mendoza: A Family Autobiography* (Houston: Arte Público, 1993).

74. For insightful accounts of the relationships between these media during this period, see Michele Hilmes, *Hollywood and Broadcasting: From Radio to Cable* (Urbana: University of Illinois Press, 1990); and Mark Glancy and John Sedgwick, "Cinemagoing in the United States in the Mid-1930s: A Study Based on the *Variety* Dataset," in Maltby, Stokes, and Allen, *Going to the Movies*, 155–195.

75. García Riera, *Historia documental*, 1:253.

76. For *¡Ora Ponciano!*, see the advertisements for the California, Eléctrico, and Roosevelt Theaters, *La Opinión*, July 1, 1937, 4. For *Allá en el Rancho Grande*, see ibid., August 15, 1937, sec. 2, p. 3.

77. Advertisements for the California and Eléctrico Theaters, *La Opinión*, August 29, 1937, sec. 2, p. 3.

78. For these and other examples, consult the Frontera Collection of Mexican-American Music, Chicano Studies Research Center, UCLA, accessed July 23, 2014, http://digital.library.ucla.edu/frontera/.

79. "Estrenan 'La cucaracha,'" *La Opinión*, December 30, 1934, sec. 2, p. 3. Both the Warner Bros. and RKO theaters downtown had premiered *La cucaracha* on November 15,

advertising the event in *La Opinión* as "Noche Mexicana" (Mexican night). See *La Opinión*, November 15, 1934, 4.

80. "Formula de éxito," sec. 2, p. 6.

81. Tom Gunning, "An Aesthetic of Astonishment: Early Film and the (In)Credulous Spectator," in *Film Theory: Critical Concepts in Media and Cultural Studies*, ed. Philip Simpson, Andrew Utterson, and K. J. Sheperdson, 291–310 (New York: Routledge, 2004), 86.

82. A. Patiño Gómez, "La película 'Alla en el Rancho Grande' marca una nueva era en la producción de México," *La Opinión*, November 27, 1936, 4.

83. Fidel Murillo, "Una opinión sobre 'Allá en el Rancho Grande,'" *La Opinión*, February 14, 1937, sec. 2, p. 3.

84. X. Campos Ponce, "Hay entusiasmo nacionalista en la producción mexicana," *La Opinión*, June 10, 1937, 4.

85. "Teatrales," *La Opinión*, July 7, 1937, 4.

86. Paul J. Crawford, "Movie Habits and Attitudes of the Under-Privileged Boys of the All Nations Area in Los Angeles" (master's thesis, University of Southern California, 1934), 40.

87. Eric Schaefer, *Bold! Daring! Shocking! True! A History of Exploitation Films, 1919–1959* (Durham, NC: Duke University Press, 1999), 391–392.

88. Herbold, "Sociological Survey," 1, 7–8.

89. Blaise Cendrars, *Hollywood: Mecca of the Movies* (Berkeley: University of California Press, 1995), 193.

90. "Abrirán nuevo teatro típico en Broadway," *La Opinión*, August 22, 1937, sec. 2, p. 3.

91. See "Latin Stars to Appear at Mexican Music Hall," *Los Angeles Times*, September 15, 1937, A16.

92. "Fouce habla y dice . . . ," *La Opinión*, September 19, 1937, sec. 2, p. 3.

93. Dina Berger and Andrew Grant Wood, "Introduction: Tourism Studies and the Tourism Dilemma," in *Holiday in Mexico: Critical Reflections on Tourism and Tourist Encounters*, ed. Dina Berger and Andrew Grant Wood (Durham, NC: Duke University Press, 2010), 6.

94. Lockhart, "Cinema Attendance."

95. "Gran éxito de Rancho Grande en su retorno," *La Opinión*, August 15, 1937, sec. 2, p. 3.

96. Harry Carr, *Los Angeles: City of Dreams* (New York: Appleton-Century, 1935), 10.

97. For Lydia Mendoza's account of performing at the Mason, see Strachwitz and Nicolopulos, *Lydia Mendoza*, 131–138.

98. Advertisement for the Mason Theater, *Los Angeles Times*, May 8, 1940, 27.

99. Salvador Baguez, "Spanish Play Elaborate," *Los Angeles Times*, May 13, 1940, 11.

100. X. Campos Ponce, "El cinema en México," *La Opinión*, October 4, 1937, 4.

101. See X. Campos Ponce, "El Bajío es una inagotable fuente musical de temas para el cinema mexicano," *La Opinión*, October 31, 1937, sec. 2, p. 6.

102. X. Campos Ponce, "Un defecto del cinema en México," *La Opinión*, April 10, 1938, sec. 2, p. 6.

103. Gabriel Navarro, "Dignifiquemos al cinema mexicano," *La Opinión*, June 26, 1938, sec. 2, p. 6.

104. "El cine mexicano," *La Opinión*, September 28, 1937, 2.

105. Higson, "Concept of National Cinema," 36.

106. Joanne Hershfield, *Mexican Cinema/Mexican Woman, 1940–1950* (Tucson: University of Arizona Press, 1996), 119.

107. Ernesto R. Acevedo-Muñoz, *Buñuel and Mexico: The Crisis of National Cinema* (Berkeley: University of California Press, 2003), 80.

CHAPTER 5 — NOW WE HAVE MEXICAN CINEMA?

1. Alberto Sandoval-Sánchez, *José Can You See? Latinos On and Off Broadway* (Madison: University of Wisconsin Press, 1999), 21.

2. "Lo que ha dado; lo que dará la 'Azteca Films," *La Opinión*, January 2, 1938, sec. 2, p. 3.

3. "Vienen muchos estrenos para el año actual," *La Opinión*, February 13, 1938, sec. 2, p. 3.

4. Alfonso Pulido Islas, *La industria cinematográfica de México* (Mexico City: México Nuevo, 1939), 83.

5. Tamara Falicov, "Hollywood's Rogue Neighbor: The Argentine Film Industry during the Good Neighbor Policy, 1939–1945," *Americas* 63, no. 2 (2006): 247.

6. Matthew B. Karush, "The Melodramatic Nation: Integration and Polarization in the Argentine Cinema of the 1930s," *Hispanic American Historical Review* 87, no. 2 (2007): 298.

7. Hortensia Elizondo, "Voz de alarma a la industria cine-mexicana," *La Opinión*, August 18, 1940, sec. 2, p. 6.

8. Hortensia Elizondo, "Exhiben una película de Tito Guízar," *La Opinión*, February 9, 1941, sec. 2, p. 6.

9. James Lockhart, "Exhibition Stems Mexico's Decline," *Motion Picture Herald*, April 1, 1939, 55.

10. For an account of the various factors contributing to this anxiety in Hollywood during this period, see Catherine Jurca, *Hollywood 1938: Motion Picture's Greatest Year* (Berkeley: University of California Press, 2012).

11. "Pix Eye Latin America," *Hollywood Reporter*, November 19, 1937, 1.

12. Jarvinen, *Rise of Spanish-Language Filmmaking*, 147–152.

13. Catherine Benamou, *It's All True: Orson Welles's Pan-American Odyssey* (Berkeley: University of California Press, 2007), 11.

14. Ana M. López, "Are All Latins from Manhattan? Hollywood, Ethnography, and Cultural Colonialism," in *Unspeakable Images: Ethnicity and the American Cinema*, ed. Lester D. Friedman (Urbana: University of Illinois Press, 1991), 406–409.

15. Allen L. Woll, *The Latin Image in American Film* (Los Angeles: UCLA Latin American Center, 1980), 65. See also Keller, *United States Film*, 111–149.

16. López, "Are All Latins from Manhattan?," 405. See also Shari Roberts, "'The Lady in the Tutti-Frutti Hat': Carmen Miranda, a Spectacle of Ethnicity," *Cinema Journal* 32, no. 3 (1993): 3–23.

17. A. A. Loyo, "Notas cineloyicas," *La Opinión*, September 20, 1940, 4.

18. Sandoval-Sánchez, *José Can You See?*, 24.

19. Angel Villatoro, "Notas del cine mexicano," *La Opinión*, June 2, 1941, 4.

20. Brian O'Neil, "The Demands of Authenticity: Addison Durland and Hollywood's Latin Images during World War II," in *Classic Hollywood, Classic Whiteness*, ed. Daniel Bernardi (Minneapolis: University of Minnesota Press, 2001), 368, 375.

21. See advertisements for the California and Eléctrico Theaters, *La Opinión*, June 9, 1938, 4.

22. See advertisement for Teatro Roosevelt, *La Opinión*, June 9, 1938, 4.

23. "Una reposición de 'Allá en el Rancho Grande," *La Opinión*, June 19, 1938, sec. 2, p. 3.

24. See, for instance, Gabriel Navarro, "Ante la crisis!," *La Opinión*, July 9, 1939, sec. 2, p. 6; "La realidad del cine mexicano," *La Opinión*, August 6, 1939, sec. 2, p. 6.

25. "Problemas de distribución," *Cinema Reporter* 2, no. 99 (1940): 1. See also "Al margen de nuestros problemas," *Cinema Reporter* 2, no. 100 (1940): 1.

26. Roberto Cantú Robert, "Nuestros problemas al exterior," *Cinema Reporter* 2, no. 101 (1940): 3.

27. "El Sr. Frank Fouce, de California, opine sobre la producción cinematográfica mexicana," *Cinema Reporter* 2, no. 102 (1940): 102.

28. Romo, *East Los Angeles*, 81, 65.

29. A church theater group, for instance, performed *La jaula de la Leona* there in 1932. "Función en el Teatro 'Unique,'" *La Opinión*, October 28, 1932, 4.

30. The newspaper *Belvedere Citizen* offers the most complete listings for these theaters during the course of the decade.

31. "Teatrales," *La Opinión*, September 15, 1933, sec. 2, p. 5.

32. Advertisement for Teatro Bonito, *Belvedere Citizen*, July 1, 1938, 2.

33. See "Los teatros," *La Opinión*, September 21, 1939, 4.

34. Advertisement for Unique Theater, *Belvedere Citizen*, August 4, 1939, 3.

35. "Ten Thousand Protest Nazi Persecutions," *Eastside Journal*, November 28, 1938, 1.

36. See advertisement for Brooklyn Theater, *Eastside Journal*, December 15, 1938, 2.

37. See advertisement for National Theater, *Eastside Journal*, July 20, 1939, 2.

38. See advertisement for Joy Theater, *Eastside Journal*, June 8, 1939, 2.

39. "Un mensaje a la colonia de habla española," *Belvedere Citizen*, February 14, 1941, 2.

40. Advertisement for Nuevo Teatro México, *La Opinión*, April 29, 1939, 4.

41. "'Perjura' sera estrenada en el teatro 'México' el próximo Cinco de Mayo," *La Opinión*, April 30, 1939, sec. 2, p. 3.

42. "Nuevo teatro para la colonia: El 'México' en la Calle Main," *La Opinión*, April 29, 1939, 5.

43. "Al público cinematográfica," notice published by Azteca Films Distribution, *La Opinión*, May 7, 1939, 8.

44. "Don Rubén Calderón habla sobre los proyectos de la 'Azteca Films Dist. Co.,'" *La Opinión*, May 7, 1939, sec. 2, p. 4.

45. See "Se estrenará 'Perjura' el Martes en el 'California,'" *La Opinión*, July 7, 1940, sec. 2, p. 3.

46. A. A. Loyo, "Teatrales," *La Opinión*, March 17, 1940, sec. 2, p. 3.

47. "El gran problema mexicano," *La Opinión*, March 24, 1940, sec. 2, p. 1.

48. Gabriel Navarro, "El cine de aquí y el cine de allá," *La Opinión*, June 19, 1938, sec. 2, p. 6.

49. Miguel de Zárraga, "Las películas españolas hechas en Hollywood," *La Opinión*, July 3, 1938, sec. 2, p. 6.

50. Ibid.

51. Gabriel Navarro, "Lo que olvidó el Señor de Zárraga," *La Opinión*, July 3, 1938, sec. 2, p. 6.

52. See Gabriel Navarro, "*Verbena trágica*: La vida en su peor tragedia; La desleatad," *La Opinión*, August 28, 1938, sec. 2, p. 6.

53. Miguel de Zárraga, "Punto final: El defensor del cine hispano en Hollywood halla el camino de Damasco," *La Opinión*, July 10, 1938, sec. 2, p. 6.

54. "Jaime Salvador expresa su sentir sobre el cine," *La Opinión*, June 12, 1938, sec. 2, p. 6.

55. Douglas W. Churchill, "Hollywood's Formula for Diplomacy," *New York Times*, April 3, 1938, 157.

56. "War Changes All Prod. Plans," *Hollywood Reporter*, October 17, 1939, 1.

57. Press book for *The Llano Kid*, Paramount press sheets, August 1, 1939–July 31, 1940, Paramount Collection, Margaret Herrick Library, Academy of Motion Picture Arts and Sciences, Los Angeles, 1–2, 4.

58. "La función de mañana en el T. 'California,'" *La Opinión*, June 19, 1938, sec. 2, p. 3.

59. "Tito Guízar irá a la tardeada," *La Opinión*, July 29, 1938, 4.

60. Fidel Murillo, "Un delicioso absurdo que dignifica a los nuestros," *La Opinión*, July 24, 1938, sec. 2, p. 6.

61. Gabriel Navarro, "Como vimos la reciente cinta de Tito Guízar," *La Opinión*, August 21, 1938, sec. 2, p. 6.

62. Gabriel Navarro, "Por Fin! Cinema hispano dirigido por hispanos," *La Opinión*, October 2, 1938, sec. 2, p. 6.

63. A. A. Loyo, "Película española; técnica americana," *La Opinión*, December 4, 1938, 4.

64. De Zárraga, quoted in Gabriel Navarro, "Analfabetos de Hollywood," *La Opinión*, November 27, 1938, sec. 2, p. 6.

65. Navarro, "Analfabetos de Hollywood," sec. 2, p. 6.

66. "H'wood Pix Can Hit Spanish Market with Keyed Prod'n," *Hollywood Reporter*, November 22, 1938, 3.

67. Brian O'Neil, "Yankee Invasion of Mexico, or Mexican Invasion of Hollywood? Hollywood's Renewed Spanish-Language Production of 1938–1939," *Studies in Latin American Popular Culture* 17 (1998): 91.

68. Roberto Cantú Robert, "Ramón Peón: Enemigo num. 1 del cine hispano," *Cinema Reporter* 1, no. 21 (1938), 3.

69. See, for instance, "La union de trabajadores se preocupa por el exodo de nuestros elementos a Hollywood," *Cinema Reporter* 1, no. 25 (1939): 3.

70. "¿Está en peligro nuestra industria?" *Cinema Reporter* 1, no. 22 (1938): 1.

71. O'Neil, "Yankee Invasion of Mexico," 88–89.

72. Gabriel Navarro, "Tempestad en un vaso de agua," *La Opinión*, January 8, 1939, sec. 2, p. 6.

73. Fernando Soler and Arturo de Cordova, quoted in Gabriel Navarro, "La embajada artística mexicana en Hollywood," *La Opinión*, January 22, 1939, sec. 2, p. 6.

74. Navarro, "Tempestad en un vaso," sec. 2, p. 6.

75. Ibid.

76. "De Los Angeles, CAL, se nos envia una carta . . . ," *Cinema Reporter* 1, no. 50 (1939): 3.

77. O'Neil, "Yankee Invasion of Mexico," 94.

78. See Sánchez, *Becoming Mexican American*. For "third space" or "borderlands" discourse, see David G. Gutiérrez, "Migration, Emergent Ethnicity, and the 'Third Space': The Shifting Politics of Nationalism in Greater Mexico," *Journal of American History* 86, no. 2 (1999): 481–517.

79. See advertisements for the California and Roosevelt Theaters, *La Opinión*, March 4, 1942, 3.

80. Garcia, *Mexican American Middle Class*, 252.

81. Sánchez, *Becoming Mexican American*, 229.

82. See William Wallace, "The Stars Invade Mexico," *Movie-Radio Guide*, May 17, 1941, 1.

83. Significativa distinción a Francisco Fouce," *La Opinión*, July 6, 1941, sec. 2, p. 3.

84. See Francisco Fouce, "A la colonia mexicana," *La Opinión*, September 12, 1942, 8.

85. Richard Houdek, "Sleeping Beauties," *First Run*, suppl., *Los Angeles Times*, June 4, 1978, 34.

86. Darrell Dawsey, "Once-Glamorous Film Palace to Fall to Wrecking Ball," *Los Angeles Times*, September 5, 1990, B4.

87. Jean Bruce Poole and Tevvy Ball, *El Pueblo: The Historic Heart of Los Angeles* (Los Angeles: Getty Conservation Institute/Getty Museum, 2002), 85.

88. Jay Rounds, quoted in Dawsey, "Once-Glamorous Film Palace," B4. See also "California Theater," *Los Angeles Times*, September 20, 1990, 7; "Stand on Theater Altered after $10,000 Gift," *Los Angeles Times*, September 28, 1990, 3; and "Conservancy Donation," *Los Angeles Times*, October 20, 1990, 6.

89. In a two-part series, film historian Robert G. Dickson presented a detailed history of the theater and its importance to Mexican cultural life in Los Angeles. See "El Teatro California: Una tradición cultural de Los Angeles vencida por el espíritu de la modernidad," *La Opinión*, March 1, 1992, E1; and Dickson, "El Teatro California y el legado de Francisco Fouce," *La Opinión*, March 8, 1992, E3.

CONCLUSION

1. Robin Menken, "¡Adios Clichés! ¡Hola México! The 2012 Hola México Film Festival," Cinema without Borders, May 26, 2012, http://cinemawithoutborders.com/festivals/3079-hola-mexico-2012-film-festival.html.

2. Reed Johnson, "Hola Mexico Film Festival Comes to L.A.," *Los Angeles Times*, June 9, 2006.

3. Samuel Douek, quoted in Afroxander, "¡Adiós Clichés! Hola Mexico Film Festival Returns to L.A.," Remezcla, May 21, 2012, www.remezcla.com/2012/latin/hola-mexico-film-festival-returns-to-1-a/.

4. Reed Johnson, "Festival a Reminder of Mexican Films' Reach," *Los Angeles Times*, June 9, 2009.

5. Douek, quoted in Johnson, "Hola Mexico Film Festival."

6. "Adios Cliches—Hola México Film Festival. Los Angeles 24–30 Mayo, 2012," YouTube video, 1:00, May 15, 2012, www.youtube.com/watch?v=3vAVT3cvdo8.

7. Liz Czach, "Film Festivals, Programming, and the Building of a National Cinema," *Moving Image* 4, no. 1 (2004): 82.

8. Julian Stringer, "Global Cities and the International Festival Economy," in *Cinema and the City: Film and Urban Societies in a Global Context*, ed. Mark Shiel and Tony Fitzmaurice (Malden, MA: Blackwell, 2001), 137.

9. Cindy Hing-Yuk Wong, *Film Festivals: Culture, People, and Power on the Global Screen* (New Brunswick, NJ: Rutgers University Press, 2011), 2.

BIBLIOGRAPHY

Abel, Richard. "G. M. Anderson: 'Broncho Billy' among the Early 'Picture Personalities.'" In *Flickers of Desire: Movie Stars of the 1910s*, edited by Jennifer M. Bean, 22–42. New Brunswick, NJ: Rutgers University Press, 2011.

———. *The Red Rooster Scare: Making Cinema American, 1900–1910*. Berkeley: University of California Press, 1999.

Acevedo-Muñoz, Ernesto R. *Buñuel and Mexico: The Crisis of National Cinema*. Berkeley: University of California Press, 2003.

"Adios Cliches—Hola México Film Festival. Los Angeles 24–30 Mayo, 2012." YouTube video, 1:00. May 15, 2012. www.youtube.com/watch?v=3vAVT3cvdo8.

Afroxander, "¡Adiós Clichés! Hola Mexico Film Festival Returns to L.A." Remezcla. May 21, 2012. www.remezcla.com/2012/latin/hola-mexico-film-festival-returns-to-1-a/.

Agrasánchez, Rogelio, Jr. *Guillermo Calles: A Biography of the Actor and Mexican Cinema Pioneer*. Jefferson, NC: McFarland, 2010.

———. *Mexican Movies in the United States: A History of the Films, Theaters, and Audiences, 1920–1960*. Jefferson, NC: McFarland, 2006.

Aldama, Arturo J. *Disrupting Savagism: Intersecting Chicana/o, Mexican Immigrant, and Native American Struggles for Self-Representation*. Durham, NC: Duke University Press, 2001.

Allen, Robert C. "From Exhibition to Reception: Reflections on the Audience in Film History." In *Screen Histories: A Screen Reader*, edited by Annette Kuhn and Jackie Stacey, 13–21. Oxford: Clarendon, 1998.

———. "Manhattan Myopia; or, Oh! Iowa! Robert C. Allen on Ben Singer's 'Manhattan Nickelodeons: New Data on Audiences and Exhibitors.'" *Cinema Journal* 35, no. 3 (1996): 75–103.

———. "Motion Picture Exhibition in Manhattan, 1906–1912: Beyond the Nickelodeon." *Cinema Journal* 18, no. 2 (1979): 2–15.

"Al margen de nuestros problemas." *Cinema Reporter* 2, no. 100 (1940): 1, 7.

Alonzo, Juan J. *Bad Men, Bandits, and Folk Heroes: The Ambivalence of Mexican American Identity in Literature and Film*. Tucson: University of Arizona Press, 2009.

Anderson, Benedict. *Imagined Communities: Reflections on the Origin and Spread of Nationalism*. London: Verso, 1983.

Arredondo, Gabriela F. *Mexican Chicago: Race, Identity, and Nation, 1916–1939*. Urbana: University of Illinois Press, 2008.

Avila, Eric. *Popular Culture in the Age of White Flight: Fear and Fantasy in Suburban Los Angeles*. Berkeley: University of California Press, 2004.

Balderrama, Francisco E. *In Defense of la Raza: The Los Angeles Mexican Consulate and the Mexican Community, 1929–1936*. Tucson: University of Arizona Press, 1982.

Balderrama, Francisco E., and Raymond Rodríguez. *Decade of Betrayal: Mexican Repatriation in the 1930s*. Albuquerque: University of New Mexico Press, 2006.

Barber, Stephen. *Projected Cities: Cinema and Urban Space*. London: Reaktion Books, 2002.

Beltrán, Mary C. *Latina/o Stars in U.S. Eyes: The Making and Meanings of Film and T.V. Stardom*. Urbana: University of Illinois Press, 2009.

Benamou, Catherine. *It's All True: Orson Welles's Pan-American Odyssey*. Berkeley: University of California Press, 2007.

Berger, Dina, and Andrew Grant Wood. "Introduction: Tourism Studies and the Tourism Dilemma." In *Holiday in Mexico: Critical Reflections on Tourism and Tourist Encounters*, edited by Dina Berger and Andrew Grant Wood, 1–20. Durham, NC: Duke University Press, 2010.

Bernardi, Daniel. "The Voice of Whiteness: D. W. Griffith's Biograph Films (1908–1913)." In *The Birth of Whiteness: Race and the Emergence of U.S. Cinema*, edited by Daniel Bernardi, 103–128. New Brunswick, NJ: Rutgers University Press, 1996.

Bertellini, Giorgio. *Italy in Early American Cinema: Race, Landscape, and the Picturesque*. Bloomington: Indiana University Press, 2010.

Bogardus, Emory. *The Mexican in the United States*. Los Angeles: University of Southern California, 1934.

Bordwell, David, Janet Staiger, and Kristin Thompson. *The Classical Hollywood Cinema: Film Style and Mode of Production to 1960*. New York: Columbia University Press, 1985.

Brewer, Arthur L. *West Coast Theaters, Inc.: A Sketch of the Company and the Motion Picture Exhibiting Business from the Stand Point of the Bond House and the Conservative Investor*. Los Angeles: Banks, Huntley, 1925.

Bruce-Novoa, Juan. "*La Prensa* and the Chicano Community." *Americas Review* 17, nos. 3–4 (1989): 150–156.

Butsch, Richard. "Changing Images of Movie Audiences." In Maltby, Stokes, and Allen, *Going to the Movies*, 293–306.

Carr, Harry. *Los Angeles: City of Dreams*. New York: Appleton-Century, 1935.

Carrillo, Leo. *The California I Love*. Englewood Cliffs, NJ: Prentice Hall, 1961.

Cendrars, Blaise. *Hollywood: Mecca of the Movies*. Berkeley: University of California Press, 1995.

Cheung, Hye Sung. *Hollywood Asian: Philip Ahn and the Politics of Cross-Ethnic Performance*. Philadelphia: Temple University Press, 2006.

Cohen, Lizabeth. *Making a New Deal: Industrial Workers in Chicago, 1919–1939*. New York: Cambridge University Press, 1990.

Conolly-Smith, Peter. *Translating America: An Immigrant Press Visualizes American Popular Culture, 1895–1918*. Washington, DC: Smithsonian Books, 2004.

Crawford, Paul J. "Movie Habits and Attitudes of the Under-Privileged Boys of the All Nations Area in Los Angeles." Master's thesis, University of Southern California, 1934.

Czach, Liz. "Film Festivals, Programming, and the Building of a National Cinema." *Moving Image* 4, no. 1 (2004): 76–88.

Danan, Martine. "Hollywood's Hegemonic Strategies: Overcoming French Nationalism with the Advent of Sound." In Higson and Maltby, *Film Europe*, 225–248.

Dávila, Arlene. *Latinos, Inc.: The Marketing and Making of a People*. Berkeley: University of California Press, 2001.

_____. *Latino Spin: Public Image and the Whitewashing of Race*. New York: New York University Press, 2008.

Decherney, Peter. *Hollywood and the Culture Elite: How Movies Became American*. New York: Columbia University Press, 2006.

DeCordova, Richard. "Ethnography and Exhibition: The Child Audience, the Hays Office, and Saturday Matinees." In Lewis and Smoodin, *Looking Past the Screen*, 229–245.

De la Vega Alfaro, Eduardo. "Origins, Development, and Crisis of the Sound Cinema (1929–1964)." In Paranaguá, *Mexican Cinema*, 79–93.

"De Los Angeles, CAL, se nos envia una carta . . . ," *Cinema Reporter* 1, no. 50 (1939): 3.

De los Reyes, Aurelio. *Con Villa en Mexico: Testimonios sobre camarógrafos norteamericanos en la revolución, 1911–1916*. Mexico City: Universidad Nacional Autónoma de México/Instituto de Investigaciones Estéticas, 1985.

_____. "El gobierno mexicano y las películas denigrantes, 1920–1931." In Durán, Trujillo, and Verea, *México Estados Unidos*, 23–35.

_____. "'Goodbye to the Greaser': Mexico, the MPPDA, and Derogatory Films, 1922–1926." *Journal of Popular Film and Television* 12, no. 1 (1984): 34–41.

_____. *Medio siglo de cine mexicano (1896–1947)*. Mexico City: Trillas, 1987.

Delpar, Helen. *The Enormous Vogue of Things Mexican: Cultural Relations between the United States and Mexico, 1920–1935*. Tuscaloosa: University of Alabama Press, 1992.

_____. "'Goodbye to the Greaser': Mexico, the MPPDA, and Derogatory Films, 1922–1926." *Journal of Popular Film and Television* 12, no. 1 (1984): 34–40.

De Orellana, Margarita. *Filming Pancho: How Hollywood Shaped the Mexican Revolution*. New York: Verso, 2009.

_____. *La mirada circular: El cine norteamericano de la revolución mexicana, 1911–1917*. Mexico City: Artes de México, 2010.

De Usabel, Gaizka S. *The High Noon of Films in Latin America*. Ann Arbor: UMI Research Press, 1982.

Deverell, William. *Whitewashed Adobe: The Rise of Los Angeles and the Remaking of Its Mexican Past*. Berkeley: University of California Press, 2004.

Dickson, Robert G. "California Theater in the 1930s." *Marquee* 26, no. 4 (1994): 6.

_____. "Los orígenes y desarrollo del cine hispano." In Durán, Trujillo, and Verea, *México Estados Unidos*, 135–146.

Di Stefano, Onofre. "*La Prensa* of San Antonio and Its Literary Page, 1913–1915." PhD diss., University of California, Los Angeles, 1983.

D'Lugo, Marvin. "Aural Identity, Genealogies of Sound Technologies, and Hispanic Transnationality on Screen." In Ďurovičová and Newman, *World Cinemas, Transnational Perspectives*, 160–185.

Durán, Ignacio, Iván Trujillo, and Mónica Verea, eds. *México Estados Unidos: Encuentros y desencuentros en el cine*. Mexico City: Universidad Nacional Autónoma de México, 1996.

Ďurovičová, Nataša. "Vector, Flow, Zone: Toward a History of Cinematic *Translatio*." In Ďurovičová and Newman, *World Cinemas, Transnational Perspectives*, 90–120.

Ďurovičová, Nataša, and Kathleen Newman, eds. *World Cinemas, Transnational Perspectives*. New York: Routledge, 2010.

Ervin, J. McFarline. *The Participation of the Negro in the Community Life of Los Angeles.* San Francisco: R and E Research Associates, 1973.

Escobar, Edward J. *Race, Police, and the Making of a Political Identity.* Berkeley: University of California Press, 1999.

España-Maram, Linda. *Creating Masculinity in Los Angeles's Little Manila: Working Class Filipinos and Popular Culture, 1920s–1950s.* New York: Columbia University Press, 2006.

"¿Está en peligro nuestra industria?" *Cinema Reporter* 1, no. 22 (1938): 1, 7.

Estrada, William David. *The Los Angeles Plaza: Sacred and Contested Space.* Austin: University of Texas Press, 2008.

Falicov, Tamara. "Hollywood's Rogue Neighbor: The Argentine Film Industry during the Good Neighbor Policy, 1939–1945." *Americas* 63, no. 2 (2006): 245–260.

Fein, Seth. "Hollywood and United States–Mexico Relations in the Golden Age of Mexican Cinema." PhD diss., University of Texas, 1996.

Fogelson, Robert M. *The Fragmented Metropolis: Los Angeles, 1850–1930.* Berkeley: University of California Press, 1993.

Fox, Claire. *The Fence and the River: Culture and Politics at the U.S.-Mexico Border.* Minneapolis: University of Minnesota Press, 1999.

Gamio, Manuel. *El inmigrante mexicano: La historia de su vida; Entrevistas completas, 1926–1927.* Edited by Devra Weber, Roberto Melville, and Juan Vicente Palerm. Mexico City: Porrúa, 2002.

———. *The Life Story of the Mexican Immigrant.* New York: Dover, 1971.

Garcia, Desirée J. "'The Soul of a People': Mexican Spectatorship and the Transnational *Comedia Ranchera.*" *Journal of American Ethnic History* 30, no. 1 (2010):72–98.

Garcia, Matt. *A World of Its Own: Race, Labor, and Citrus in the Making of Greater Los Angeles, 1900–1970.* Chapel Hill: University of North Carolina Press, 2001.

Garcia, Richard A. *The Rise of the Mexican American Middle Class: San Antonio, 1929–1941.* College Station: Texas A&M University Press, 1991.

Garcia Berumen, Frank Javier. *The Chicano/Hispanic Image in American Film.* New York: Vantage, 1995.

García Riera, Emilio. *Historia documental del cine mexicano.* Vols. 1–12. Guadalajara, Mexico: Universidad de Guadalajara, 1992.

———. "The Impact of *Rancho Grande.*" In Paranaguá, *Mexican Cinema,* 128–132.

Gerow, Aaron. *Visions of Japanese Modernity: Articulations of Cinema, Nation, and Spectatorship, 1895–1925.* Berkeley: University of California Press, 2010.

Glancy, Mark, and John Sedgwick. "Cinemagoing in the United States in the Mid-1930s: A Study Based on the *Variety* Dataset." In Maltby, Stokes, and Allen, *Going to the Movies,* 155–195.

Gomery, Douglas. *The Coming of Sound.* New York: Routledge, 2005.

González, Gilbert G. *Culture of Empire: American Writers, Mexico, and Mexican Immigrants, 1880–1930.* Austin: University of Texas Press, 2004.

Grieveson, Lee. *Policing Cinema: Movies and Censorship in Early Twentieth Century America.* Berkeley: University of California Press, 2004.

Griswold del Castillo, Richard. *The Los Angeles Barrio, 1850–1890: A Social History.* Berkeley: University of California Press, 1979.

Guerin-Gonzales, Camille. *Mexican Workers and American Dreams: Immigration, Repatriation, and California Farm Labor, 1900–1939.* New Brunswick, NJ: Rutgers University Press, 1996.

Gunckel, Colin. "Ambivalent Si(gh)tings: Stardom and Silent Film in Mexican America." *Film History* (forthcoming).

Gunning, Tom. "An Aesthetic of Astonishment: Early Film and the (In)Credulous Spectator." In *Film Theory: Critical Concepts in Media and Cultural Studies*, edited by Philip Simpson, Andrew Utterson, and K. J. Sheperdson, 291–310. New York: Routledge, 2004.

Gurza, Agustín. *The Arhoolie Foundation's Strachwitz Frontera Collection of Mexican and Mexican American Recordings.* With Jonathan Clark and Chris Strachwitz. Los Angeles: UCLA Chicano Studies Research Center, 2012.

_____. "A Cultural Treasure for the Ages." In Gurza, *Strachwitz Frontera Collection*, 1–6.

_____. "El Mariachi: From Rustic Roots to Golden Era." In *Strachwitz Frontera Collection*, 109–126.

Gutiérrez, David G. "Migration, Emergent Ethnicity, and the 'Third Space': The Shifting Politics of Nationalism in Greater Mexico." *Journal of American History* 86, no. 2 (1999): 481–517.

_____. *Walls and Mirrors: Mexican Americans, Mexican Immigrants, and the Politics of Ethnicity.* Berkeley: University of California Press, 1995.

Gutiérrez, Ramón A. "Hispanic Identities in the Southwestern United States." In Katzew and Deans-Smith, *Race and Classification*, 174–193.

Haenni, Sabine. *The Immigrant Scene: Ethnic Amusements in New York, 1880–1920.* Minneapolis: University of Minnesota Press, 2008.

Hagener, Malte. "*Prix de beauté* as a Multiple Intersection: National Cinema, Auteurism, and the Coming of Sound." *Cinema et Cie*, no. 4 (2004): 102–116.

Halleck, DeeDee. "Las imágenes contradictorias del México de Gene Autry: Un análisis de dos películas: *South of the Border* y *Down Mexico Way*." In Durán, Trujillo, and Verea, *México Estados Unidos*, 37–40.

Haney, Peter C. "*Carpa y teatro, sol y sombra*: Show Business and Public Culture in San Antonio's Mexican Colony, 1900–1940." PhD diss., University of Texas at Austin, 2004.

Hayes, Joy Elizabeth. "National Imaginings on the Air: Radio in Mexico, 1920–1950." In Vaughan and Lewis, *Eagle and the Virgin*, 243–258.

Heinink, Juan B., and Robert G. Dickson. *Cita en Hollywood: Antología de las películas habladas en castellano.* Bilbao, Spain: Mensajero, 1990.

Heinze, Andrew R. *Adapting to Abundance: Jewish Immigrants, Mass Consumption, and the Search for American Identity.* New York: Columbia University Press, 1990.

Henriques, Donald Andrew. "Performing Nationalism: Mariachi, Media, and the Transformation of a Tradition (1920–1942)." PhD diss., University of Texas, 2006.

Herbold, Paul. "Sociological Survey of Main Street, Los Angeles, California." Master's thesis, University of Southern California, 1936.

Hershfield, Joanne. *The Invention of Dolores del Rio.* Minneapolis: University of Minnesota Press, 2000.

_____. *Mexican Cinema/Mexican Woman, 1940–1950.* Tucson: University of Arizona Press, 1996.

Higashi, Sumiko. "Manhattan's Nickelodeons: Sumiko Higashi on Ben Singer's 'Manhattan Nickelodeons: New Data on Audiences and Exhibitors,'" *Cinema Journal* 35, no. 3 (1996): 72–74.

Higson, Andrew. "The Concept of National Cinema." *Screen* 30, no. 4 (1989): 36–47.

_____. "Polyglot Films for an International Market: E. A. Dupont, the British Film Industry, and the Idea of a European Cinema, 1926–1930." In Higson and Maltby, *Film Europe*, 274–301.

Higson, Andrew, and Richard Maltby, eds. *"Film Europe" and "Film America": Cinema, Commerce, and Cultural Exchange, 1920–1939.* Exeter: University of Exeter Press, 1999.

Hilmes, Michele. *Hollywood and Broadcasting: From Radio to Cable.* Urbana: University of Illinois Press, 1990.

Hjort, Mette. "On the Plurality of Cinematic Transnationalism." In Ďurovičová and Newman, *World Cinemas, Transnational Perspectives,* 12–33.

Jarvinen, Lisa. *The Rise of Spanish-Language Filmmaking: Out from Hollywood's Shadow, 1929–1939.* New Brunswick, NJ: Rutgers University Press, 2012.

Jones, Willis Knapp. *Behind Spanish American Footlights.* Austin: University of Texas Press, 1966.

Jurca, Catherine. *Hollywood 1938: Motion Picture's Greatest Year.* Berkeley: University of California Press, 2012.

Kanellos, Nicolás. "A Brief History of Hispanic Periodicals in the United States." In *Hispanic Periodicals in the United States, Origins to 1960: A Brief History and Comprehensive Bibliography,* edited by Nicolás Kanellos, with Helvetia Martell, 8–136. Houston: Arte Público, 2000.

_____. *A History of Hispanic Theater in the United States: Origins to 1940.* Austin: University of Texas Press, 1990.

_____. "An Overview of Hispanic Theater in the United States." In *Hispanic Theater in the United States,* edited by Nicolás Kanellos, 7–23. Houston: Arte Público, 1984.

_____. "Recovering and Re-constructing Early Twentieth-Century Hispanic Immigrant Print Culture in the US." *American Literary History* 19, no. 2 (2007): 438–455.

_____. "Two Centuries of Hispanic Theater in the Southwest." In *Revista Chicano Riqueña: Mexican Theater Then and Now,* edited by Nicolás Kanellos, 17–36. Houston: Arte Público, 1983.

Karush, Matthew B. "The Melodramatic Nation: Integration and Polarization in the Argentine Cinema of the 1930s." *Hispanic American Historical Review* 87, no. 2 (2007): 293–326.

Katzew, Ilona, and Susan Deans-Smith, eds. *Race and Classification: The Case of Mexican America.* Stanford, CA: Stanford University Press, 2009.

Keller, Gary D. *Hispanics and United States Film: An Overview and Handbook.* Tempe, AZ: Bilingual Press/Editorial Bilingüe, 1994.

Khor, Denise. "Asian Americans at the Movies: Race, Labor, and Migration in the Transpacific West, 1900–1945." PhD diss., University of California, San Diego, 2008.

_____. "'Filipinos Are the Dandies of the Foreign Colonies': Race, Labor Struggles, and the Transpacific Routes of Hollywood and Philippine Films, 1924–1948." *Pacific Historical Review* 81, no. 3 (2012): 371–403.

Kibler, M. Alison. *Rank Ladies: Gender and Cultural Hierarchy in American Vaudeville.* Chapel Hill: University of North Carolina Press, 1999.

Klein, Norman M. *The History of Forgetting: Los Angeles and the Erasure of Memory.* New York: Verso, 1997.

Knight, Alan. "Weapons and Arches in the Mexican Revolutionary Landscape." In *Everyday Forms of State Formation: Revolution and the Negotiation of Rule in Modern Mexico,* edited by Gilbert M. Joseph and Daniel Nugent, 24–66. Durham, NC: Duke University Press, 1994.

Knopf, Robert. Introduction to *Theater and Film: A Comparative Anthology,* edited by Robert Knopf, 1–20. New Haven: Yale University Press, 2005.

Koegel, John. "Crossing Borders: Mexicana, Tejana, and Chicana Musicians in the United States and Mexico." In *From Tejano to Tango: Latin American Popular Music*, edited by Walter Aaron Clark, 97–125. New York: Routledge, 2002.

Koszarski, Richard. *An Evening's Entertainment: The Age of the Silent Picture*. Berkeley: University of California Press, 1990.

Kropp, Phoebe S. "Citizens of the Past? Olvera Street and the Construction of Race and Memory in 1930s Los Angeles." *Radical History Review*, no. 81 (Fall 2001): 35–60.

Lanigan, Mary C. "Second Generation of Mexicans in Belvedere." Master's thesis, University of Southern California, 1932.

Lastra, James. *Sound Technology and the American Cinema: Perception, Representation, Modernity*. New York: Columbia University Press, 2000.

Levine, Lawrence W. *Highbrow/Lowbrow: The Emergence of Cultural Hierarchy in America*. Cambridge, MA: Harvard University Press, 1988.

Lewis, Jon, and Eric Smoodin, eds. *Looking Past the Screen: Case Studies in American Film History and Method*. Durham, NC: Duke University Press, 2007.

Lewthwaite, Stephanie. *Race, Place, and Reform in Mexican Los Angeles: A Transnational Perspective, 1890–1940*. Tucson: University of Arizona Press, 2009.

Longstreth, Richard. *City Center to Regional Mall: Architecture, the Automobile, and Retailing in Los Angeles, 1920–1950*. Cambridge, MA: MIT Press, 1997.

López, Ana M. "Are All Latins from Manhattan? Hollywood, Ethnography, and Cultural Colonialism." In *Unspeakable Images: Ethnicity and the American Cinema*, edited by Lester D. Friedman, 404–424. Urbana: University of Illinois Press, 1991.

———. "A Cinema for the Continent." In *The Mexican Cinema Project*, edited by Chon A. Noriega and Steve Ricci, 7–12. Los Angeles: UCLA Film and Television Archive, 1994.

Maltby, Richard. "Introduction: 'The Americanisation of the World.'" In *Hollywood Abroad: Audiences and Cultural Exchange*, edited by Melvyn Stokes and Richard Maltby, 2–20. London: British Film Institute, 2004.

———. Introduction to *Identifying Hollywood's Audiences: Cultural Identity and the Movies*, edited by Melvyn Stokes and Richard Maltby, 1–22. London: British Film Institute, 1999.

———. "New Cinema Histories." In *Explorations in New Cinema History: Approaches and Case Studies*, edited by Richard Maltby, Daniel Biltereyst, and Phillipe Meers, 3–40. Malden, MA: Wiley-Blackwell, 2011.

Maltby, Richard, and Melvyn Stokes. Introduction to Maltby, Stokes, and Allen, *Going to the Movies*, 1–22.

Maltby, Richard, Melvyn Stokes, and Robert Allen, eds. *Going to the Movies: Hollywood and the Social Experience of Cinema*. Exeter: University of Exeter Press, 2007.

Maltby, Richard, and Ruth Vasey. "'Temporary American Citizens': Cultural Anxieties and Industrial Strategies in the Americanisation of European Cinema." In Higson and Maltby, *Film Europe*, 32–55.

Marez, Curtis. *Drug Wars: The Political Economy of Narcotics*. Minneapolis: University of Minnesota Press, 2004.

———. "Subaltern Soundtracks: Mexican Immigrants and the Making of Hollywood Cinema." *Aztlán: A Journal of Chicano Studies* 29, no. 1 (2004): 57–82.

May, Lary. *Screening Out the Past: The Birth of Mass Culture and the Motion Picture Industry*. Chicago: University of Chicago Press, 1980.

McEuen, William Wilson. "A Survey of the Mexicans in Los Angeles." Master's thesis, University of Southern California, 1914.

McLean, Adrienne L. *Being Rita Hayworth: Labor, Identity, and Hollywood Stardom*. New Brunswick, NJ: Rutgers University Press, 2005.

McWilliams, Carey. *North from Mexico: The Spanish-Speaking People of the United States*. New York: Greenwood, 1968.

―――. *Southern California: An Island on the Land*. Salt Lake City: Gibbs-Smith, 1973.

Medeiros, Francine. "*La Opinión*, a Mexican Exile Newspaper: A Content Analysis of Its First Years, 1926–1929." *Aztlán: A Journal of Chicano Studies* 11, no. 1 (1980): 65–87.

Menken, Robin. "¡Adios Clichés! ¡Hola México! The 2012 Hola México Film Festival." Cinema without Borders. May 26, 2012. http://cinemawithoutborders.com/festivals/3079-hola-mexico-2012-film-festival.html.

Merlín, Socorro. *Vida y milagros de las carpas: La carpa en México, 1930–1950*. Mexico City: Instituto Nacional de Bellas Artes/Centro Nacional de Investigación y Documentación Teatral Rodolfo Usigli, 1995.

Meyer, Doris. *Speaking for Themselves: Neomexicano Cultural Identity and the Spanish-Language Press, 1880–1920*. Albuquerque: University of New Mexico Press, 1996.

Miquel, Angel. *Disolvencias: Literatura, cine y radio en México (1900–1950)*. Mexico City: Fondo de Cultura Económica, 2005.

Miyao, Daisuke. *Sessue Hayakawa: Silent Cinema and Transnational Stardom*. Durham, NC: Duke University Press, 2007.

Molina, Natalia. *Fit to Be Citizens? Public Health and Race in Los Angeles, 1879–1939*. Berkeley: University of California Press, 2006.

Monroy, Douglas. *Rebirth: Mexican Los Angeles from the Great Migration to the Great Depression*. Berkeley: University of California Press, 1999.

Montejano, David. *Anglos and Mexicans in the Making of Texas, 1836–1986*. Austin: University of Texas Press, 1987.

Mraz, John. *Looking for Mexico: Modern Visual Culture and National Identity*. Durham, NC: Duke University Press, 2009.

Mullen Sands, Kathleen. *Charrería Mexicana: An Equestrian Folk Tradition*. Tucson: University of Arizona Press, 1993.

Musser, Charles. "Towards a History of Theatrical Culture: Imagining an Integrated History of Stage and Screen." In *Screen Culture: History and Textuality*, edited by John Fullerton, 3–20. Eastleigh, UK: Libbey, 2004.

Nájera Ramírez, Olga. "Engendering Nationalism: Identity, Discourse, and the Mexican Charro." *Anthropological Quarterly* 67, no. 1 (1994): 1–14.

Navarro Tomás, T. *El idioma español en el cine parlante*. Madrid: Tipografía de Archivos, 1930.

Navitski, Rielle. "The Tango on Broadway: Carlos Gardel's International Stardom and the Transition to Sound in Argentina." *Cinema Journal* 51, no. 1 (2011): 26–49.

Nicolaides, Becky M. *My Blue Heaven: Life and Politics in the Working-Class Suburbs of Los Angeles, 1920–1965*. Chicago: University of Chicago Press, 2002.

Nornes, Abé Mark. *Cinema Babel: Translating Global Cinema*. Minneapolis: University of Minnesota Press, 2007.

North, C. J., and N. D. Golden. "The Latin-American Audience Viewpoint on American Films." *Journal of the Society of Motion Picture Engineers* 17, no. 1 (1931): 18–25.

Oberdeck, Kathryn J. *The Evangelist and the Impresario: Religion, Entertainment, and Cultural Politics in America, 1884–1914*. Baltimore: Johns Hopkins University Press, 1999.

O'Brien, Charles. *Cinema's Conversion to Sound: Technology and Film Style in France and the U.S.* Bloomington: Indiana University Press, 2005.

Ogihara, Junko. "The Exhibition of Films for Japanese Americans in Los Angeles during the Silent Film Era." *Film History* 4, no. 2 (1990): 81–87.

Olsson, Jan. "Hollywood's First Spectators: Notes on Ethnic Nickelodeon Audiences in Los Angeles." *Aztlán: A Journal of Chicano Studies* 26, no. 1 (2001): 181–195.

_____. *Los Angeles before Hollywood: Journalism and American Film Culture, 1905 to 1915.* Stockholm: National Library of Sweden, 2008.

O'Neil, Brian. "The Demands of Authenticity: Addison Durland and Hollywood's Latin Images during World War II." In *Classic Hollywood, Classic Whiteness*, edited by Daniel Bernardi, 359–385. Minneapolis: University of Minnesota Press, 2001.

_____. "Yankee Invasion of Mexico, or Mexican Invasion of Hollywood? Hollywood's Renewed Spanish-Language Production of 1938–1939." *Studies in Latin American Popular Culture* 17 (1998): 79–104.

Paranaguá, Paulo Antonio. *Mexican Cinema.* London: British Film Institute, 1995.

Parle, Dennis J. "The Novels of the Mexican Revolution Published by the Casa Editorial Lozano." *Americas Review* 17, nos. 3–4 (1989): 163–168.

Peiss, Kathy. *Cheap Amusements: Working Women and Leisure in Turn-of-the-Century New York.* Philadelphia: Temple University Press, 1986.

Petit, Arthur G. *Images of the Mexican American in Fiction and Film.* College Station: Texas A&M University Press, 1980.

Pick, Zuzana. *Constructing the Image of the Mexican Revolution: Cinema and the Archive.* Austin: University of Texas Press, 2010.

Pilcher, Jeffrey. *Cantinflas and the Chaos of Mexican Modernity.* Wilmington, DE: Scholarly Resources, 2001.

Poole, Jean Bruce, and Tevvy Ball. *El Pueblo: The Historic Heart of Los Angeles.* Los Angeles: Getty Conservation Institute/Getty Museum, 2002.

"Problemas de distribución." *Cinema Reporter* 2, no. 99 (1940): 1, 10.

Pulido Islas, Alfonso. *La industria cinematográfica de México.* Mexico City: México Nuevo, 1939.

_____. *Latinos Images in Film: Stereotypes, Subversion, and Resistance.* Austin: University of Texas Press, 2002.

Ramírez, Elizabeth C. *Chicanas/Latinas in American Theatre: A History of Performance.* Bloomington: Indiana University Press, 2000.

_____. *Footlights across the Border: A History of Spanish-Language Professional Theater on the Texas Stage.* New York: Lang, 1990.

Ramírez Berg, Charles. "Colonialism and Movies in Southern California, 1910–1934." *Aztlán: A Journal of Chicano Studies* 28, no. 1 (2003): 75–96.

_____. *Latino Images in Film: Stereotypes, Subversion, Resistance.* Austin: University of Texas Press, 2002.

Reyes de la Maza, Luis, ed. *El cine sonoro en México.* Mexico City: Universidad Nacional Autónoma de México, 1973.

_____. Introduction to Reyes de la Maza, *Cine sonoro en México*, 11–30.

Rezutko Bokar, Camille Naomi. "A Historical Study of the Legitimate Theater in Los Angeles, 1920–1929, and Its Relation to the National Theatrical Scene." PhD diss., University of Southern California, 1973.

Ríos-McMillan, Nora. "A Biography of a Man and His Newspaper." *Americas Review* 17, nos. 3–4 (1989): 136–149.

Robert, Roberto Cantú. "Nuestros problemas al exterior." *Cinema Reporter* 2, no. 101 (1940): 3.

_____. "Ramón Peón: Enemigo num. 1 del cine hispano." *Cinema Reporter* 1, no. 21 (1938): 3.

Roberts, Shari. "'The Lady in the Tutti-Frutti Hat': Carmen Miranda, a Spectacle of Ethnicity." *Cinema Journal* 32, no. 3 (1993): 3–23.

Rodríguez, Clara E. *Heroes, Lovers, and Others: The Story of Latinos in Hollywood.* Washington, DC: Smithsonian Books, 2004.

Romo, Ricardo. *East Los Angeles: History of a Barrio.* Austin: University of Texas Press, 1983.

Ross, Robert Howard. "Social Distance as It Exists between the First and Second Generation of Japanese in the City of Los Angeles and Vicinity." Master's thesis, University of Southern California, 1939.

Ross, Steven J. "How Hollywood Became Hollywood: Money, Politics, and Movies." In *Metropolis in the Making: Los Angeles in the 1920s,* edited by Tom Sitton and William Deverell, 255–276. Berkeley: University of California Press, 2001.

Ruiz, Vicki L. "'Star Struck': Acculturation, Adolescence, and the Mexican American Woman, 1920–1950." In *Building with Our Hands: New Directions in Chicana Studies,* edited by Adela de la Torre and Beatríz M. Pesquera, 109–129. Berkeley: University of California Press, 1993.

Sánchez, George J. *Becoming Mexican American: Ethnicity, Culture, and Identity in Chicano Los Angeles, 1900–1945.* New York: Oxford University Press, 1993.

Sandoval-Sánchez, Alberto. *José Can You See? Latinos On and Off Broadway.* Madison: University of Wisconsin Press, 1999.

Schaefer, Eric. *Bold! Daring! Shocking! True! A History of Exploitation Films, 1919–1959.* Durham, NC: Duke University Press, 1999.

Schwartz Seller, Maxine. Introduction to *Ethnic Theater in the United States,* edited by Maxine Schwartz Seller, 3–17. Westport, CT: Greenwood, 1983.

Segre, Erica. *Intersected Identities: Strategies of Visualization in Nineteenth- and Twentieth-Century Mexican Culture.* New York: Berghahn Books, 2007.

Serna, Laura I. "'As a Mexican I Feel It's My Duty': Citizenship, Censorship, and the Campaign against Derogatory Films in Mexico, 1922–1930." *Americas* 63, no. 2 (2006): 225–244.

_____. "Exhibition in Mexico during the Early 1920s: Nationalist Discourse and Transnational Capital." In *Convergence Media History,* edited by Janet Staiger and Sabine Hake, 69–80. New York: Routledge, 2009.

Serna, Laura Isabel. *Making Cinelandia: American Films and Mexican Film Culture before the Golden Age.* Durham, NC: Duke University Press, 2014.

_____. "'We're Going Yankee': American Movies, Mexican Nationalism, Transnational Cinema, 1917–1935." PhD diss., Harvard University, 2006.

Sheehy, Daniel. "Popular Mexican Musical Traditions: The Mariachi of West Mexico and the Conjunto Jarocho of Veracruz." In *Music in Latin American Culture: Regional Traditions,* edited by John M. Schechter, 34–79. New York: Schirmer Books, 1997.

Shiel, Mark. "Cinema and the City in History and Theory." In Shiel and Fitzmaurice, *Cinema and the City,* 1–18.

_____. *Hollywood Cinema and the Real Los Angeles.* London: Reaktion Books, 2012.

Shiel, Mark, and Tony Fitzmaurice, eds. *Cinema and the City: Film and Urban Societies in a Global Context.* Malden, MA: Blackwell, 2001.

Sides, Josh. *L.A. City Limits: African American Los Angeles from the Great Depression to the Present.* Berkeley: University of California Press, 2003.

Singer, Ben. "Manhattan Melodrama: A Response from Ben Singer." *Cinema Journal* 36, no. 4 (1997): 107–112.

_____. "Manhattan Nickelodeons: New Data on Audiences and Exhibitors." *Cinema Journal* 34, no. 3 (1995): 5–35.

_____. *Melodrama and Modernity: Early Sensational Cinema and Its Contexts.* New York: Columbia University Press, 2001.

_____. "New York, Just Like I Pictured It . . ." *Cinema Journal* 35, no. 3 (1996): 104–128.

Smoodin, Eric. "Introduction: The History of Film History." In Lewis and Smoodin, *Looking Past the Screen,* 1–34.

Snyder, Robert W. *The Voice of the City: Vaudeville and Popular Culture in New York.* New York: Oxford University Press, 1989.

"El Sr. Frank Fouce, de California, opine sobre la producción cinematográfica mexicana." *Cinema Reporter* 2, no. 102 (1940): 3.

Staiger, Janet. "The Future of the Past." *Cinema Journal* 44, no. 1 (2004): 126–129.

_____. *Perverse Spectators: The Practices of Film Reception.* New York: New York University Press, 2000.

Stanfield, Peter. *Horse Opera: The Strange History of the 1930s Singing Cowboy.* Urbana: University of Illinois Press, 2002.

Stern, Alexandra Minna. "Eugenics and Racial Classification in Modern Mexican America." In Katzew and Deans-Smith, *Race and Classification,* 151–173.

Stewart, Jacqueline Najuma. *Migrating to the Movies: Cinema and Black Urban Modernity.* Berkeley: University of California Press, 2005.

Strachwitz, Chris, and James Nicolopulos, eds. *Lydia Mendoza: A Family Autobiography.* Houston: Arte Público, 1993.

Stringer, Julian. "Global Cities and the International Festival Economy." In Shiel and Fitzmaurice, *Cinema and the City,* 134–144.

Tenorio-Trillo, Mauricio. *Mexico at the World's Fairs: Crafting a Modern Tradition.* Berkeley: University of California Press, 1996.

"To the Motion Picture Producers," *Hollywood Filmograph* 10, no. 5 (1930): 19.

Turino, Thomas. "Nationalism and Latin American Music: Selected Case Studies and Theoretical Considerations." *Latin American Music Review* 24, no. 2 (2003): 169–209.

Ulff-Moller, Jens. "Hollywood's 'Foreign War': The Effect of National Commercial Policy on the Emergence of the American Film Hegemony in France, 1920–1929." In Higson and Maltby, *Film Europe,* 181–206.

"La union de trabajadores se preocupa por el exodo de nuestros elementos a Hollywood." *Cinema Reporter* 1, no. 25 (1939): 3.

Uricchio, William, and Roberta E. Pearson. "Manhattan's Nickelodeons: New York? New York! William Uricchio and Roberta E. Pearson Comment on the Singer-Allen Exchange." *Cinema Journal* 36, no. 4 (1997): 98–101.

_____. *Reframing Culture: The Case of Vitagraph Quality Films.* Princeton, NJ: Princeton University Press, 1993.

Urquijo-Ruiz, Rita E. "Las figuras de la peladita/el peladito y la pachuca/el pachuco en la producción cultural chicana y Mexicana de 1920 a 1990." PhD diss., University of California, San Diego, 2004.

Valdivia, Angharad N. *Latina/os and the Media.* Malden, MA: Polity, 2010.

Vasey, Ruth. *The World according to Hollywood, 1918–1939.* Madison: University of Wisconsin Press, 1997.

Vaughan, Mary Kay, and Stephen E. Lewis, eds. *The Eagle and the Virgin: Nation and Cultural Revolution in Mexico, 1920–1940.* Durham, NC: Duke University Press, 2006.

_____. Introduction to Vaughan and Lewis, *Eagle and the Virgin,* 1–20.

Venegas, Daniel. *The Adventures of Don Chipote; or, When Parrots Breast-Feed.* Houston: Arte Público, 2000.

Vincendeau, Ginette. "Hollywood Babel." *Screen* 20, no. 2 (1988): 24–39.

Vivian, Octavia B. *The Story of the Negro in Los Angeles.* San Francisco: R and E Research Associates, 1970.

Warnke, Nina. "Immigrant Popular Culture as Contested Sphere: Yiddish Music Halls, the Yiddish Press, and the Process of Americanization, 1900–1910." *Theatre Journal* 38, no. 3 (1996): 321–335.

"White Opens California as Spanish Theater: This Will Be Tryout Here for Spanish Made Pictures." *Hollywood Filmograph* 10, no. 10 (1930): 14.

Wild, Mark. *Street Meeting: Multiethnic Neighborhoods in Early Twentieth-Century Los Angeles.* Berkeley: University of California Press, 2005.

Woll, Allen L. *The Latin Image in American Film.* Los Angeles: UCLA Latin American Center, 1980.

Wong, Cindy Hing-Yuk. *Film Festivals: Culture, People, and Power on the Global Screen.* New Brunswick, NJ: Rutgers University Press, 2011.

Ybarra-Frausto, Tomás. "'I Can Still Hear the Applause': La farándula chicana; Carpas y tandas de variedad." In Kanellos, *Hispanic Theater*, 45–61.

_____."Rasquachismo: A Chicano Sensibility." In *CARA: Chicano Art; Resistance and Affirmation,* edited by Richard Griswold del Castillo, Teresa McKenna, and Yvonne Yarbro-Bejarano, 155–162. Los Angeles: UCLA Wight Art Gallery, 1991.

INDEX

Page references in bold indicate figures.

accent issues. *See under* Hollywood
Spanish-language films, early 1930s;
Hollywood Spanish-language films,
late 1930s
Acuña, Manuel, 35
Adamic, Louis, 47
Addams, Jane, 23
admission prices, 57–59, 77, 120–121
advertising. *See* intermedial strategies;
nationalism in publicity; *Opinión,
La* (newspaper), publicity in; *specific
theaters and newspapers*
African Americans, 3, 7, 14–15, 17, 38
Agrasánchez, Rogelio, Jr., 56
Aguila, Guz, 78–79
Aguilas frente al sol (Antonio Moreno,
1932), 127
Alaska Airlines, 196
Alba, Luz, 117
Alberich, Salvador, 106, 107
Aldama, Arturo J., 85, 86
Alegría (theater), 57
Allá en el Rancho Grande (Fernando de
Fuentes, 1936): analysis of transna-
tional identity formation in, 124–
125, 158; as comedia ranchera genre
foundation, 11, 124, 137–138, **138**,
143–144; exhibition practices, 166,
169; Guízar's career and, 140, 180, 183;
as Mexican public relations, 11, 125,

148; musical and folkloric elements,
136, 147; narrative analysis, 138–139,
156–157, 158; origins/history, 139–
140; publicity, 143–144, **152**; reproductions, 144, **145, 146**; success, 124,
137, 141, 143, 156
Allá en el trópico (Fernando de Fuentes,
1941), 181
Alonso, Miguel, 87
Amapola del camino (Juan Bustillo Oro,
1937), 143, 153–155, 183
Americanization: of cinema, 29, 30–31,
90, 93; cultural authorities' resistance,
9, 33, 34; English language and, 92, 93;
Hollywood's domination of global film
industry and, 29, 53–54, 60; mainstream conceptions, 23, 27, 68; sound
cinema and, 89, 110; theater and, 51,
53, 80, 84. *See also* de-Mexicanization;
Hollywood, domination of film industry by; youth/children
amores de Ramona, Los (González), 82
Amores perros (Alejandro González
Iñárritu, 2000), 194
Anahuac Film Corporation, 55
Anderson, Gilbert M. "Broncho Billy,"
29–30
Argentina, 165
Argentine national cinema, 118, 160,
161, 162–163, 166, 181

ABOUT THE AUTHOR

COLIN GUNCKEL is an assistant professor of screen arts and cultures, American culture, and Latina/o studies at the University of Michigan. His work has been published in *Aztlán: A Journal of Chicano Studies*, *Film History*, and the *Velvet Light Trap*. He is also the associate editor of A Ver: Revisioning Art History series published through the UCLA Chicano Studies Research Center.